JOE CALZAGHE

with Brian Doogan

NO ORDINARY JOE

THE AUTOBIOGRAPHY OF THE GREATEST BRITISH BOXER OF OUR TIME

arrow books

Published in the United Kingdom by Arrow Books in 2008

9 10 8

Copyright © Joe Calzaghe 2007

First published in Great Britain in 2007 by Century

Arrow Books
The Random House Group Limited
20 Vauxhall Bridge Road, London SW1V 2SA

Addresses for companies within The Random House Group Limited
can be found at: www.randomhouse.co.uk

The Random House Group Limited Reg. No. 954009

www.rbooks.co.uk

A CIP catalogue record for this book
is available from the British Library

ISBN 9780099509356

The Random House Group Limited supports The Forest Stewardship
Council (FSC), the leading international forest certification organisation. All
our titles that are printed on Greenpeace approved FSC certified paper carry
the FSC logo. Our paper procurement policy can be found at
www.rbooks.co.uk/environment

Typeset by SX Composing DTP, Rayleigh, Essex
Printed and bound in Great Britain by
CPI Bookmarque, Croydon CR0 4TD

To Mum and Dad, for always being there for me
And to my sons, Joe and Connor

CONTENTS

ACKNOWLEDGEMENTS

Thank you Brian Doogan, Tim Andrews and Random House for helping put this book together and for sharing a few laughs along the way.

Thanks to all those who have helped me in my career down the years, from the sparring partners to my gym mates, Enzo, Gavin, Bradley and Nathan, thanks for being real mates. Frank Warren has done a great job in guiding my career through twenty successful defences of the WBO super middleweight title and to him, Ed, Andy, Dennis, Richard, Emma and all at Sports Network, a special word of thanks. My dad introduced me to boxing and he has been my trainer all my life. You know how much you mean to me, Dad, for without you we would never have shared this incredible journey. Mum, I know you've always worried but you won't have to worry much longer, I'll be retired soon, which might not please my boys, Joe and Connor, but I'm more proud of you than you are of me. My sisters Melissa and Sonia, and my girlfriend, Jo-Emma, thanks for being there and John Salerno, I may still need you one day for sparring, mate. My godfather Uccio, Uncle Serge, and my cousins Andre and Sergio, thanks for accompanying me on the road, and thank you, Grandad, for beginning it all.

Brian Doogan would like to thank Joe Calzaghe, Enzo Calzaghe, Tim Andrews, Jackie Calzaghe, Jo-Emma, Patrick Myler, Steve Farhood, Nigel Collins, Alex Butler, Neil Bramwell, Frank Warren, Richard Maynard, Nigel Benn, Chris Eubank, Ron Bodie, Dave Smith, Pat Sheehan, John Wragg, Russell Padmore, Gerry Hand, David Moore, Chris Moore, Janine Self, Neil Moxley, Dave Harrison, Ray Matts, John Curtis, Adria Milledge, Ralph Ellis, David Walsh, Kevin Palmer, Nick Pitt, John Rawling, Colin Hart, Hugh McIlvanney, Barry McGuigan, Steve Bunce, the late Martin Woods, Alan Hubbard, Matthew Prior, Gareth Evans, Daniel Herbert, Claude Abrams, Bob Mee, Peter Watts, James Mossop, Jeff Powell, Alan Hunter, Terry Smith, Jay Larkin, Fred Burcombe, Frank Wiechula, Mike Lewis, Ron Lewis, all his colleagues on the boxing beat, and the crew who helped him through this project, Steve, Jag, Gerry, Dorothy, Mark, Paul, May and John, Tom and Cokey, Michelle, Thomas, Anne, Kevin, Mary, Margaret, and Michael and Celia.

LIST OF ILLUSTRATIONS

Calzaghe v Trevor French © PA/EMPICS

Calzaghe v Wilson © Sean Dempsey/PA/EMPICS

Calzaghe v Delaney © Sean Dempsey/PA/EMPICS

Calzaghe v Eubank © John Giles/PA/EMPICS

Calzaghe v Eubank © PA/EMPICS

Calzaghe v Reid © PA Photos

Calzaghe v Giminez © PA Photos

Calzaghe v Sheika © Getty Images Sport/Getty Images

Calzaghe v Woodhall © Owen Humphreys/PA/EMPICS

Calzaghe v Jimenez © Nick Potts/PA/EMPICS

Calzaghe v Mitchell © David Davies/PA/EMPICS

Calzaghe v Ashira © Nick Potts/PA/EMPICS

Calzaghe and Lacy © Jon Super/PA/EMPICS

Calzaghe v Lacy © Nick Potts/PA/EMPICS

Calzaghe v Lacy © Nick Potts/PA/EMPICS

Calzaghe v Lacy © Nick Potts/PA/EMPICS

Calzaghe v Bika © South Wales Argus

Calzaghe v Bika © South Wales Argus

Calzaghe v Bika © South Wales Argus

Calzaghe and Jones © Sports Network

Joe Calzaghe – at a glance © boxrec.com

FOREWORD

Friends don't always make the best judges. I remember sitting ringside at Caesars Palace in Las Vegas with Michael J. Fox for Marvin Hagler's fight against John 'The Beast' Mugabi. Marvin was a guy I watched religiously. I knew he'd fought two tough fights against Tommy Hearns and Roberto Duran and I knew he was getting older, then against Mugabi I could see that the fights were taking their toll. He beat Mugabi but he was slowing down. I turned to Michael – we were drinking a few beers – and I told him, 'I can beat this guy.' Michael looked at me like I was crazy. 'Ray,' he said, 'have another beer.' The rest is history.

Exactly twenty years later I was in Eddie Murphy's home in Los Angeles to watch Joe Calzaghe fight Jeff Lacy. Eddie follows the fights and, like Michael, he's a great actor, but he should stick to acting. Lacy got in the ring, Eddie took one look at his big barrel chest, his muscular torso and six-pack, and announced with a huge grin, 'Man, this Calzaghe guy, he has no chance.'

In fairness to Eddie, he wasn't alone in picking Lacy. I had never seen Joe fight before. Of course, I'd heard about him, but the way the fight was billed in the United States he was the opponent and Jeff Lacy was the superstar. I must have watched Lacy in half a dozen or more of his fights and I could see why he generated excitement. He could punch, and some people, commentators in the business, were comparing him to a young Mike Tyson. He was going through opponents with blazing speed. Pure destruction. Not having seen Joe, not knowing him, I figured that Lacy's manager and promoter had set up their hot young property to look good against an ageing thirty-three-year-old fighter with a good record, as is frequently the case. So it wasn't just Eddie, I figured Lacy would win too.

Within two rounds, however, I was a Joe Calzaghe supporter. I was stood up in front of the TV, shouting, 'Wow, holy shit, look at this guy!' The performance he produced was amazing. It was artistic, a demonstration of pure boxing. Joe would have beat anyone with that style, that mindset. What he performed was a boxing clinic, masterful. I'm a fan too and it gives me enormous pleasure to see my peers succeed, especially in a way that is awe-inspiring. This was Joe's great accomplishment, to reach that level, to scale that peak.

We met for the first time in a London hotel two days after he fought Sakio Bika. This was his second title bout of 2006 and a completely different kind of fight, which I was able to view while in Britain and Ireland on a speaking tour. I had the same type of fight against Duran the first time we met. I'll never forget, he had eyes like Charles Manson, the serial killer, he was one scary-looking man and, psychologically, he got to me. He took me out of my game and I found myself fighting a different kind of fight, toe-to-toe, mano-a-mano with the Hands of Stone. It wasn't the brightest decision I ever made. My cornermen tried frantically to get me to box but I was like a racehorse with the blinkers on. I fought Duran in a way I thought I could beat him and, even though I lost the decision after fifteen rounds, I gained a different kind of respect for engaging this man in such a tough, physical battle, almost a street fight. We fought three times in total, the second time I humiliated him and he quit, the third time I had sixty stitches after the fight, twenty inside my mouth. So Joe coming out against Bika with only six stitches around his eye did pretty well. What he was made to do – and what I did against Duran – was show his versatility and his resilience.

Against Lacy, we saw Joe at his consummate best, displaying his all-round boxing skills. Bika brought out the fighter in him, as Duran did to me, but years from now people will remember the Lacy fight long after Bika has been forgotten.

I really admire Joe for being the fighter he is but as we

sat down and talked I quickly realised that he has a very appealing personality. The reason people celebrate my career and look up to me is down to the way I was brought up by my parents. They always told me to respect people: 'You give respect, you see respect.' Joe has the same values. He's a humble guy and this is why we hit it off so well. We talked like we were brothers and I'm glad we had that time together because now I admire the person he is also and I'm honoured to have been asked to write this foreword to his life story.

With his looks, his humility, his natural charm and his ability, he has the potential to become larger than life in the American sports market and I'd really like to see him do this. The top fighters around his weight – Jermain Taylor, Winky Wright, even Bernard Hopkins – Joe beats them all, if he fights the way he fought against Lacy. I keep coming back to that fight because in those twelve rounds Joe made such an impact. We need that. We need those moments. We need action that lingers in the memory, be it Muhammad Ali coming off the ropes against George Foreman to knock him out or Hearns knocking out Duran or Sugar Ray climbing off the canvas to win against Donny Lalonde. I won the WBC super middleweight title that night, which kind of gets me thinking about how today's super middleweight king might have done against me. I'll go to my grave believing I could have beaten Mike Tyson, so Joe and me? Even

Eddie Murphy and Michael J. Fox could tell you the winner of that mythic match-up.

Right, guys?

Sugar Ray Leonard
Los Angeles, March 2007

ROUND ONE
Winning is Everything

It was quiet on the train out of London Paddington. A pile of newspapers lay on the table but I couldn't concentrate. The pain in my hand and the shit in my head were too intense, I was in no mood for reading. My mobile phone rang and I picked it up to resume a conversation which got interrupted when the train back to Newport entered a tunnel, even though I wasn't much in the mood for talking either. A Harley Street doctor had just shot cortisone into the carpal bone in my left wrist, which I'd damaged in sparring three weeks ahead of the biggest fight of my life. 'You won't be able to punch with the hand for a week,' he told me. I knew what this meant. No way would I be fighting Jeff Lacy with one good hand, no way. Lacy was twenty-eight-years old and the IBF super middleweight title-holder. He had a 22–0 record and knockout power in both his fists. In America he was being hyped as the second coming of Mike Tyson. He even had the *Sports Illustrated* 'Six-Pack of the Year'. Of course, the voice on the other end of the phone didn't give a monkey's for his six-pack or his unbeaten record or my doom-and-gloom attitude.

'Joe, listen, if you don't want to fight, it's up to you. Pull out of the fight if that's what you want, but you have to realise that you're going to be a fucking laughing stock if you do.'

'What are you talking about? My hand's not right. You want me to get in the ring and box Jeff Lacy with a bad hand? Fight him one-handed?'

'You will beat the crap out of Jeff Lacy. Believe me because you don't believe in yourself. It doesn't matter about your wrist. It doesn't matter that you haven't sparred. Listen to me, it doesn't fucking matter. You're going to smash this guy. The guy is nothing but you're going to be a laughing stock if you cry off with your wrist injury.'

'What are you on about? I can't fucking hit the bag, never mind get in the ring and fight. Anyway, how could anyone fight with one hand in the biggest fight of his life? I'll fight him in a couple of months when I'm 100 per cent fit. OK?'

'Forget it, Joe. If you don't fight this fight now, it won't happen. It won't come around again and you'll never get another fight like this. Besides, this will be the easiest fight you ever had because he's made for you.'

'Why are you saying that? I can't win this fight with one hand.'

'Joe, if you're not going to fight this fight, you might as well retire. You'll lose all credibility. Lacy won't come back. He won't touch you. You'll be damaged goods. You are going to be a laughing stock. You won't get another big fight for the rest of your career. This is your fight, and this is going to make you. If you fight this fight, you'll get respect. Win it and you will have everything you ever wanted to achieve from the time you first put on a pair of boxing gloves. Even if you lose, people will respect you for fighting the guy. You need to fight this fight or you know what people will remember you as? They'll remember you as a fucking chicken. Is that what you want?'

'A fucking chicken? What are you on about?'

'. . .'

'Are you there? . . . Are you still there, Dad? . . . Fucking tunnels . . .'

Sometimes I get up in the morning and I ask myself, 'Why am I doing this? Why am I in boxing? I don't want to box. I'm bored with it all. I really don't want to do this any more.' The politics makes boxing a shit sport and it can be horribly cruel. I can't believe that Muhammad Ali was allowed to fight against Larry Holmes and Trevor Berbick in his last two fights. I watched him being interviewed by Michael Parkinson after the Holmes fight and his words were heavy and slurred. He didn't sound like the Ali the whole world had come to know. And he still had one more fight. How sickening is that? When I listen to Evander Holyfield speak I feel sad. Holyfield won the world heavyweight championship, regained it and he's made over £100 million in his career. Yet, at the age of forty-four, he's still boxing, continuing to get his head punched in, and I listen to him speak in interviews and his words are slurred. Why is he doing it? How can he be allowed to box when we know what happened to Ali and countless others who fought too long? Will they let him fight until he's walking and talking like Ali? In ten years' time Holyfield might not know his own name.

Mickey Duff once told me a story about Joe Bugner. He was sitting in a sauna back at his hotel after challenging Ali for the world heavyweight title and Mickey asked him why he hadn't really tried to win, he had only tried to survive. 'Making the money is one thing,' Joe replied. 'Then I've got to be able to count it.' When I'm retired I want to be able to do the same.

Would I retire now if I was financially secure? Possibly. I don't miss boxing when I'm not fighting. I don't miss the training. It's the boredom that gets the better of me. I miss doing 'something', and the reality is that I've been doing this since I was eight years old. What else am I going to do? Boxing is what I know. When I'm in training and my weight is down I love it. I love running up and down the hills I've trained on since I was a boy, building up my fitness and stamina. I love going about my work in the gym and hitting the bags and the pads. *Bah-bah-bah-bah-bah.* The sound, the smell, the sweat dripping onto the floor, this is who I am. This is me. I find myself when I'm in the ring. I find contentment. It's what I'm good at and it gives me satisfaction knowing that I can make other people happy too. My kids are especially proud. Connor, my youngest son, says to me, 'Dad, I don't want you to retire. I want you always to be world champion.' As far as he's concerned, I'm the best fighter in the world. Superman.

But I don't always think about winning. I could lose, and that's what I think about which is why I've pulled out of fights when I felt that, with the injuries, I was leaving myself with too much to do. I wanted to pull out of the fight with Lacy. I didn't want to fight him. My hand was gone and I was convinced there was no way I could box with one hand. I could get battered. That's when my dad's psychology came into play. He's been my trainer since the day I first put on a pair of boxing gloves. He's also a great judge of fights and fighters. He's my best pal, a total pain in the arse sometimes but I love him to bits. He knew exactly what was going on in my head and he laid everything on the line.

'It was one of those fights – even if Joe had lost, just the fact that he went in the ring would have been an achievement. Not getting in there would have destroyed his career. He would have had no legacy.

He had performed badly in recent fights. He had also pulled out of fights twice or three times. Now Lacy? People are gullible and they would have drawn their own conclusions. Joe's unbeaten record would have meant nothing. This was the fight he needed to leave people with no option but to recognise that he's a special fighter. He had no choice. "Pull out of the fight and you'll be a laughing stock for the rest of your life," I told him. "Whether you get knocked out or not, it doesn't matter. Just by fighting him, you're proving all that you need to prove. If you're not in that ring on 4 March, you're history. But believe me, Joe Calzaghe will always fight a good fight. You're good enough to destroy this guy. Box your fight, you'll destroy him because he's just Jeff Lacy, a guy who is made for you. From the first round you'll out-think this guy and you'll outbox him. It will be the easiest fight of your career. He has to go through five different moves just to throw one punch because he's so muscle-bound and laboured but you can throw five punches in one single movement. It will be easy, Joe, believe me." I had a few of these conversations with him and so did Frank Warren. Barry McGuigan came down to the gym to film some footage for ITV and he told him the same. Eventually, it began to sink in.' – Enzo Calzaghe

Four days before the fight we travelled to Manchester by train. That morning I woke up, looked out across the garden and saw a blanket of snow outside. Suddenly, I had this very calm feeling. I love snow, always have since I was a kid, and the scene outside that morning convinced me this was my destiny. Throughout the build-up I'd been nervous. I wasn't sleeping well. I tried to get my body clock adjusted to the scheduled time of the first bell, so I was staying awake until 2 a.m. I'd train for an hour and go to bed, hoping to wake up again at midday. But it never worked out that way. I was waking up at 8 a.m., unable to get back to sleep, then I was becoming knackered from trying to stay awake at night, but I just couldn't stay in bed any morning past nine. I woke up dreaming about the fight and I was worried. Yet on the morning we set out for Manchester this total calm came over me. All of my demons were gone. I was totally relaxed. It was like every bit of pressure was taken off me. My dad couldn't believe how calm I was. Normally, I'm uptight in the days before a fight but the two of us played cards on the train with my uncle Sergio and joked and laughed all the way into Manchester Piccadilly. It was as if we were going on our holidays.

Winning is everything, it's all that matters to me. This is why I've made my career in boxing. I could have earned more money if I had fought in the Nigel Benn and Chris

Eubank era in the early 1990s but I could have taken some beatings then too. Look at what happened to Michael Watson, and to Gerald McClellan and the state Benn was in after his savage fight with McClellan at the London Arena, pissing blood, unable to get out of a bathtub without being helped. I wouldn't want to be in a fight like that or in some of the wars Eubank was in. I haven't had the same rivalry but only because I've proved myself to be so much better than everyone else in the super middleweight division in the past decade.

To me, boxing is a sport. I don't step in the ring to damage my health or to do damage to someone else. I have no desire to come out pissing blood just so I can say that I fought in a war. I've had hard fights, I've had to go down in the trenches. Eubank gave me hell for twelve rounds, but I don't fight to get beaten up. I don't fight to get hit with a thousand punches on my head just so I can say, 'Look at what a hard man I am.' What does that mean? What kind of boast is that? The reason I fight is simple: I like to win. I see boxing as an art. Hit and not be hit. Yes, I can take a hard punch to the chin, I've been cut and I've been knocked down, but I would never quit. I have the heart of a fighter. I don't crave to be in a war, however, for the sake of being in a war. It is simply about winning.

People would look sometimes and say, 'There's Joe Calzaghe in another shit fight,' without knowing the circumstances. They didn't think about the psychological problems of going through a divorce as I'm in the ring struggling and getting knocked down by Kabery Salem. They didn't realise that my hands were so bad that I wasn't able to spar for fights against David Starie, Rick Thornberry and Robin Reid. I won those fights and I'm proud of those wins. Fighters like Charles Brewer, Byron Mitchell, Richie Woodhall were all world champions. They were former world champions when I fought them and in some people's minds that's what seemed to count but your destiny is not always in your hands. Did I want to fight Robin Reid when he held the WBC super middleweight belt? Of course I did. I was screaming for the fight but Reid didn't want it and then he was beaten by Sugarboy Malinga. The belt rapidly changed hands between Woodhall, Markus Beyer and finally Glen Catley, whose promoter, Chris Sanigar, said he didn't even want Catley to spar me, never mind fight me. This is what can happen in boxing and, for me, that always left something missing, a single fight to look back on to show everybody exactly who I am. I needed the right opponent to prove myself and, finally, get the public acclaim.

It was frustrating that fights against Roy Jones and Bernard Hopkins, two of the great names in and around my weight division, never happened. I was too dangerous for my own good and I began to think that I would never get my career-defining fight. The fight with Hopkins was actually agreed in 2002 but he pulled out and I got used to that kind of disappointment. It seemed I wasn't a big enough name in America for the likes of Jones and Hopkins to take the risk. I accepted it but I always hoped that the recognition would come eventually. I used to look at my situation and compare it to Marvelous Marvin Hagler, a great champion who didn't have his biggest fights against Roberto Duran, Tommy Hearns and Sugar Ray Leonard until he was in his thirties. The same with Hopkins. His situation was similar to mine. He was a long-reigning title-holder in the middleweight division, not really given a lot of credit. He'd never beaten any great fighters until well into his thirties when he got big fights against Felix Trinidad and Oscar De La Hoya and won them both. So I realised, as I reached my thirties, that there was still hope. All I could do was fight and keep winning.

I established myself as the legitimate world champion at super middleweight. The WBO title, which I won from Eubank, may be considered the least of the four major belts in America but the fighter makes the belt. I've defended against six world champions and I've outlasted the fighters who won other belts during my reign. What more could I have done? Yet until Lacy came across from America I was never given my dues. Maybe I needed to feel fear to bring out my best. I wasn't scared of Lacy but I was fearful of what he could do. This was a fight I could really lose and the fear of defeat spurred me on. It was the fear of losing and the pain that would bring. Every time I was defeated as an amateur I cried. It hurt me that bad. I hope I wouldn't cry now that I'm a grown man but even today I would be crushed by defeat. Failure is a horrible feeling and the fear of failure motivates me. I don't fear anything about getting hurt, that's nothing, it goes with the territory. I just don't think that it's all right to fail. It's not about what other people think. It's about how I feel. I know that almost everybody will lose some time and there's no shame in that but I'm a winner. This is who I am. Every person has to be honest and true to himself or herself and the one thing I would hate above anything else is being in a fight in which I didn't give my all. That's why I was so concerned about the injury to my wrist. That's why I didn't want to fight. I didn't want to beat myself. I wouldn't be able to live with that.

Every man who climbs through the ropes into a boxing ring deserves respect. From the journeyman who fights in the small halls to the guy whose name goes up in lights on the Strip in Las Vegas, anybody who has that courage to do what we do. Some fighters fall and we say that they swallowed it but I can't judge them. They have mortgages to pay and children to feed. Maybe they're being clever by not take a beating, but I'm a different creature. I'm a champion. I'd have to be nailed to the floor because my nature is to fight to the end. I have a tremendous amount of belief in myself but before every single fight I think about the big 'what if'. What if I lost?

Three weeks before stepping into the ring with Lacy I went out for a meal in Cardiff with my girlfriend, Jo-Emma. I had tested my wrist that day and it was knackered. I'd had the injection but I still couldn't punch and I told myself that I wouldn't be fighting. I drank a bottle of wine with my meal, came home and had another glass.

The next day I didn't train and I told my dad that I wasn't fighting. 'I'm not fighting. I'm not going to fight this guy and risk everything,' I said. I felt that I needed to be 100 per cent. 'This is meant to be my hardest week of sparring and I haven't sparred. I can't even punch the bags.' My wrist was hurting and I sent my sparring partners home. There was no way back.

For some reason I still went jogging at 2 a.m. on Kendon Hill, five miles in the freezing cold, the ground all covered in snow. My dad followed me in his car with the fog lights turned on. 'You are fitter than you've ever been, Joe,' he shouted out. 'You will beat this guy.' I wasn't listening but I ran at the same time the next night and again the night after that, through the snow with my dad following me. 'Just be Joe Calzaghe,' he shouted. 'Joe Calzaghe and Jeff Lacy will not even be a contest.'

In the evenings I was watching tapes of Lacy, rewinding them over and over, watching this guy destroy Scott

Pemberton in two rounds and knock Robin Reid through the ropes. In my mind I was building him up into the bloody Predator but I was underestimating myself and making Lacy into something more than he was. 'I watched one of those Lacy fights last night too,' my dad would say. 'Two rounds, that was enough. Then I took out the tape and I put on Joe Calzaghe and I had a smile on my face. Joe, you are going to pin this boy against the wall. It will be the easiest fight you've ever had.'

I still hadn't sparred. The last time I didn't spar properly was ahead of my fights with Reid, Thornberry and Starie and I looked awful. Then I got a sparring partner in two weeks before the fight, my last week of training, to do some light work. My wrist wasn't 100 per cent. It wasn't even 75 per cent but it was OK. So I made up for the week of sparring that I missed three weeks before the bout. I did six or eight rounds a day but it was light, almost tap-sparring. I didn't want to risk my wrist because it was still sore and I was still stressed. This horrible anxiety had built up because I felt that I wasn't ready and I thought that Lacy was going to eat me up if I wasn't prepared. I thought I would fail. I was making things worse than they really were.

I've said to Joe many times that getting him in the ring is a real pain but when he's in the ring he's an animal. They would have to kill him to beat him. Then it's not a problem. But getting him in there can be a big problem. – Enzo Calzaghe

The thought of losing was making me feel ill. Everything I had worked for my whole life was riding on this fight. I sparred every day of that week, two weeks out from the fight, just tapping with my left hand because I couldn't punch hard but at least I was able to throw it. I wrapped loads of tape around it, so that I almost had a cast underneath my glove. Slowly the hand improved and so did my head.

'I'm going to fight this fight,' I said to my dad towards the end of the week, eight or nine days before we got in the ring. It was almost 3 a.m. and we were just back from a run. 'Joe,' he replied with a big smile, 'I never thought that you weren't.'

Lacy and his promoter, Gary Shaw, thought that I was washed up. They underestimated me because I had struggled so badly fighting one-handed against Evans Ashira after I broke my left hand in the fourth round. So the Lacy fight had to be postponed and they thought I was scared.

Joe Calzaghe is a disgrace. I don't believe this injury is legit. He never, ever wanted to fight Jeff Lacy. I suspected all along that Calzaghe didn't want any of this. I never thought they'd fight us, I always suspected it was all a bluff. There are some fighters who are willing to fight anyone, any time, and there are fighters who just don't fit in that warrior category. Joe Calzaghe is one of the latter.

– Gary Shaw, 12 September 2005

Showtime, the American cable TV network which broadcast the fight in the United States, thought they had another Tyson on their hands and Lacy reckoned he would just turn up and walk right through me. He came to Manchester with a false sense of security, then something hit him. We came face to face at the pre-fight press conference and he saw my confidence and suddenly he was faced with the truth. He could sense at that moment the size of his task. He wasn't in Florida any more with Gary Shaw tapping him on his back and all his homies and friends telling him, 'You're the man!' He was in a bloody cold city in the north of England a long way from home where no one gave a shit about Jeff Lacy, me least of all. I knew what I had to do, I had to step up to the plate on the most important night of my life. It didn't matter that I was going to pull out less than three weeks before the fight because I'd injured my hand. It didn't matter that I'd actually made the decision and had to be talked round by my dad. None of that was relevant. The only thing that people were going to take away from this was how I did. A whole career came down to one fight. A lesser man might have crumbled under the pressure, but I produced the performance of my life. I did it when the chips were down, and not many people can say that.

All who watched Calzaghe outspeed, outthink and punishingly outbox the American through every one of 12 rounds had no option – regardless of how far the ability to make comparisons stretched into the past – but to recognise what they were seeing as one of the greatest displays of superb technique, confidence and fighting intelligence a British boxer has delivered in a major contest. Lacy came in with the IBF title and a reputation for overwhelming aggression. He left chastened, knowing and cruelly persuaded that the unbeaten 33-year-old who had tormented him is the best 12-stone fighter in the world.

– Hugh McIlvanney, *Sunday Times*, 12 March 2006

Some people told me it was the best night of their lives and doors suddenly opened for me. I was even asked to compete on *Strictly Come Dancing* shortly afterwards, but that's not me. I'm not into the celebrity scene and going to big movie premieres. I'm a boxer, a guy from the Welsh valleys. That's not to say I lock myself in solitude, I socialise but I don't go out of my way to be seen. Being seen with this person or that person just doesn't interest me. I'm not into being a superstar. I'm just a champion fighter. That's all that matters to me. When people get the two confused, that's when they mess up and get distracted. I keep my feet on the ground, I live in the same area in which I grew up and I train like I've always trained. I train like the challenger, even after twenty title defences, because every fight is still another challenge to me.

When I stick that gumshield in my mouth and they ring the bell it's all about pride. I have a ferocious will not to get beaten and that's what keeps driving me. You have to be a special sort of person to be undefeated for seventeen years in any discipline, especially boxing, but this is what I was born to do and sometimes it seems like it was all mapped out for me.

ROUND TWO
Fighting Men Through and Through

Giuseppe Calzaghe was fourteen years old and fearless. His father was a builder and Giuseppe grew up in that environment, in the village of Bancali, outside Sassari, on the island of Sardinia, working with mortar and stones for much of his life. People in the village called him an animal because he was strong as an ox. It was said that he could carry five big bags of cement on his back and he was tough. When the Second World War broke out he decided that he wanted to fight for his country, even though he was still a boy.

His father, Antonio, refused him permission to go to war but young Giuseppe was stubborn. He went to his uncle Comitto who forged his brother's signature on identity papers and presented the papers to the authorities to enlist in the Italian navy, two years before he was the legal age. He never spoke much of his experiences in battle but he was captured in Spain and spent more than a year as a prisoner of war in Majorca before he returned home. He lives in Sassari today, eighty-two years old, no longer as big or as strong as he was but he still has thick wrists and shovel-like hands. I'm proud of my grandfather. The soldiers of Sassari are renowned for their courage, immortalised in the stories of the Sassari Brigade, and my grandad, I know, is a fighting man through and through.

After the war he became a policeman in Torino, where he met my grandmother, Victoria. At that time in Italy a policeman wasn't allowed to marry before the age of twenty-eight but when my nan became pregnant they had to bring forward the wedding. Unfortunately, it leaked out and he was discharged from the police force. He was twenty-one and my nan was seventeen and they needed some means to support a family. Many Italians had come to England at the end of the war, some to the coal mines in Wales and Scotland as well, but a lot of them ended up in Bedford, where there is still a large Italian population. There they worked in the brickworks, which is what my grandad set his hands to, having travelled from Sardinia, where he and Nan and their small family had lived for a couple of years back in his home village.

My dad was two years old when they sailed across, my uncle Antonio was four and my uncle Uccio was a baby. They settled easily in Bedford, where my aunt Alba was born, yet my grandad and nan always thought of Sardinia as home and after eleven years they returned home to Bancali with their young family. Dad had become

19

friendly at school with a boy called Joe Bugner, the former British and European heavyweight champion from the seventies, whose family had moved over from Hungary at the same time. Joe's sister, Margaret, was in Dad's class and Joe was in Uccio's class and was always over at the house, messing around with Dad and his brothers. In fact, Dad used to kick his ass in the schoolyard all the time. Another brother, Sergio, was born shortly after my grandparents returned to Sardinia and it's funny that today Dad and his three brothers all live in England or Wales while Alba, the only one in the family born here, lives back in Sardinia. Gianfranco Zola, the former Chelsea and Italy footballer, used to stay regularly in her house, after games, when he was a young lad playing for Torres before he moved to Cagliari. For a short time uncle Manlio, Alba's husband, was president of Torres, who played in the Italian Serie C, something like the Conference here, and Dad was an apprentice at the club, playing in the youth team with Communardo Niccolai, who featured in the 1970 World Cup in Mexico. As a kid, his dream was always to become a footballer, but my grandad preferred to have him box at every party in the village, entertaining the grown-ups by fighting other kids. He never had to fight though. He was too clever and beat his opponents by outboxing them.

Dad never went to school in Italy and he couldn't speak a word of Italian when he first returned to Bancali, but at the age of fourteen he found work as a butcher. There was no such thing as signing on the dole. Over the next few years he did a number of jobs – barman, chef, cleaner, clothes shop assistant; he even took up singing and playing bass guitar with his uncle Vicenzo – before he went off to do his national service in the air force. Dad was almost twenty when he left his station in Milan. It was the hippy era, late sixties, early seventies, he grew his hair long and decided to see a bit of the world. With his guitar on his back and a small suitcase in his hand, he left Bancali and set out on a tour of Europe over the next couple of years, busking on the streets wherever he went, sleeping out on park benches whenever he had to. Music was something he hated at first because his father had pushed him into playing in his uncle Vicenzo's band, but he had a talent for it and he got to see cities like Paris and Amsterdam. He enjoyed life on the road and, eventually, he made it to England to visit his aunt Nina who lived in Bournemouth. Not long after that he met my mum.

I arrived in Bournemouth late at night and, by chance, bumped into my brother, Antonio, who I hadn't seen for two years. He gave me directions to Auntie's house and when I got there she and Uncle Peppino were loading up their Austin car. 'We're leaving tonight for Sardinia. Come home with us,' she said. I told her I couldn't. 'No way. I promised my dad I'd be a millionaire when I went back to Bancali.' She was able to fix me up with a little job at the Double O Egg restaurant and I ate and slept there, but Bournemouth wasn't for me. I headed for Southampton, got the boat to Le Havre and started hitch-hiking, intending to go back to Italy. Somehow I ended up in a little French village on the outskirts of Dijon – I'd been drinking and had no idea how I got there – and got woken up under a lamp post by a gendarme. I told him I was on my way to Italy and he pointed me in the general direction. So I started thumbing again, still the worse for wear, and finished up all the way back in bloody Le Havre! For some reason I decided to get the boat back across to Southampton, finished up again in Bournemouth and met a guy there who said he was going to Cardiff, so off I went with him. We arrived in the afternoon, pulled into a Wimpy restaurant to get ourselves something to eat and that's where I met Jackie Phillips. She took our order and got cheesed off with me because I kept changing my mind about having coffee or tea but, for me, it was love at first sight. She looked Italian with her dark hair and I just got the feeling that she was familiar. So I got cheeky and I asked her out and we met that evening after she finished work. I met her mum after a couple of weeks and we were married four weeks later. Everything just felt right. – Enzo Calzaghe

My mum is from Markham, a village in south Wales, which is about three miles from where I now live in Blackwood. Markham was a mining town here in the valleys and, although the colliery was closed in 1986, it still has that same sense of community. People know one another and their roots are here and in the surrounding area. My mum's dad was a miner. He died when she was nine years old after suffering an illness that probably came from working down the pits for years. My nan, Rebecca, was a lovely woman. Sadly, she died before I won anything in my professional boxing career, a few months before my first son, Joe, was born in 1995. She took a real interest in everything going on around her and I'd always pop round to her house, which was here in Blackwood, the day after a fight. 'I didn't see you boxing last night,' she'd say. All she had was a little black-and-white television with one channel that worked, and, bless her, if she could, she would have enjoyed following my career.

For a while after they got married Mum and Dad moved to Sardinia but Mum didn't settle, so they came back, to Bournemouth and then to London. Dad worked in a factory, making nails and screws, and had a waiting job at the B&B they lived in, on St Mark's Road in

Hammersmith. Mum was a secretary at the offices of Twentieth Century Fox and they continued to live in London after I was born in Hammersmith Hospital on 23 March 1972 in the same ward where a certain Frank Bruno first saw daylight. 'Son of My Father', a song which was originally written in Italian, had just been knocked off number one in the charts.

Dad decided to move back to Sardinia towards the end of 1972 and for a year or more we lived in my grandad's house in Bancali, which he'd built with his own hands. I'm very proud of my Italian heritage. I love Italian food and I love the culture and the way the people dress. Rome has to be the most beautiful city I've ever seen and I'm fascinated by the history, the Colosseum, the old glory of the Eternal City. There's not much of the Colosseum left but I've often imagined what it must have been like for the gladiators fighting one another to the death and facing the lions in that great amphitheatre. Sardinia has its own separate identity. It even has its own flag. The island was attacked and raided for centuries, so Sardinians are resilient and proud and sentimental. I've been back to Sardinia every year of my life and it will always have a special place in my heart. In my grandad's house is the little cupboard drawer that was used as my cot when I was a baby and pride of place goes to my World Boxing Organisation (WBO) belt that I brought back and presented to my grandad after I had made my ninth title defence against Will McIntyre in Copenhagen. Family and roots have always been important to me. I'm proud to be Welsh and to represent Wales but I have Italian blood too. I'm proud of my name – it's such an unusual name – and I'm proud to be Italian and Sardinian especially. My grandad's little house in Bancali was really my first home.

I don't know if my fiery character comes from the Italian side of my family or the Welsh side but my mum can be more fiery than my dad. I'm sure he's not the only person who has thought she might be Italian! When Mum said that she wanted to move back home my dad didn't argue and agreed to return to Markham. We moved in with my nan and lived with her for three years before the council built a new housing estate in Pentwynmawr, where we were the first family to move in. Mum and Dad still live there, on the edge of the village, about thirty miles from Cardiff. Over the years the house has been renovated and it's a better place to live now but I was happy growing up in the area. Like most kids, I was very active and the surrounding countryside meant that I was heavily involved in outdoor activities. I was at my happiest playing football, which was my first love. I used to play all day in the summer months, from first thing in the morning until it got dark. Left side of midfield was my position and I was pretty skilful with a good engine. I could run all day but I lacked pace, unlike my dad, who was an out-and-out winger when he was young, with great acceleration. My strength was my stamina and I built up a tremendous level of fitness. If you've sat on your arse for most of your life, you'll probably never reach the same peak of physical fitness as someone who has been active throughout. I was active all the time – if I wasn't on the football pitch, I was playing hide-and-seek with my friends – and my heart and lungs developed a tremendous capacity for physical exercise.

Of course, there wasn't much in the way of PlayStations or computers in those days, which helped too. Everything was basic. My dad worked as a conductor on the buses and my mum was a housewife. She stayed at home to bring up me and my two sisters, Sonia and Melissa, and it was hard, as it was for a lot of people in those days. There were no silver spoons in Pentwynmawr but we never went hungry. My mum cooked delicious steak and kidney pies and other great food and Dad proved more than a match. He used to come home and rustle up a curry out of nothing. I never asked him what the ingredients were and, if I'd known, I probably wouldn't have eaten what he served up but they were great curries. Most days however, we had pasta with a beautiful sauce. My uncle Sergio went to catering college to train as a chef, yet he cannot make the same kind of meal as my dad. He just always had the knack. Actually,

Sergio, Uccio and my dad are all great cooks. They take after my grandad, another brilliant cook. Unfortunately, although I don't make a bad pasta, I've been unable to continue the family tradition. What can I say? I must have missed those lessons.

I don't know why but I cried my eyes out on my first day at Pentwynmawr Primary School. I was a big baby, the only kid in the class who didn't stop crying all day long. Mrs Watson, the teacher, tried to settle me down, putting me into one of those cars we had that were made out of red wooden boxes, but I just kept crying, like a mummy's boy. Perhaps I had a premonition of a painful episode that was soon to come.

I wasn't a loud kid. I was actually shy and timid. My sisters and I fought a lot but that was mainly because I was outnumbered. We loved each other. Every Christmas we went carol singing together and we could harmonise beautifully. Those were different times. We were able to go around to houses not having to worry about who would open the door or what type of person they were. I would never allow my kids to go carol singing or trick-or-treating now but back then it was all more innocent. It was beautiful.

My dreams were played out on the football pitch. I played at school and started to train with Pentwynmawr Under 10s. Whenever I wasn't picked and was left on the subs' bench I cried. I just loved the game so much that it was a real loss for me not to be playing when I had the chance. 'Why do you keep leaving me out of the team?' I would ask the coach, and if I see him now I nearly always tell him, 'Vid, you left me mentally scarred as a kid,' and I'm only half kidding. I was always a sub. Then Gordon Phillips took over and I started to make the team, so the next big challenge was to score my first goal. It took me a while but it was my holy grail. Dad would tell me on the morning of a game that if I got a goal, he'd give me 50p. I used to pray, 'Please, God, get me a goal, just one goal.' It meant so much to me to score and I remember my first goal vividly. We were playing a team called Cefn Forest and it was a scrappy, goalmouth scramble. I managed to toe-poke the ball into the net but I might as well have scored the greatest goal ever. Suddenly, I was off celebrating like Tardelli at the World Cup. I must have run half the length of the pitch before I heard a voice from the sidelines: 'Joe, what are you doing? Get back. Get back.' But it was too late. By the time I looked round the other team had scored – their fourth in a 6–1 win. But I didn't give a monkey's. I'd scored a goal. That's all that mattered. I should have realised then that I'm not a team player.

I scored twenty goals in my first full season as a regular player for Pentwynmawr Under 10s and fourteen the following season, a good return for a midfield player. I looked forward to every game like it was Christmas morning. I remember staring out the window one morning and everywhere was covered in snow. There must have been a foot of snow on the ground and anyone would have been able to tell you that there wasn't going to be a game of football played. But off I went to Gordon's house, almost two miles away, just to make sure. I had a thin pair of socks on my feet and trainers that had holes in the bottom of them and by the time I got to Gordon's my toes were so cold they were numb and my fingers were the same. Needless to say, Gordon told me there would be no game, so I turned round and ran home, crying as I was running because my feet were freezing. No matter the weather, if there was a game to be played, I didn't want to miss it.

But much as I loved football, I discovered that my real talent was in my hands. I was eight years old when Dad bought me one of these Sugar Ray Leonard punchballs. I was still more into football then but I began to punch this ball and I liked the feeling. My first 'bag' was actually a piece of rolled-up carpet that my dad had brought into the house one day. I used to stand there and punch it, left hooks, right hands, uppercuts, crosses, shifting my weight on my feet, ripping into it like I imagined Hagler would do but always with Leonard's speed. Leonard, Hagler and Ali were the fighters that my dad most admired. Football and boxing were his big sports and he kept encouraging me and after a while he began to notice that I had some

29

skill. I would move around the boxing ball as if it was an imaginary opponent, just as you're supposed to do.

The first boxer I remember was Sugar Ray Leonard. I couldn't say his name properly and called him Sugar Ray Lemon. I can recall clearly in my mind the '*No Mas*' fight when Leonard made Roberto Duran quit in the eighth round of their rematch in New Orleans. *No mas*, he said. No more. I couldn't believe what Leonard did. He was like a clown, winding up the bolo punch with his right hand and hitting Duran in the face with his left. He made me laugh because I didn't understand the psychology. I just saw a guy pulling faces and sticking his chin out while the other guy was unable to hit him. Duran just gave up in the end and it was unbelievable.

Marvelous Marvin Hagler was another fighter I liked. I used to watch him and get my gloves on and start punching the walls. While Leonard was a showman, Hagler brought out the aggression in me. I'd still never been to a boxing gym so I used to get out a cushion and Dad taught me how to stand and how to punch. I was ten when Dad took me to the gym for the first time, Newbridge Amateur Boxing Club. The trainer was Paul Williams and he had an assistant trainer called Dennis Rogers. The boxing gym was a big blue shed and the first thing I saw was these men punching the bags and what struck me was the loud *boom boom boom* as the fighters hit those bags and sparred in the ring. The noise scared me. I couldn't skip so they gave me a pair of gloves and I started punching the bag. Dennis tried to show me how to hit it, but I was already into it and within a couple of minutes Paul Williams walked over and said to my dad, 'Where has your son been boxing then?' He thought I had come from another gym and that I'd already had some fights because of the way I could hit and move but I'd learnt everything I knew from my dad. People think my dad knows nothing about boxing. That's what they believe. But from the first day I went to the boxing gym in Newbridge, where Paul Williams took training Mondays, Wednesdays and Fridays, my dad trained me every day of the week. At home he would take the cushion off the settee and put it around his waist and I would hit it as if he was holding the pads. As I got older, he used to have me punch his hand and, until I was seventeen and really began to grow, he was my best sparring partner. I used to have more trouble sparring him than anybody because he knew my style. He'd wear a protective cup and when I started getting bigger he put a headguard on and he was busy, throwing good combinations. I've never been one to bash up sparring partners, so with my dad it was more feinting and fencing, picking him off and parrying. We would tap each other really, neither of us hitting hard, but it certainly helped to hone skills and reflexes.

People are amazed whenever they see us working on the pads. We used to do our own combinations and I get my hand speed from the work rate I've always kept up on the pads with my dad. From the age of eleven, I've always had fast hands. I've got my own style and sometimes I throw so many punches, like Roy Jones does, like Leonard used to do, two incredibly fast fighters. But you can't turn over your hand and add power to every punch, if you're throwing them in fast bunches. When you're throwing ten punches in two seconds it's just impossible.

The first sparring I had was with Jason Rogers, Dennis's son. I gave him a bleeding nose and I was hooked. I loved sparring and I was good at it. I didn't like the skipping and the hitting the bags as much.

I played for the Under 10s on a Saturday morning and sometimes on a Wednesday. In the summer I had training in Newbridge on a Wednesday but when we had a match I wanted to play football. 'I don't want to box,' I would say, 'I want to play football.' One Wednesday night I skipped boxing training for an evening game. At the end of the trial I realised that I was never going to be an exceptional footballer. I was winning fights and doing well in boxing, so I decided I would stick with that. I loved football but after Under 12s I gave up. I wouldn't have made it as a top-flight footballer because I didn't have enough pace. Perhaps I could have been a half-decent footballer but I wouldn't have made the top grade. Yet what I lacked in my feet I gained in my hands. I knocked football on the head and threw all my energy into boxing.

*

I can see it and hear it still, the name-calling and kids in the classroom chucking things at me and laughing. I can feel the sweat rolling down my back and the humiliation. I was embarrassed and I just sat in the corner and bottled everything up. At break times, when the other kids went to play football, I would sit on a wall, completely by myself. It was one kid who caused all the trouble but, eventually, no one in the class would speak to me and it lasted for months. I was tormented. Now I'd just laugh it off, but to a young teenager, being bullied can seem like the end of the world.

There was never any problem at Pentwynmawr Primary. I liked school, did my homework and I made friends easily. The bother began when I changed schools at the age of eleven and instead of staying in Newbridge, where all of my friends were going to the local school, I was sent to Oakdale Comprehensive, about six miles away. It was outside my catchment area and I never really wanted to go but our next-door neighbour's son went there and Mum thought Oakdale was a better school. I enjoyed my first and second years, the second year even better than the first. I was a bit unruly when I started, messing about with a couple of kids, giving them dead arms because I was an amateur boxer, I guess. But I wasn't bullying them or threatening them. That was never my way. It was just a laugh. I did quite well at my studies when I concentrated and I was beginning to settle in when, in my third year, my friends just deserted me. It was like an exodus. It was horrible. Even my next-door neighbour stopped speaking to me, a boy I'd grown up with and known my whole life. Dave, a friend of mine through the boxing, wasn't speaking to me either. Something happened involving a new kid from South Africa but I've never understood what really went on. All I know is that all of a sudden no one in my class was talking to me and I hadn't a clue why. My nightmare at school had begun.

The abuse was mostly verbal, not physical, but it tore away at me. In reality, it was petty stuff but it was also an orchestrated campaign and it got to me. Even though I was boxing, I was small for my age and skinny, matchstick-thin, and I was quiet, therefore an easy target. Physically, I was sixteen or seventeen before I really developed and was always smaller than the other kids in my year. Occasionally, older and bigger guys would try it on because I was a boxer, so I became like a little hermit and just sat away in the corner. I couldn't bond with anybody. I stayed within myself all the time. If I'd grown up more quickly, probably none of it would have happened and my schoolwork went completely down the pan as a result. I just sat in the class unable to concentrate, worried all the time, completely stressed out and I couldn't take in anything that I was being taught. I just retreated into a shell, for the only way I could handle it was to shut myself off.

'What's wrong? What's happened here?' I asked Dave, the young boxer. 'I thought you were a good friend of mine.' But he didn't want to know. Then a short kid called Miller came up out of the blue and said that he wanted to fight me.

'Meet me after school,' he said.

'I don't want to fight you,' I told him.

'I'll come to your house.'

'Well, come to my house then and have a go.'

The next thing I knew, there were thirty kids who had turned up on bikes outside the front of our house one weekend, all of them looking for me. My dad went out and took me and this kid Miller, said that we were going for a walk and told the rest of the kids to stay there. I found out later that their plan was to jump me, so Miller wouldn't walk anywhere on his own. He needed the protection of his mates, if he was going to fight me.

Joe was being bullied for a long time before we knew anything about it. He never came home and told us anything that suggested he was feeling so low. He just kept it to himself. Then one weekend morning a large group of boys came down on their bikes. Me and his dad were here and, at first, Joe said they wanted him to come out to play but what

35

they wanted to do was hurt him. Enzo realised what was happening and went out and said, "OK, one by one," but they all just scarpered. Before that incident I never could have told that Joe was being bullied. Boys go through their teenage years and sometimes they're not too keen to open up. – Jackie Calzaghe

Mum and Dad both asked me if I wanted to change schools but I said I didn't and decided to just stick it out. When I look back now I ask myself, 'Why didn't I just move schools?' To this day I don't understand why I put myself through that hell. I never skipped school either, even though I had to walk almost three miles just to get the bus. Why didn't I? I was learning nothing anyway because my mind was switched off but I made a masochist of myself. Thinking back, I should have gone to the other school in Newbridge when I had the chance, but maybe it's just not in me to be a quitter.

This went on for the whole of my third year but the people who were behind it all didn't bother me so much in my fourth year because they got no reaction any more. I kept myself to myself and stayed away from the kids who pissed me off. But the abuse affected me to such an extent that I didn't devote any time or energy to my schoolwork and didn't sit any GCSE exams. It was 1988 and the European football championships were being held in Germany that year so I just stayed at home and watched the games. The headmaster had written on one of my school reports: 'If Joe put half as much effort into school as he does into his boxing, he would be one of our top students.' But I was only ever able to go through the motions in class because of the stress of my third year. I just wasn't interested and lost so much during that time at school. I never recovered from it. I wasn't listening to the teachers because I still thought that someone was going to say something about me and, as soon as they would, I'd start churning up inside. In the end it made me stronger as a person and now I speak out about bullying. It can be a devastating position for a young person to be in but I tell kids that it happened to me, a guy who went on to become a world boxing champion, so maybe my experience will help some of the victims of bullying today. A lot of children are embarrassed and ashamed to tell anyone but it can happen to anybody.

I also tell kids, my own included, that they should never throw all their eggs in one basket though that's what I did. Boxing was escape. When I went to the gym, started sparring and hitting the bags, I was a different guy. I was left to concentrate on my training and my boxing. I had friends. So I was like two different characters, an introvert at school where no one would have guessed I was a boxer just to look at me, and outgoing and happy in the evening, joking with my friends from my old primary school as usual. I don't really know what lasting

37

psychological effects that bullying had on me but I went in for a very flamboyant style of boxing from a young age and, strangely, the ring was always a stress-free zone. I knew I had talent and my goal, my burning ambition, was to be a world champion. Dad could see that desire in me, almost from the start, and he always gave me confidence. Even as an amateur, I developed an aggressive, professional style. I planted my feet and threw hard uppercuts and body shots. In boxing you don't see many aggressive, come-forward southpaws. Normally, south-paws are quite cautious but I've always wanted to move in and fight. When the bullying was at its worst I remember that I went to see my careers teacher one day and she asked me how I wanted to earn a living. I told her I was a boxer and I was going to become a world champion. I was full of confidence, but she looked at me and laughed.

I never had many friends growing up but my best friend has always been my dad. He didn't drive a car for years, so most people in the valleys came to know him as 'the running man' because he walked and jogged everywhere and he still would, despite having a car now, if it wasn't for his knees. Dad has always been fit and if he had to go to Blackwood, three miles away from our home in Pentwynmawr, he would often have walked there and I was always with him. If I had a penny for every mile we've run and jogged and walked side by side over the years, I wouldn't still be boxing for a living. When I joined the boxing gym in Newbridge we used to walk the mile and a half there and back. I probably walked and ran ten miles most days, between going to the gym and getting out for the school bus, and this built up a good level of fitness and stamina. I didn't start driving until I was twenty-one, taking after Dad.

My earliest memories are of my dad playing in a little band with my uncle Uccio. They were always into music and used to practise in an upstairs bedroom, Dad on lead guitar, Uccio on vocals, and every weekend they went out to do a gig. Uccio lived just up the road in Blackwood, but he often stayed over when they came home. Uccio was a big part of my life growing up and so was music. Saturday night was 'Teddy boy' night, with Dad wearing a pair of those bloody awful winkle-picker boots, which had metal taps on the soles and long, pointed toes. Their only redeeming feature was that I could always hear him coming home. I'd be lying in bed and I'd hear this distinctive clicking sound along the road. 'Dad's almost home,' I'd say before running down the stairs to meet him and he'd let me stay up to watch *Match of the Day* or maybe a fight.

Eventually Uccio moved with his family to Milton Keynes, and this meant that Dad was away a lot with the band. Calling themselves 'Foreign Legion' and then 'Burgundy', they were working on a record contract and regularly played as supporting acts for bands like Bucks Fizz, the Barron Knights and Edwin Starr. There were times when I might see Dad only one day a week and I used to get lonely when he wasn't around. I was the only boy in the house, both my sisters were closer to Mum and, because of what was happening at school, sometimes I had a problem dealing with the loneliness. The boxing gym became a refuge and I took up hunting with a mate of mine called Kevin and got myself a ferret, which my mum hated because he stank the house out even though his cage was in the back garden. I used to go to the butcher's to get him bits of livers and lungs that were going to be chucked out and at the weekend me and Kevin would go into the fields looking for rabbit holes, throw down the nets and send in the ferret. We killed the rabbits by grabbing them and breaking their necks. Kevin had no problems killing and skinning the rabbits. He might even say he enjoyed it. My pleasure came from eating them and escaping from Jackson's farm, which was one of our favourite haunts, as Farmer Jackson came running and screaming after us. We often had to leave the ferret behind because he could be hours down the rabbit hole. When Dad came home he'd grill the rabbit and throw salt on it and we ate it like that, although never in front of Mum who hated the rabbits more than the ferret.

Funny, when I grew out of hunting rabbits I got myself a pet rabbit and cried when the wee thing died after only a couple of months. Dad was the same. He didn't like dogs and would never allow one about the house, but one day Mum brought home a beautiful dog, a cross between a sheepdog and a Lassie, who we called Bruce. The first time Dad came home and saw him he shouted, 'This is an outside animal.' He whacked Bruce to get him off the bed and cut his hand on his teeth. 'Serves you right, Dad,' I thought. It took a while for Dad to grow affectionate towards old Bruce. He wasn't one to sit down and stroke the dog or take him for walks. Instead he used to give out about him all the time, yet when Bruce died a couple of years ago Dad cried for him more than my mum did. Really we must be big softies at heart, me and Dad.

We spent some of our best days back then hitch-hiking between home and Milton Keynes. Dad might thumb a lift in the morning back home to see us and head up the road again the same day, so I used to love it when he took me with him. There could be snow lying by the sides of the road, both of us freezing, but we still made the journey, which we could sometimes do in as little as three or four hours. We always tried to stop by an orchard near Bristol, so that we could grab ourselves some big cooking apples to eat along the way. That was our lunch. Dad liked to take me because passing drivers would be more likely to take pity on a guy who had a young kid with him. Back then there would be a line of hitch-hikers by the side of the road, all looking to be taken somewhere. I went up a couple of times a month and enjoyed the trip. It was an adventure and I was with my dad, spending time with him, and I loved listening to him and Uccio and Serge performing onstage.

At one point Dad was going to move us all up to Milton Keynes to make life easier and so that we could be a family again. We were even ready to pick up the keys to our new house before Mum phoned the solicitors and told them that we wouldn't be moving. So Dad continued to do the commute and I kept going with him as often as I could. He played at the Apollo Theatre in London and supported Shirley Bassey. He even recorded with Paul Young just before Paul Young made it big. I thought he was going to make it into the charts and I told my friends but it just never happened for him. He made no money from it but that's what he wanted to be and that's what I wanted for him and me. However, soon we embarked on a new dream, one we've shared together every step of the way, most of it in a decrepit old shed in Newbridge where we've rowed, fallen out and not spoken to one another and forgotten it ever happened within minutes. Because we created something special in that place too.

ROUND THREE
Ti Faccio un Culo Cosi!

Nobody would ever have confused it with Emanuel Steward's Kronk Gym in Detroit or the Fifth Street Gym in Miami, where Muhammad Ali trained. Newbridge Amateur Boxing Club was unique and fighters everywhere should thank God for that.

My old gym was like a shack, there is just no other way to describe it. People used to come inside and ask, 'How the hell can a world champion train in a place like this?' Honestly, it was the mangiest little building you could possibly imagine. The ring wasn't even a proper ring, just a carpeted area on the floor, and it was tiny. You could nearly stand in the centre of it and touch all four corners. It wasn't even put up in a safe place. The river ran underneath the floor and the building, which went up in the 1920s and was made from wood and tin, was falling down. The rugby club wanted us out for years because they wanted to extend the car park but we had nowhere else to train, so we stayed put.

Four years ago we were able to buy a new building on a

site just a mile or two away. The council gave us a grant to renovate the building, which again was situated at an old rugby ground, and we were able to buy all the equipment and a proper boxing ring. Until then, I'd always trained on that carpeted bit of floor, with ropes around it that were held up by broom handles. The ropes were only there for effect. If you fell into them, you almost landed on the floor, which was slippery and dangerous because of all the condensation and moisture. There was no heating, the toilets were bad and there were no showers. Dad had to put down several rolls of square carpet and nail it to the floor to stop us from sliding all about the ring. It must have been terrible for my lungs, training there from the age of nine. Coming out of the gym, I used to have to cough up all the dust I'd inhaled. The building was so old and the smell inside was something else. It was the pungent smell of leather from the battered old gloves that you get in all boxing gyms and you could also smell the sweat, but mixed in with that was an aroma from all the dampness and the wet and the place was so small and run-down that the stench of all those years could not escape. People think I must have been gutted when we moved away and they knocked the place down but no way. I'm hardly a prima donna but that was no place for anyone to have to spend a lot of time in. When they finally demolished it we were told that we were lucky the floorboards hadn't given way a long time before. They just had to hit it once and the whole place fell, like a pack of cards. At least we'd have had a soft place to land in the river below and what a knock-down that would have been.

I was never able to move around the heavy bag, so my footwork had to evolve naturally. It wasn't something I was able to develop in training. I'd clatter into the wall and it's no wonder I picked up elbow injuries and all sorts from tripping over the buckets that had been left to catch the rain that leaked in. The gym I'm in now feels like a palace because I have a proper ring and I'm able to move inside it. I can even move around the bags. But I won a world title training out of the old gym and, for all its faults, there was definitely something about the place. I'll always remember the day a really well-dressed business-man drove up in a Mercedes and popped his head in the door. He was wearing a dark suit and a light-coloured tie and all he did was close his eyes and take a deep breath. 'That's what I came for,' he said and went straight back out the door. I didn't know him and I never saw him again. He had probably trained in the gym years before, but that incident captured an essential element for me: for all the money that man had made, he never wanted to forget the smell or the memories.

From a young age, maybe twelve years old, I was being trained like a professional by my dad and I developed a huge desire to succeed. I just knew I was going to be a fighter and I believed that one day I could be world champion. The first time I went in the ring was an exhibition bout and I boxed well, confidently, and couldn't wait for my first real fight. The first time I knocked anyone down in sparring was completely by accident. I had closed my eyes to swing a big hook and I caught the lad on the chin, a skinny little boy, and he fell over. His trainer told me off and I started to cry. 'Did he not slip?' I said. I was just so shocked by what I'd done that I didn't know how to react. There were never many boys to spar with in our gym, so Paul Williams, the coach, used to have me skip over in one corner. I skipped so much that I grew to hate it, so I never do skipping now. 'Why am I doing this?' I used to ask. 'I'm a boxer, not a skipper.' I'd do four rounds of shadow-boxing followed by two more on the bags and that was my training, three days a week, along with the work I did with Dad, and at times I got frustrated. What I wanted more than anything was to do some boxing.

But I lost my first ever amateur bout by a majority decision against a guy called Chris Stock from Harlequins Boxing Gym in Newport. When the decision was announced I went over to the other corner, shook his trainer's hand and stayed in the ring with my hands over my face, crying my eyes out against the ring post. Paul had to come and get me out of the ring after he'd finished shouting at the judges. I hated to lose and it broke my heart. Being a champion is never about finishing second, for there is no second place. Winning is what's driven me all these years, though I've never forgotten the feeling of losing. I had four more bouts against Chris Stock and I beat him every time.

I did lose my fourth fight and I lost my ninth fight and after twenty fights I'd lost five times but out of 110 in total I lost only six more and I never got stopped or even put on the canvas in all that time. I took one standing count as an amateur against a guy I managed to knock out. In the beginning I put too much pressure on myself and fought wildly, putting my head down and firing bolo punches and big shots over the top. But I improved, became more poised, and almost every fight I lost as an amateur you could have made a case for me winning because they were all split decisions. I've never lost a fight clearly in my whole career and I've never come out of the ring having accepted that I was beaten, even in those early amateur contests.

Referees were always giving me public warnings and taking points away because of my crude style and constant showboating. I boxed a boy in Cardiff called John Lonsborough, who was about seven pounds heavier than me, and I stuck out my tongue at him, pointed to my chin, did the Ali shuffle and laughed, just like Leonard against Duran. The crowd loved it but the referee threatened to disqualify me. 'Stop it now or I'll throw you out,' he warned and he very nearly did. I actually lost fights through showboating but the people in the hall enjoyed seeing a scrawny little lad being cheeky and having fun and this made me believe in myself a little more. When you get a positive reaction from a crowd of people it doesn't half fill you with confidence. The flamboyance and entertaining only stopped when I realised I was getting penalised too much. Maybe I should have kept up the gimmicks, as these tend to get you noticed.

After I lost several of my early fights no one really gave me a chance of succeeding, but I won the Welsh schoolboys' title in 1985 at the age of thirteen and this qualified me for the Amateur Boxing Association schoolboys' championship at 36kg, the Junior A. My dad was on the road a lot at this time, playing in the band, and he missed the quarter-final and the semi-final but he was at the final at the Assembly Rooms in Derby with Uccio and Serge. Mine was the third bout on and I faced a boy from London called Ian Raby. I had lost in the Welsh final the year before but I'd been training really hard for the Junior A and my heart was set on winning. I boxed the quarter-final up in Worcester and won easily on points, but my semi-final bout had gone to a majority decision. Hardly any Welsh boxers won schoolboys' titles, even the best ones, so I was a heavy underdog. A couple of more experienced boys said to me, 'You'll never win a British

ABA title, you can't win in England. They're brilliant.' I thought the kid I was facing was good too but I rushed out of my corner, completely overwhelmed him with my first flurry of punches and stopped him in thirty-five seconds, the quickest fight of the night. Unbelievable. I was wearing an old pair of orange-coloured shorts and a pair of trainers, as I had forgotten my boxing boots and I was the proudest boxer on the planet. Apart from winning the world title, I still regard it as my most satisfying moment in the ring. Dad and my uncles were ecstatic and it was just the kind of boost that any young kid needs. For taking part in the ABA finals, we got £7 spending money, which to me was a fortune. An official from the Welsh ABA would give you the money as you stepped on the bus from Newport and just staying in a hotel room, away from home, I thought I had it made.

Boxing was not just my passion now, I felt like I was a fighter and I trained twice a day, throwing all my energy into making myself the best I could possibly be. I would come home from school and my dad and me would go running together. Even in the snow, if I had to make weight for a fight, I'd go for my normal four-mile run after school, come back home and head straight to the gym. Every single day. Even when I left school, although we didn't have much money, I didn't go looking for a job because I already had one. That's how much boxing mattered to me. My mum actually got me a job once in the bakery where she worked, putting stickers on these cakes, like a robot. It got to eleven o'clock on my third day there and I went on a tea break. 'Don't be long,' the supervisor shouted after me, but I never returned. I did a week on top of that, sticking leaflets through letter boxes for my dad, who was selling windows at the time. I knocked on people's doors but was too shy to speak to them, so I quickly kicked that into touch and went to work on a building site and lasted three days. I just didn't want to work, I wanted to box and I allowed nothing else to get in the way.

The *Rocky* films inspired me and when he was in the slaughterhouse, punching the sides of beef, I was in a corner of the living room, punching the back of the settee. You use your imagination when you're a kid, so I used to go in the kitchen, cut up some oranges and stick the peel in my mouth for a gumshield, come back to the living room and punch the settee again. It took more abuse than Jake LaMotta, our settee. I even drank a glass of five raw eggs after seeing Rocky do it in the movie.

'I gave up after one glass, I thought it was disgusting,' I told Sylvester Stallone when I met him last year at the premiere of *Rocky Balboa* in London.

'Me too,' Stallone said, smiling.

The only time I was ever worried about an opponent was in my second year as a schoolboy boxer in the final of the

Junior B. I lost, mainly because of the way the other guy looked. Darren Blumsom had muscles coming out of his muscles, a moustache and a bit of beard, he had big shoulders and arms and I was just a skinny little runt of fourteen who weighed 42kg. I psyched myself out and I hardly threw a punch in the first round. I had the flu as well and runny eyes and I couldn't stop blowing my nose, but I overcame my fear to win the third round, though Blumsom got the decision. I'd felt a bit vulnerable that night and put it down to experience.

I was trying to accumulate as much experience as I could in club shows and championships, and I boxed in exhibition bouts, even one against Robbie Regan, who was also a schoolboy ABA champion who would later enjoy a successful professional career. We were supposed to be tapping one another but he started trying to beat me up and land a big bomb on my chin, so our 'exhibition' turned into a proper war. Regan had knocked someone out in an exhibition bout two weeks before, so I knew I had to watch him and I wasn't going to just stand and take it. I hit him as hard as I could in retaliation and after two rounds the referee had warned us so frequently that his patience snapped. 'That's enough,' he said before chucking both of us out of the ring.

Everything began to click into place with my boxing. I suddenly changed from being about wild, unbridled power to being more of a thinking boxer, jabbing, moving, considering all kinds of different strategies and settling down on my punches. The hardest part was making weight. I had to starve myself to make the 36kg limit for my first schoolboys' title when my 'walking around' weight was 40kg. Even 4kg is a lot of weight to shift when you're thirteen years old and only skin and bones. The constant struggle made me binge, whenever I could, on junk food, burgers and soda drinks, which was terrible for my system. It was ten times worse for me then than it is now as an adult. Back then I was growing and the craving for food was something terrible. I also had to box a couple of hours after stepping on the scales, whereas in the pros I get up to thirty-six hours to refuel my body and make sure that I'm physically ready.

The worst experience I had making weight was in my senior year as a schoolboy when I had to lose 13lb in a week. A year earlier, aged fifteen, I had boxed in the ABA Intermediate final at 51kg with a cracked rib against Nicky Bardell. I'd suffered the injury in sparring when a bigger guy caught me with a left hook in the short ribs and really got his meat into it. I could just about punch with the pain but if I'd got hit in the ribs, I'd have been all over the floor. I still went for it, that's the kind of desire I had and I won the fight, flooring Bardell twice and stopping him in the second round. Now, in the same position, I'd probably just say, 'Listen, it may be the ABA finals but you can always fight another day.' The tiniest tap in the right area could have left me in excruciating pain. Bardell was in the opposite corner again when I boxed in the final of the National Association of Boys' Clubs championships. I was sixteen years old and growing, and because of my nightmare getting back down to 51kg, I was in an even worse state. For the ABA championships, which were overlapping, I was able to weigh 54kg and later in the season I boxed at 57kg in the Gaelic Games in Nova Scotia, Canada, so making 51kg was just murder.

For two whole days I ate nothing, not a morsel. It was horrible at school because I went without taking breakfast and I couldn't eat dinner even though I was starving. Everybody else was gorging themselves on chips and sausages or whatever and the smell from the canteen was killing me. I was almost in tears with the hunger. The days I was able to eat I had mostly salad, four leaves of lettuce, a tomato and no dressing and that was my dinner. I went running wearing bin bags beneath my tracksuit to make me sweat and then I went training in the gym. When I came home I had something light, maybe just a sip of soup or a little cabbage. I don't know how I got down to the weight but I did and as soon as I stepped off the scales I went out to McDonald's and got a burger and a Lucozade and I bought a big chocolate Swiss roll in a shop nearby and stuffed my face with it. I was as weak as a robin and nearly sick when I lay down in the back of the car to rest myself before the fight. I couldn't move. My stomach was bloated and for days afterwards I was recovering from diarrhoea because I'd binged and didn't have my strength. If I'd been boxing the boy I beat by a majority decision several weeks earlier in the semi-finals, Matthew Hall, a short stocky guy, I might have lost. I was terribly weak and light-headed, and nearly passed out when I got in the ring, but I had Bardell's measure and just a few hours after getting down to the weight I won on points. The next morning I bought a giant box of Weetabix and ate the whole bloody pack.

There were no dieticians to consult then, I knew nothing about nutrition and the damage I must have been doing to myself I'd rather not think about. It was never as bad as it was for that NABC final any other time but my diet was incredibly bad for the demands I was making of my body. I'd eat a sandwich or a burger along with a Mars bar and guzzle down a bottle of Lucozade to try to build up my energy after weighing in, then I'd get sick before going to the ring – and I did that for years. If I didn't get sick, I'd worry about being hit by a body shot because everything would have come up and probably landed on some old dear in the second row. Still, I was winning and I took my third ABA schoolboys' title that year, as a senior, by beating a lad called Ian McShane convincingly on points. My dad was the second in the corner alongside Paul Williams but, to me, he was always my trainer. Dad was in the band a lot so he couldn't be in the gym as often as he wanted to be, but when I needed a kick up the arse he was always the one to swing the boot. There were many times when he pissed me off and it was only in retrospect that I was able to see exactly where he was trying to get me but I hated him sometimes. I guess I was going through the normal teenage rebellious streak at the time but we had loads of arguments about all the training he was making me do. I thought he was a fool and that he was being cruel.

Dad would write down on little cards all the different exercises and runs that I had to do each week. It could have been snowing but he still had me out running, even though it might have been a foot deep in places. I would pull on my wellies and run with heavy sweaters on and two pairs of trousers. The hills around here, like Kendon Hill which is really steep, are all perfect for building up stamina. What I've had all these years, right on my doorstep, is something similar to the training camps that the old-school fighters used to locate to in the countryside. If I was going out with friends all the time, doing stupid things, I'd need to go away to camp, but that's really never been an issue with me. Even today I can start my run at the back door of my house and turn straight up into the hills from the end of the lane. I'm surrounded by fresh air and some of the most beautiful countryside in Britain and I get left alone, no hassle. There's a solitude and tranquillity here, a calm before the storm, and it's just ingrained in me now because I'm going up hills that I've been running on since I was twelve years old. Doing the runs became a habit and my running tracks have remained much the same through all these years. If it's not broke, don't fix it, as the saying goes, and this is one of the secrets of my success. This is what works for me, so Dad knew what he was doing all right, I just didn't realise it when I was a kid.

'Dad, I'm not going out running in the snow,' I'd tell him.

'Well, forget about boxing then,' he'd reply. 'Rain, hail, snow or tornadoes, which you're lucky we don't get here, if you don't train, you won't make it.'

My dad made me run even when I was starving myself, trying to make weight for fights. I could be in absolute agony, crying, but he'd be there pushing me.

'You have to keep running, Joe. Come on. Run.'

We sparred all the time, tap sparring, but it frequently became heated. He could catch me more than anyone else was able to do, so I would go for him. I think it was probably me who squashed his nose. He'd piss me off and I'd start landing some big shots on him and sometimes, if I was hitting him too much, he'd go berserk.

'Come on then,' he'd shout at the top of his voice, his blood boiling. 'Come on, let's go outside and we'll make it a fucking street fight.'

The list of things he had for me to do was the last thing

I wanted to have shoved in my face sometimes and the battles of will began.

'I want you to do fifty press-ups, Joe, and fifty sit-ups.'

'Fuck off, I'm tired, I'm not doing that.'

'What did you just say?'

Many times the rows escalated from there. Even to this day, I hate to do exercises. I do sit-ups and press-ups but I don't do any circuit training. I have a strong stomach because I do a lot of body work, which hardens up the muscles. My dad used to have me on fifty press-ups, fifty sit-ups, squat thrusts and whatever else. I had to do ten rounds of shadow-boxing at home and maybe all I'd have eaten was a salad because I had to make weight. Then I had to go to the gym, come home and he might take me on the pads, the cushions off the settee. It was ten o'clock at night maybe and I'd be punching those cushions; but I was a kid, I wanted to see my friends and do other things.

'I'm not boxing any more,' I told him more than once.

'What do you mean you're not boxing any more?' he'd say back. 'I'll tell you when you're not doing it any more.'

'I want to do my own thing, Dad. I want to go over to my friend's house.'

'Well, you can't.'

'Why not?'

'You're not going over to your friend's place and that's the end of it.'

Psychologically, all the training and making weight

was just draining. I used to get a headache from it, the constant grind and monotony. I had many heart-to-heart chats with my dad. I used to cry in front of him and tell him that I didn't want to go through this any more. Mainly, I was rebelling against him because he wanted me to box. He saw the talent I had and he wanted me to reach my potential, so he'd call my bluff and say to me that if I didn't want to box, that was OK. I had won the argument, I thought, so the next day, of course, I would be back at the gym, content that I wasn't being told what to do. That's why I have such a tight relationship with my dad. He knows how far to push and when to push and he's always known how to get the best out of me.

The Gaelic Games, contested by Wales, Ireland, Scotland and Canada, were the final championships of 1988 and a trip to Nova Scotia was the perfect way for the season to end. Gareth Pugh was the hardest puncher I ever fought as an amateur. He came charging out of his corner and whacked me on the side of the head in the opening round and I felt like a mountain had come down on me. I was able to weather the storm, though, and Gareth quickly blew himself out from his efforts. His vision wasn't the best, so he wasn't the most accurate puncher, which was just as well for me. In the final minute of the round I gave him a count and finished him off. But the only boxer in the amateurs who ever gave me a count by the referee was the Scottish lad in the final of the Gaelic Games called Andrew Borland. In the second round he hit me with a combination of punches that stunned me. I didn't go down, but if you were hit with three good punches and maybe got staggered a little, the referee would step in and count and that's what he did. The guy waded back in and I held on to him and got a public warning, so I needed to stop him in the third round to win. Years later I faced a similar scenario against Byron Mitchell, a dangerous American one-time world champion, who had put me down in the second round. I needed to strike back fast and I did, totally overwhelming him and forcing the referee to stop the fight, which is exactly what happened in the third round in Nova Scotia. The referee issued two counts and waved it over.

We had a couple of free days when the tournament was over and on the second day I thought I'd have a few drinks and join the party with the older boys, one of whom had brought a flagon of cider. 'Get some cider into you,' he said and laughed. I thought I'd be one of the boys and get a bit tipsy. It was 2 p.m. and we were flying home at 8 p.m. I only had one drink, but it was twelve per cent proof and I'd never before had even a whiff of a drink, so within seconds I was paralytic, dangerously paralytic, almost ready to be hospitalised. All I remember after speaking to this boy was banging my head on the floor and then nothing. Complete blank. When I came to again in my room everything was in slow motion. I was sick and felt awful. I was properly gone, had no control of my bowels and even shat in the shower when the other lads chucked me in underneath it to try to bring me round. I collapsed and banged my head again, so they put me in bed for a couple of hours, got me up and managed to get me into my clothes when it was time to leave. Someone put the rest of my clothes in my bag and I was able to head to the airport but I was still ill and was even sick on the plane, to the point where nothing more was coming up. I'd enjoyed the flight on the way over – it was the first time I had ever been on a plane – but the flight back was one of the most awful experiences of my life and it seemed like it would never end. I didn't touch another drink for a while.

The season had been a real success with my wins in the NABC championships, the ABA schoolboys and, finally, a gold medal in the Gaelic Games. Though I didn't know it at the time, I had boxed my last bout for a whole year and a specialist was soon to tell me that I would never box again.

There was nobody left in Wales for me to fight but I had finished school the previous summer, so I began sparring early for the 1989 season and it was in a local boxing club in Cwmbran that I suffered the injury which threatened to end my career. I've had various problems and injuries with my hands over the years, but this was different. The sparring session itself was harmless until I threw a right hand in the second round and a sharp, searing pain suddenly developed in my wrist, as if a knife had been put through it. I was immediately in agony and had to be taken to the Royal Gwent Hospital in Newport where my wrist was X-rayed before the doctor came back to tell me that I had suffered an injury which would leave me with chronic, recurrent pain in my wrist. 'I don't think you'll ever be able to box again,' he said, which was the second knife to be suddenly plunged in.

I'm not familiar with all the medical jargon but what became clear from the X-ray was that there was extensive tissue damage in what is known as the interosseous membrane, which holds the bones in proper position. Once this happens, it fails to stabilise the position of the bones and this will recur when force is applied, leading to further pain and injury. I went home and told my dad and he was as devastated as I was, but I refused to believe the doctor. I kept trying to put the pain out of my head and still went to the gym to train, strapping my wrist up heavily with bandages, but there was nothing I could do with it. I couldn't box. I couldn't even shadow-box. I would wince with the pain. Ultrasound and different treatments were carried out in the hospital over the following weeks and months but the problem wouldn't go away. Even now I can't press on my wrist or do press-ups properly. I have to do them on my knuckles. Eventually, I overcame the problem with willpower, shutting out the pain and putting so much strapping and tape on my hands inside big gloves that it looked like I was punching with cushions. But for the time being there was nothing to do but take a complete rest and put boxing as well as the pain to the back of my mind.

At the same time my dad was going back to Sardinia to work as a chef in a little bar and restaurant business, which my grandad was leasing. It was next to the beach, half an hour out of Sassari, so I went out and stayed for four months. It was a chance for my dad to make some money and my uncles Uccio and Sergio were also going across. I tagged along to do odd jobs around the place but mostly to get over my disappointment, which I did. I went to the beach every day, swam in the beautiful Mediterranean and made friends. Every morning I ran on the sand to keep myself fit and all of us ate like kings. My dad and grandad cooked lobster and the finest fish and pizza, pasta, beautiful food and everything was fresh. I was meeting different people and I really had the time of my life. I went over to be a waiter but my main jobs were collecting the bread in the morning and taking out the bins and I did little else.

'Joe!' I'd often hear my grandad shout. 'Where's he gone? What does he do?' He had to come looking for me all the time because I was spending my time in the pool swimming or chatting up a girl on the beach.

'On my way, Grandad,' I shouted back as soon I saw him.

'You're never going to work, Joe. You're lazy, never going to work.'

My grandad's a lovely man but he's stern. One morning I was running to collect the bread because I was late when I brushed past a short, stocky Italian guy with a baldish head. He stayed in the same chalet as me and my dad but he took real exception to me bumping him accidentally on my way past.

'*Vaffanculo*,' he said, which means 'Fuck off'.

'*Vaffanculo? Perché* ?'

The guy just walked on but I told my uncle Sergio when I got back and he muttered something in Italian.

'*Ti faccio un culo cosi!*'

'What does that mean, Serge?'

Serge spread his arms wide and said, 'It means I'm going to make your arse that big!'

So I decided to take the matter into my own hands by waiting for him on his lunch break.

'*Ti faccio un culo cosi!*' I said as he approached along the path.

He was a strong man and his eyes suddenly opened wide as he lifted this huge log, the size of an oar, and swung for me. I made a very sensible decision and ran.

But the guy had gone berserk and he set off after me, roaring like a lunatic, waving this Captain Caveman log. He was far too fat to catch me but for a while he gave it a good go. The road went through sands and trees about a quarter of a mile from the chalets to the restaurant and I managed to lose him and take cover round a corner. But he saw me and started to chase me again and it must have been a comical sight. I was shouting at him, 'Come on then, you bastard,' which aggravated him more, but he was too slow and eventually gave up. Later in the day, however, he saw my grandad.

'Your grandson tried to kill me,' he told him, so Grandad sent for me and ordered me to apologise. I went to shake the guy's hand but took mine away at the last split second. My grandad's face turned red with rage so, very quickly, I completed the handshake. I'd rather swallow my own pride than risk Grandad's wrath.

I had still packed my boxing gloves and Dad had brought along the pads and now and again he stuck them on and I did a bit of work on them but it was very light. The wrapping had to be thick and solid over my wrist but after a couple of months I could feel that it was getting stronger. So, twice a week, we began to do it regularly, tip-tapping, but slowly this was building up my confidence and reinforcing my belief that I would box again. When the tourist season died off I decided to come home, though Dad was staying in Sardinia for another month or two. For all the fun I had out there, I got a bit homesick after a while and it was good to be back. Of course, after a week of feeling the cold again I wanted to return to Sardinia but I'm a homebird at heart and I don't think I'll ever be torn away.

Dad came home but I still didn't know what I was going to do or whether I'd even be able to box again, so I began to hit the social scene with my mates. We'd go out drinking and clubbing and a lot of the time come home well plastered. When you're a kid you can't hold your drink, I certainly couldn't hold mine. I used to roll in at whatever hour of the morning and head straight for the toilet to puke up my guts.

'You're a disgrace,' my dad would tell me. 'Look at yourself.'

Once when I'd had too much to drink I didn't even make it home before I was sick along the side of the road. At the same time a cop car drew up and one of the cops hopped out and chucked me in the back seat.

'Just drop me off,' I said to him but, of course, he took me to the station.

A bit sheepishly, I had to call my dad to come and pick me up.

'You are a fucking disgrace, Joe, and you better start sorting out your life,' he told me on the way home. 'You're seventeen years old, almost a man, and look at you. If you carry on like this, you're headed nowhere. Listen to me: nowhere.'

Dad didn't say it but he didn't need to, for the only way I knew how to get back on track was to start boxing again.

ROUND FOUR

What Might Have Been

The Barcelona Olympics were two years away when I got back into training, and making the British team for the Games provided even more incentive. In my year out of boxing I had a growth spurt, to a height of six feet, but I was still a couple of years away from shaving and was built like a young Tommy Hearns, long and lean, without the muscle definition. I was a slow developer, maybe I'd stunted my growth through all the years of making weight. My walking-around weight now was 11st 5lb but I was able to boil down to 10st 7lb to compete as a welterweight. The problems with my right wrist especially and also my hands were still a concern but the only way I was going to find out how everything would hold up was by getting back in the ring. I did take extra precautions, like putting a thick sponge over the knuckles and the back of my hand and using extra wadding as well inside the bandages. I wore big gloves, 16oz or 18oz, in sparring and even when working the pads and bags and ball, and all of this reduced the force of the impact and I felt ready to put myself to the test again, physically and mentally.

My first two fights were against Germans and I won the first easily, suffering no ill effects from the wrist injury, but the second bout, on another club show, put me in with a class opponent, Otkay Urkal, a naturalised Turk who fought for the world light welterweight title as a professional. He was clever, moved well in the ring and he beat me on points, but it was only my second fight back after almost eighteen months. I was a senior now, seventeen going on eighteen, but I didn't have the full strength of a man yet.

This was the crucial difference when I came up against Michael Smyth in the final of the Welsh championships. In my semi-final bout I stopped Gareth Pugh, a farmer from North Wales who was short but strong and wore thick-rimmed glasses. When the bell rang he charged me like a lunatic and probably hit me with the hardest punch I've ever been nailed by. I was buzzed by it but I came back to stop him before the end of the first round. Sadly, he hanged himself not long after we fought. Smyth came through on his side of the draw and after winning his semi-final he looked at me and said, 'You're next,' turning it into a real grudge match.

Smyth was older than me and strong and he brought loads of supporters from Barry, his home town, to cheer him on. When he came into the ring he walked straight to the centre and stood there, looking straight at me, trying to intimidate me. I was quite nervous but I boxed beautifully in the first round, dropped my hands and ripped in uppercuts and bolo punches, so many that I blew myself out. All he kept throwing were little, short blows but he kept catching me. The second round was competitive until I became knackered. It was man against boy. I was the classier fighter and I hit him with good shots but they were having no impact. I had sparred with men from the age of fifteen but this was different. Smyth was able to stun me a little with some good shots and in the clinches I could really feel his strength. He won the third round and, even though a lot of people thought I deserved it, he got the majority decision.

On my way back to the changing room I chucked my runners-up trophy in the bin because I was so disgusted about losing to the guy, but it could have been a blessing in disguise. In his next bout he was knocked out by Adrian Dodson, who was a very exciting amateur. Looking back, perhaps I wouldn't have been good enough to win the ABA title that year. Almost certainly, I wouldn't have been strong enough to beat Dodson at that time. Everything happens for a reason. 'You should turn pro,' Smyth suggested when we met some time later. I told him, 'No, I'm staying at welterweight.' He knew with the extra year of growing and gaining strength I would beat him. He was twenty-one years old but had a wise old head on him. Smyth turned pro instead.

Despite being eligible for senior competition, I still qualified through my age to take part in the European junior championships in Prague, where I won my first fight against a Hungarian boxer. That performance led a lot of people to say that I was going to win the gold medal, but I just couldn't get used to the Eastern European style of boxing. We were in the old Czechoslovakia and the referees and judges were all Eastern European as well. This was also the first bout in which I wore a headguard, which I couldn't get used to either. They weren't compulsory then in amateur boxing and even now I rarely wear a headguard in sparring. I just don't like them. They're uncomfortable and unnecessary and the one I wore in my next bout against Adrian Opreda of Romania wasn't tight enough on my head and kept coming down over my eyes. He frustrated the hell out of me by putting his left foot on my right foot and just tapped away like a fencer. All I kept thinking during the whole of the first round was, 'Would you stop doing that to my headguard, you moron?' He was clever and could see what was happening, so as soon as I stepped in he moved round to the side and tapped me some more and the headguard moved again and I couldn't see. I lost the round but it was the frustration that was beating me as much as Opreda.

The second round was pretty even, but I beat him in

the third round by staying on top of him the whole way – I had finally got inside his long arms and fathomed him out. But for two rounds this guy had just waited until I stepped in and then stepped to the side to tap me on the head with just a gentle, scoring tap. To me, that wasn't boxing and it's all he did, but it was enough to win it for him with the judges. I lost on a close decision and Opreda went on to win the gold medal and he also won silver at the world junior championships. There was the usual outcry about judging, for the East European judges were notorious for handing down dubious decisions and three of them were ordered out of the tournament, but this did me no favours. My biggest handicap, however, was the bloody headguard and, to this day, I blame Opreda for the fact that I don't like wearing one and I think of him whenever I do. The defeat left me in tears because I'd set my heart on winning the gold medal. The Welsh ABA, who weren't in the habit of sending boxers to a lot of places because of the money it cost, didn't send me then to the world junior championships even though another boxer, Alan Vaughan, lost his first fight in the Europeans and went to Lima. Why wasn't I given a second chance? I can remember all of my losses as an amateur but I vowed after the bout with Opreda that I would never lose again. I was seventeen years old and in the subsequent seventeen years I've stayed unbeaten, so maybe some good did come out of it.

At the time, though, I didn't think so and I became disillusioned with all the politics in the sport. I got more into my music, all the 1970s and 80s rock music, and I always remember going down to a pub in Blackwood called the Beer Keller one day with my mate Johnny, and we heard this song, 'Still of the Night' by Whitesnake. What a song. The next day I bought the album, got their posters and put them up on my bedroom wall, and grew my hair long into a bit of a mullet. I was such a huge fan of heavy metal that I never even stuck up boxing posters or football posters. David Coverdale, the lead singer of Whitesnake, was my idol. I used to go around with a mate of mine in his Mark One Escort and we'd stick their music on, pick up a few girls and get drunk. I loved boxing and that was still my dream, but the two setbacks I'd suffered since coming back just left me wanting to get away from it for a while to do my own thing. I went to Donington Park in the summer of 1990 to see Whitesnake and managed to avoid drinking any of the Bacardi that my mates had started on from about eight o'clock in the morning. I've never been into spirits. To me, they're disgusting, though a lot of people are able to down them like there's no tomorrow. Sometimes I might drink vodka with Red Bull but I always dilute it down and I'm far more appreciative of a good bottle of wine. That day I was too interested in listening to Whitesnake in any case and I got myself to the very front to see them.

It was a boiling hot day but I kept on my leather jacket and big boots anyway and didn't cheer for any other band until Whitesnake came on at ten o'clock that night. People were passing out, dozens of them, and there was a real crush at the front but I put up with it all just to watch Whitesnake in action and they were incredible. If I wasn't a boxer, I would have been onstage with Whitesnake, no question. I really thought they were the best thing.

I actually wanted to be a musician at one time and I asked my dad to teach me to play the guitar but he wouldn't. 'Stick to boxing,' he said. 'It'll take you too much time to learn.' He just didn't want me to become distracted from the boxing, though I used to mess about on my dad's guitar and play air guitar when I blasted my music up. I have my own instrument now and I can play a few chords that Dad did teach me, A minor and all the useless ones, but I'm going to start learning properly. I asked him recently if he'd give me some lessons and he said, 'Yeah, no problem.' He never said that when I was a kid big into rock. I've always loved music, which is something that runs in the family. I sing like a drain, unlike my dad and my uncles, but I'm not bad on the drums and my drum kit's down in our gym next to a recording studio that Dad set up. He has all the gear there. I have a karaoke machine at my home and now and again I have a blast. 'Mustang Sally' used to be my song, though someone told me recently to stick to the boxing, which was probably spot-on advice.

But right through my teenage years and my career in boxing I've always stayed into my bands, and I got to know the lads from Thunder, another group I really liked. I haven't seen any of them for a few years now, but I went to a lot of their gigs and they were at ringside several times to watch me fight. I used to be pally too with a couple of the guys out of the Manic Street Preachers and we actually went to the same school, Oakdale Comprehensive, as they're from Blackwood. James Dean Bradley, the lead singer, used to work in a pub called the Memorial Hall, which I was in many times to listen to the bands that played there on a Sunday. It's a bit mad that this little area has produced a world champion boxer and the lead singer of one of the top rock bands in the world. The guys in the group are all boxing fans and they came to see me fight Chris Eubank and Jeff Lacy and sent a massive hamper of champagne to my house to celebrate both those wins. They're down to earth, just like the boys from Stereophonics, and quite private, like me. Down the years I'd love to have gone to more concerts and gigs, but I knuckled down again once I got the loss to Opreda out of my system and I've never let anything really get in the way of what I wanted to achieve.

Paul Williams wanted me to turn professional after my

defeat by Smyth but I was still a kid, too young and too immature to join the paid ranks. It just didn't feel right. He came over to the house one day when I was on my own and tried to convince me about the route that he thought I should go down. It was hard for me because he had trained me from the age of ten every Monday, Wednesday and Friday, and I didn't really know how to say to him that I wasn't ready to turn pro yet and wanted to stay amateur. I felt grateful to him for all the work he had done with me over the years but he had never inspired me with confidence the way my dad always did and I had the feeling he would never have been capable enough to be my trainer in the pros.

He actually psyched me out of a fight against a boy called Wayne Charles at a club show back when I was an ABA schoolboys' champion. Charles hadn't won an ABA title but Paul really rated this kid. I was more than fit to handle him but by the time I got to the ring, after listening to everything Paul had said about him, I felt in my head that I was about to face Muhammad Ali. I fought like an idiot and lost the fight on a split decision. With a bit of reassurance I'd have stopped the guy, but Dad was away gigging and Paul gave me no confidence at all. There was a heavyweight who came to the gym once and Paul saw something in him and all of a sudden took him under his wing. The guy was hardly anything, he couldn't fight and only lasted a few months, but during that time, as far as I

75

could see, Paul took more interest in him than me. When the guy left I became his main focus of attention again but I never thought he was the right trainer for me. He was good at starting kids off and showing them how to box – this was his real expertise – but I don't see how I would have developed my career by continuing to work with him.

Not only was Dad away at the time, we also didn't have the telephone in. When I wanted to speak to my dad I used to have to go out to a phone box and either I would have 50p to call him or he would ring the number at a certain time. So I was in an awkward position when Paul tried to persuade me that now was the time to leave the amateur ranks and he would manage my career. But I was seventeen, there was no way I was going to turn pro and, finally, that's what I told him. A short time later he came to see my dad, handed him the keys to the gym and I never spoke to him again. That was a big development for me because Dad gave up the Milton Keynes gigs, came home and started going round local pubs and singing there instead. He had backing tracks and was a proper one-man show. From early on, a lot of people thought that the father/son relationship wouldn't work in boxing but we've done pretty well together. I had about fifty more fights as an amateur when my dad got the keys to Newbridge Amateur Boxing Club and I won them all. I've never lost a fight with my dad in the corner.

*

Trevor French, a Royal Marine, was my opponent in my first senior ABA final in 1991 in the welterweight division. This was also my first proper fight as a senior since losing to Smyth in the Welsh final the year before. I was eighteen and much stronger physically than I'd been when I was outmuscled and old-manned a bit by Smyth. I was training like a pro, so a Royal Marine's fitness didn't worry me and I turned out to be much fitter than he was. I had started to train at St Joseph's in Newport, working with Sammy Simms, who was a British featherweight champion. I used to spar with a lot of the pros there, one of them a guy called Gary Pemberton who gave me good work, but I was able to handle all of them well. It was a struggle to get down to welterweight as my body filled out. I trained very rarely wearing only a vest and a pair of shorts. I had to run, hit the bags and the pads and spar with a sweatsuit on all the time, which was really hard work, but being able to box regularly with pros was good for keeping me close to the weight and I was learning to counter different styles. Although he was strong, French didn't give me a problem. I controlled the bout all the way and in the last round I beat him badly, forcing the referee to issue a count before the judges awarded a unanimous decision. Frank Bruno and Gary Mason were ringside and I could see by the way they were interacting with one another that they had a bet on my fight. Mason bet on me because he turned to Frank when the fight was over, stretched out an open palm and mouthed the words, 'Hand it over.' Frank didn't appear to be best pleased.

I had now reached the pinnacle of British amateur boxing and was training regularly with the Great Britain squad at Crystal Palace in preparation for the Olympics. Sparring against the likes of Robin Reid, Richie Woodhall and Robert McCracken strengthened my view that I had Reid's number. I boxed well against Richie and Rob but I always handled Reid easily and I knew he was going to be the English representative for the Olympic qualifiers. These had been introduced for the first time to cope with the huge number of entries. There was some discussion about me going to fight in England, maybe because it came to a point where I only fought in the ABA championships or in internationals against the home nations. I never really boxed away, just once in Norway when I'd turned eighteen and that time against Opreda in Czechoslovakia. For the English guys, it was so much better, boxing in multi-nations tournaments every two weeks. That would have benefited me too, all that experience.

Carl Winstone, a former British champion, was another guy that we turned to for assistance. Dad's thinking at the time was that whenever I turned pro I'd need a professional trainer and he was based in Cardiff so maybe we'd try him. He trained Barry Jones and one or

Dad, Mum and me outside my nan's house in Markham where we lived after moving back from Sassari.

The Foreign Legion, Sergio, Uccio and my dad.

Picking up a football trophy for Pentwynmawr after winning an Under-10s five-a-side tournament at Cefn Forest.
I soon realised that my true talent wasn't in my feet.

Fourteen years old at Oakdale Comprehensive School.
Happy in the photograph, despite some unhappy days.

My first ever boxing trophy after an exhibition bout when I was nine years old. No one lost, so everyone's smiling.

Wearing my Welsh vest after winning my first ABA schoolboys title at 36kgs. Still looking like a matchstick.

Beating Ian Raby at the Assembly Rooms in Derby, a first-round stoppage and the quickest win of the whole day at the ABA schoolboys finals.

Triumphing in my first ABA senior final at welterweight against Trevor French, who lasted the distance despite taking a standing count in the third and final round. I've never liked wearing a headguard.

With Pat Thomas, former British light middleweight champion from Cardiff and Selwyn Evans, the only Newbridge boxer before me to win an ABA senior title.

Bouncing a right hook off the head of Stephen Wilson before winning the British title in eight rounds at the Royal Albert Hall in London.

Holding the prestigious Lonsdale belt with Dad after the bout and sharing the moment with my uncles.

I had to overcome not only Mark Delaney in Brentwood but his partisan fans, with their insulting songs about the Welsh. I had the last laugh.

Eubank on the canvas at the Sheffield Arena when I challenged for the WBO super middleweight title. Keeping him there was a different matter.

Ecstasy. Having my name announced
as the new world champion and being
carried around the ring. You can see the
resignation on the face of Eubank.

With my pal, Paul Samuels, former light
middleweight from Newport. Trying to
replenish myself after an exhausting bout.

My family have always been a part of my success and here I'm with Uccio (middle) and my cousins, Sergio (left) and Andre (right)

With my mate and old sparring partner, John Salerno, though he's not in shape to spar in this shot!

two other good fighters, but he always tried to make his boys box the same way. He started to teach me how to throw a punch in this fashion and it was altogether different from the method I'd developed since I was a kid. My way is my way, so I didn't last long with Carl. I was continuing to grow, and just couldn't make the welterweight limit any longer, so I moved up to light middleweight and intended to enter the qualifying tournament for the Olympics in that weight class, but the Welsh ABA had different ideas.

At one of their selection committee meetings it was decided that only the holder of the national title at each particular weight would be considered for putting forward to a qualifier. Dad went to a meeting of all the top officials and the situation was spelt out. 'If Joe wants to go, he's going to have to make welterweight,' he was told. But there was no way I could get down to welterweight any more. 'He's going to have to make welterweight because Matthew Turner's at light middle.' It was as simple and as ruthless as that. My dad suggested having a box-off between Turner and me but they wouldn't entertain it, so he came home and told me, and for the first time I saw him cry. The opportunity of a lifetime, to win an Olympic gold medal, was going to be denied both of us by some old farts meeting in a pub. Dad was so cut up about it because it was a horrible injustice and he had so much faith in me. He knew I was good enough to win a medal. I'd upset the apple cart by pulling out of a Wales–Ireland international through injury and I'd pulled out of a couple of other tournaments, but this was a classic case of cutting off your nose to spite your face. After all I had achieved over the years and all the tournaments I'd won from the age of thirteen up, the Welsh ABA were robbing me of the chance to go and win an Olympic gold medal and they were denying the whole country an opportunity of sharing in my quest. I've got nothing against Matthew Turner but he wasn't in my class as a boxer.

I've always said that it's a handicap for me to box out of Wales. I'm proud of where I'm from and I'm proud to represent Wales on the international stage, which I've done as an amateur and professional for the past twenty years, but it's a constant battle against the odds and you need your own people to be fighting with you and not against you. The Welsh ABA, I believe, did me few favours and sent me to very few tournaments, just internationals against England, Scotland and Ireland, and not a lot else. OK, they hadn't the same resources as the ABA in England but the set-up was only mediocre and it's still not good enough, which is making it more difficult for young Welsh boxers to succeed in the amateur ranks. Paul King is doing a terrific job with amateur boxing in England but the Welsh ABA still needs to be pulled into the twenty-first century. I'm convinced that I could have qualified for Barcelona and won an Olympic medal. Robin Reid did. I know that I'd lost in the European juniors but so had Alan Vaughan from England who went to the world juniors a month later and won gold, and the Welsh officials should have known that I had the same kind of potential. I would have beaten Opreda if I'd boxed him again, but they thought sending me would be a worthless exercise.

Matthew Turner, who lived in Cardiff, went to the Olympic qualifying tournament and got nowhere, but all he'd won was a Welsh title. He didn't have the same pedigree. I went to the Olympic squad sessions and maybe from time to time I had to pull out through injury but that happens. I was the ABA champion at welterweight, a multiple ABA champion all the way through schoolboy level, and the least I deserved after all I had given to the sport was a chance. I sparred with Matthew Turner and I handled him easily and the people who selected him must have known.

There's no way in the world that we would have overlooked Joe Calzaghe for a chance to enter the Olympic Games. Joe was very rarely available for Wales when it came to international boxing. There was always some excuse or another. That was probably the root cause of it. In 1992, for the first time, boxers who wanted to compete in the Olympics had to qualify for the tournament proper. Under the old system when we were allowed to send ten or eleven boxers and it was up to Great Britain to determine the team, Joe would certainly have gone. In present-day amateur boxing, and this took effect from 1992, you had to qualify to go to the Olympics and that is up to the Welsh ABA to pick the boxers to send. Because Joe may not have been supporting us at the time, somebody said, 'Well, why should we send him?' It costs a lot of money and I don't remember much fuss at the time about Joe not going because he just never was available for Wales. He knows that when he wanted us to support him we supported him, if it was just putting him into the ABA championships every year, and his expenses went along with that. Somebody has to pay for you to go to the ABA championships and we were funding all that, but when it came to Joe boxing for us against other nations you'll find that he was very thin on the ground.

– Terry Smith, former chairman,
Welsh ABA secretary

Sometimes I think about what might have been. Robin Reid won a bronze medal in Barcelona and came home a hero, even though the Dutch boy he lost to was nothing. Imagine if I'd won the gold medal, who knows what would have happened? Audley Harrison won the Olympic gold medal at super heavyweight in 2000 and signed a big fat £1 million deal with the BBC. Amir Khan came back with a silver medal from Athens and immediately became one of the biggest commodities in British sport. I could have turned pro after the Olympics, to be built up as the new kid on the block in the middleweight and super middleweight era of Chris Eubank, Nigel Benn and Steve Collins. I could have had the platform to be a superstar, but that's not the way it was to be, all because of a few men in a pub. *Sorry, you can't go. A box-off? No, no box-off. Can he make welterweight? No? Well, he's not going then.* That's how it is in boxing. Your destiny is in the hands of other people.

Ultimately, the route I had to take was probably a better one. Would I be the world champion today if I had gone to Barcelona and won the gold medal? Probably not. My mindset would have been different. I might have become a millionaire before I fought anybody who was good. My head might have become too big and an instant fortune of money could have changed the person I am. Who knows what way it would have gone? Nothing has ever been handed to me on a plate and I believe that's the reason I've been successful for so long. People talk about hunger, but you have to feel it in your belly, that's the feeling you need to have. I remember watching Reid at those Olympics on TV. He hadn't even won an ABA title and the way that made me feel, deep in my gut, was something awful. I had to fight my way to the top and I did it the hard way.

Was it a good thing that Joe didn't go to the Olympics? No, it wasn't. There will always be disappointment there that Joe wasn't chosen, but how a person reacts provides a window into their character. This is how Joe is in training. I'll be counting the rounds he's done on the bags and the rounds he's done shadow-boxing and I'll say, 'OK, Joe, that's nine, so one more will do you.' But he'll turn round and tell me, 'That's not nine, it's eight.' Other fighters will cheat. *The trainer thinks it's nine, I'll go along with that. Yeah, I've done nine.* Joe will never cheat. He's like a machine because he can go forever and something has got to fuel that level of determination. I'm not saying that for Joe it's been the Olympics that's provided that fuel but that whole episode started out from nothing. He was supposed to box for Wales against Norway in Newport but he damaged one of his knuckles in sparring against a boy called Andrew Gerrard. That injury recurred until he had an operation on the knuckle, but I phoned Ray Allen, who was the chairman of the Welsh ABA, and told him that Joe's hand had gone. Ray was a good man and thought so much of Joe that he meant it when he said, 'Enzo, Joe can box with one hand and he'll still win.' I made the decision to pull him out, not Joe. I'm sure that wasn't the only reason he wasn't sent to the qualifiers but it was unfair that Joe got punished and I know that terrible disappointment still lingers. – Enzo Calzaghe

I won my second ABA title, at light middleweight, in 1992, stopping every opponent I faced, including Dean Francis, who became a top professional, and in the final Glenn Catley from Bristol, who won the WBC super middleweight title in 2000. Ian Irwin, who was head coach for the British Olympic squad that competed in Barcelona, used one word to describe the Welsh ABA's decision not to send me to the qualifiers when I spoke to him. Crazy.

Late in the summer Dad organised for me to box against an Italian select on a trip to Sassari. Every few years he would take a team of Welsh boxers out there and I always felt under more pressure boxing in front of my grandad and all my other family there than I ever did in the ABA championships, perhaps because of an image that has become etched in my mind. Grandad was ringside when I first beat Catley on points at a club show and, out of the corner of my eye during one of the rounds, I saw that his face had turned purple and the veins in his neck were bulging like they were about to burst and I knew how much it mattered to him. So it's always mattered to me to put on a good performance for him. This was no easy bout, however, because my opponent, Paolo DiMasso had won a bronze medal in the world junior championships and was a very slick boxer, a national champion several times. He was a cool customer too, as he wore a pair of dark glasses into the ring. 'I hope he puts them away safe. He'll need them more when this is over,' Dad said to me and laughed.

Before the fight started my grandad's brother, Rino, came into the ring to present me with an enormous trophy. There were smiles all round but inside I was thinking, 'Bloody hell, are you trying to motivate DiMasso or me?' I couldn't lose now because family honour was at stake. DiMasso, who didn't have a mark on his face, walked around the ring with the air of a guy who thought he was going to be the next big thing and he was one of the stars on the Italian team, but this would be one of the best displays I ever put on as an amateur, the equivalent of what I would do to Jeff Lacy over a decade later. For three rounds, I boxed at my absolute best. DiMasso was strong and kept coming at me, but that's the kind of style I love and I peppered him with punches, *bah bah bah*, then moved to the side and fired again, *bah-bah-bah*, like a machine gun. He was so frustrated and overwhelmed that he nearly cried in the ring. When I'm in that kind of situation I always know what I've got to do: win in style, there's just no other way. His heart was broken in that fight, I embarrassed him so much. My dad brought me back four months later when we were supposed to box again. When I saw my opponent I said to my dad, 'What have you picked him for?' He was massive, a light heavyweight easily, but his trainer, who had been at the DiMasso fight, recognised me and he wouldn't let him fight me. I couldn't get another fight in Italy after beating DiMasso.

The worst act of surrender from any fighter I faced, however, happened in a club show against Geoff McCreesh. Geoff was tough and won the British welterweight title as a professional and he gave his all in the opening round. Just before the bell rang I started to catch him with some solid shots but it was pretty even. In the second round I stepped up the pace and shook him with a combination of punches which prompted the referee to issue a count. I moved in to finish him when all of a sudden he spat out his gumshield, kicked it across the ring, climbed through the ropes and walked straight back to his dressing room. I couldn't believe it because the hall was packed with his own supporters, who couldn't believe it either. I caught up with him later and he just shook his head. 'I was in pain and you were just too good for me. What could I do?'

Whatever Geoff felt in his head it couldn't have been as

bad as how I felt when I came back from Sassari. There was a pub in Newbridge that I would go to on a Thursday night and I went down to meet my mate John, even though I had a splitting headache and flu symptoms. I came home and took some tablets but I had this feeling that my head was going to explode. My dad told me I had a migraine but the pressure on my brain was intense and I ached all over. I was sick and just felt like death as I went to bed. The next morning I told my dad that there must be something wrong with me and he took me to the hospital where a trainee nurse had to do a lumbar puncture on me, taking a needle about six inches long to stick into my spinal cord to get fluid out which the doctors could test for bacteria. The pain was unbearable, a hundred times worse than I've ever experienced in a boxing ring. I was sweating and no matter how hard this nurse tried she couldn't get the fluid out. She kept hitting my spinal cord with the needle, right at the base of my spine, and the pain was shooting up through my body. I thought I was going to pass out. Finally, she called for help, another nurse came to do the procedure and I didn't feel a thing, but the doctors discovered that I had viral meningitis and I spent two days in the hospital, pumped full of antibiotics. When I was allowed out I called home for my dad to pick me up but he wasn't there and I had to get a bus. I was weak as a robin when I staggered out through the door of the hospital and I must have looked awful because a mangy dog went for me until the owner managed to get it under control. 'Don't worry, you won't catch anything,' she said – to the dog, not me.

The illness got me down again, for I was still gutted about missing out on the Olympics and I was ready to turn pro. But my dad had been looking through some old boxing book and he came across a record that had been set by Fred Webster of St Pancras ABC back in 1928 when he won his third consecutive ABA title in a third weight class. 'Nobody's done this since the Second World War, Joe,' he said. 'Why don't you stay amateur one more year and win your third?' I had won the ABA welterweight title in 1991, the light middleweight title in 1992 and I was growing into the middleweight division in any case, so this became my goal. I went into my fight with Jason Matthews with a bad right hand, which I couldn't throw. I could only stick it out and find the range with it, then club him with my left. Matthews was good enough to win a WBO title as a pro but he was very obliging that night, for he came straight and I couldn't miss him with a left cross that knocked him out. The only boxer who was able to go the distance with me was Darren Dorrington in the final. He was given three standing counts but he managed to hang on to the final bell as my name went into the record books. This was my last bout as an amateur.

I got a little taster of the journey I was about to embark

upon when Nicky Piper came to the gym for some sparring a couple of months after he challenged Nigel Benn for the WBC super middleweight title. When my dad told me that he wanted to come down for some work I was excited. Nicky was a fine boxer who challenged twice for the WBO light heavyweight title after Benn stopped him in the eleventh round in a terrific battle and he never lacked for heart. I have a lot of respect for him as a fighter and as a person.

Nicky had arrived at the gym in his white Mercedes and parked outside by the time I walked in, carrying my bag over my shoulder. He already had his kit on and was punching the bag. His trainer, Charlie Pearson, asked my dad if I could do eight rounds. 'I'll do eight rounds no problem,' I said. My weight was about 11st 10lbs and he was coming down from light heavyweight and, as we started, all the other fighters in the gym were skipping and watching. Straight off, he caught me with two stiff jabs that made my eyes water. 'This is serious here,' I thought. 'Don't make yourself look like a prick.' So I slipped the third left hand he threw and whacked him over the top with a hard left hand that dropped him. He fell face first, got straight back up, but he wasn't too happy.

'I thought this was supposed to be light sparring,' he said.

'Sorry, I just threw the punch.'

After three rounds the session was cut short. I'd felt

comfortable in the ring with a solid professional who was about to challenge one of the best boxers in the world for a WBC title. I was able to move in, throw body shots, drop my hands and was so delighted with myself that the money he paid me was just a bonus. I was always looking at Benn and his big rival, Chris Eubank, wanting to be just like them, and over three rounds I'd handled myself well against a man who was about to engage Benn in a really hard fight. That sparring session was invaluable in building up my confidence.

'Will we spar again next week?' I asked him.

'Yeah,' he said. But Nicky didn't come back. Now he probably laughs at it, but I had steely eyes walking home from the gym that day. I knew I was ready.

ROUND FIVE
Timing is Everything

There are many regrets I have about my career but the biggest is that I turned pro under Mickey Duff. This was a massive mistake, which I learnt the hard way. Duff's reputation was long-established in British boxing and on the international scene. John Conteh, John H. Stracey, Alan Minter, Charlie Magri and Lloyd Honeyghan, all world champions, were among the fighters whose careers were guided by Duff and his associates Terry Lawless and Jarvis Astaire. Together with Mike Barrett, they controlled British boxing for nearly thirty years, operating what became known as a 'cartel', until Frank Warren emerged with the support of ITV in the 1980s. Duff still had enough influence in the early 1990s to persuade me to sign with him when I turned pro but when I look back now I laugh at how naive I was.

Without legal representation and without even speaking to another promoter, I went with my dad to London to do the deal with Duff. We didn't really know what was what, which I now accept was our own fault. I didn't even get a signing-on fee. Duff offered me a £3,000 loan which went against my money. Actually, it was only as time went on that I realised it was a loan set against my purses. That was the way my deal was done. I got a weekly wage of £300, as I wanted to get a mortgage on a little house and at the time I thought that £300 a week was good money. But I never thought to ask how much my contracts were worth. In fact, I never would see a contract for any of my fights. I didn't have a lawyer or anyone else scrutinise the deal. I was just a kid and I knew no better. If I had spoken to somebody who knew his way around the boxing business, I might have seen my mistake. But I didn't have a clue. I was just flattered that a man like Duff would even want to talk to me. *Mickey Duff wants to sign me? Wow, He's the big fish in this business.* That was my attitude. I didn't have anyone with the savvy to take me to one side to say, 'Hold on a second, have you spoken to Frank Warren? He's interested too.' Frank was interested but he had heard that I was doing a deal with Duff and nobody else and that stopped him from making a bigger play for me. Duff had a promotional deal with Naseem Hamed at the time but he still described me as 'the best British amateur to turn pro for ten years'. I know now that I should have made more of the regard in which I was held by people in the game, but naivety can be a funny thing.

Initially, I was laughing. I came home and bought

myself a car, a burgundy Ford Sierra GL, even though I didn't have a driving licence. For a whole year I drove all over the country without a licence and I was on the road nearly every day. It's not the cleverest thing I've done but thank God I was never stopped by the police. After a year I thought that maybe I ought to go for my test, so I booked myself on a crash course and passed first time. I went and bought another car, a Ford Escort XR3i convertible and the second day I had it I got stopped. So it's not the way you drive, it's the car you drive, and so it is in boxing.

Over time I began to realise what was going on and I started to ask questions. The turning point came when Robin Reid, who turned pro after me, beat Vincenzo Nardiello of Italy to win the World Boxing Council (WBC) super middleweight title. He wasn't in my league, yet he was the champion and I remained a hidden secret. Even Henry Wharton, who was also part of Duff's stable, got a crack at Chris Eubank's WBO title before I did. Duff would say to me, 'Joe, you would destroy Henry Wharton but you have to wait your turn.' Which didn't exactly inspire me with a lot of confidence, I have to say. If I was better than Wharton, why did he get his shot at Eubank before I did? Duff was old-fashioned and he did things the old-fashioned way. The way he had everything mapped out was rigid. First you would box for the British title, then the European title, and, if you got that far, a shot at the world title would be yours. Basically, his way was that you served an apprenticeship of six, seven years, or however long it took, and you had to wait your turn. It seemed to me that Richie Woodhall suffered. Richie was another really good fighter who stayed loyal to Duff for a long time. But when he finally got his chance he had to go to America to fight Keith Holmes for the WBC middleweight belt. He had a bad elbow but I think Richie felt he had this opportunity and had to go through with the fight. He lost by a technical knockout in the twelfth round. In the end he had to switch stables and sign with Frank Warren before he got a second crack against Sugarboy Malinga, who'd beaten Nigel Benn, and this time he was successful. If I was Richie I would have been frustrated with Duff's insistence on staying in line. Wharton was ahead of me in the queue even though he'd lost to Benn. Mickey and Terry both used to tell me that I'd stand Wharton on his head but they wouldn't let me fight him and they wouldn't let me jump him in the queue. That's the way they worked.

On top of these frustrations was the fact that I never knew what the money was for any particular fight. I would ask, of course, but it was difficult to pin anyone down on the subject. Terry Lawless would hang up whenever I mentioned money. Then Mickey would ring me and tell me that I was getting X amount because my purse was going against my wages. But I never saw a contract, it was a totally ridiculous situation. Of course, I'm more clued in about these things now but back then I was just a kid from a small town with a small-town mentality. They said they'd get me a big fight and the money would come but it just wasn't happening.

The set-up was simple. I was paid a wage of £300 a week and this was set against my purses for fights. If I had been able to see a contract for each fight, which should have been the case, I would have known how much money I should have been taking in. As it was, I was just about skint after three years of boxing as a professional. I had a young kid and a mortgage to pay and I had no money worth speaking about. I was British champion at super middleweight and had defended my title twice but I was broke. Duff and Lawless acted as manager and promoter, and because I had no other job and no other income, I just couldn't go on. I was totally disheartened because I felt that my career was going nowhere. So I had a heart-to-heart chat with Dad. I needed to get out of the situation. Ironically, it was an injury that bought me a little time.

Paul Wright was due to be the second challenger for my British title. If I won, the prestigious Lonsdale belt would be mine to keep, but six days before the fight I twisted my ankle while out running. I just stuck my foot in a pothole and stretched the ligaments, badly spraining my ankle. I hobbled home in absolute agony. The doctor bandaged it up and I needed crutches to walk.

'Can you stand?' Mickey asked me down the phone.

'Yes, but –'

'You can beat this guy on one foot.'

Maybe he was joking, but I decided against trying. The injury actually prevented me from training for several weeks and this gave me further time to assess where I was going. Naseem Hamed was on his way to becoming a superstar and Robin Reid was to have his WBC showdown with Nardiello and that just made me more frustrated. Here I was, nowhere near that kind of level, even though I knew that I was good enough. I just wasn't being given the chance to prove my worth. I needed to break out and it was then that I went to see Frank Warren.

Timing is everything and the decisions you make will determine the direction of your life, even when you don't know it. I'm convinced that I would have become as big a star in boxing as Naseem Hamed if I'd been with Frank Warren from the start. Everything that Naz was doing I was doing. I was destroying opponents, most of them inside the first or second rounds. I wasn't entering the ring by flipping over the ropes but I was knocking guys out through them, knocking them cold. The difference was that Naz had exposure – first on ITV, then on Sky – and he was able to attract a large following. Meanwhile I was getting little or no TV coverage, just short clips on *Sportsnight*. Some of my fights were broadcast on

Eurosport but I was never exposed to a large mainstream audience. If you're going to make it big as a performer, you need a stage or a platform. Nigel Benn, Chris Eubank and Steve Collins all had a platform. They had over ten million viewers watching their series of fights. I didn't. Even after three years, with a record of twenty-one straight wins and twenty knockouts, I wasn't close to getting in on the act, and it became more and more frustrating. Long before push came to shove with Duff and Lawless, I was regretting not being with Frank.

It was Panix Promotions who staged my first professional fight against Paul Hanlon on 1 October 1993 at Cardiff Arms Park, on the undercard of Lennox Lewis's WBC heavyweight title battle against Frank Bruno. It was a wet and windy night, poor conditions for an outdoors venue, but I was just delighted to be making my debut on such a high-profile bill. Years before, when I was still an amateur, I had gone to Earls Court to watch Lewis fight Razor Ruddock. The seat I had was up in the heavens and Lewis looked great that night, powerful, athletic and almost unbeatable, but against Bruno he was mediocre. Frank was Frank. He did well before showing the same old vulnerability, which Lewis took advantage of. It wasn't a great fight. I remember thinking how poor they both looked but that's the heavyweights. They get big purses and most of the recognition but in my opinion not many of them can fight. Most look like big lumps to me.

Audley Harrison, a good example of what I mean, was able to turn pro for a £1 million pay cheque signed, incredibly, by the BBC, yet I was happy, even on my £300-a-week wages, because I was setting out on a dream. Of course, I was nervous and had butterflies in my stomach but I was confident. I'm always confident when I step in the ring and that night was no different.

Hanlon was trained by Nobby Nobbs, whose stable of fighters are renowned for their professionalism. If an opponent is needed, any promoter in the country can count on Nobby. We were on early, several hours before Lewis and Bruno, so it was quiet around the Arms Park. The pubs were still full around Cardiff. Hanlon had a habit of coming in with his head and in the first round he caught me with it, right on the nose. I looked at the referee, expecting him to issue a warning but nothing happened. Welcome to professional boxing. Apart from a quick Ali shuffle I didn't get much of a chance to put on a show. Hanlon didn't make it through the first round, which would become the pattern.

Joe Calzaghe made a winning start in the professional ranks with a crushing first round stoppage victory over Paul Hanlon of Birmingham. The Welsh southpaw, who won the last of his three consecutive ABA titles at middleweight, weighed in at 11st 13lb and did not look overweight. Hanlon, in contrast, had a flabby midriff at 11st 12lb. Calzaghe, with Terry Lawless in his corner, looked in no particular hurry at first but became more animated when Hanlon appeared to butt him on the nose, reddening it. He forced the Brummie to the ropes and unleashed a powerful volley that had Hanlon crouching down. Joe kept punching and landed a right to the back of Paul's neck before referee Ivor Bassett moved in to pick up the count. Hanlon got up at seven but could find no respite as Calzaghe kept the pressure on. A left cross followed by a right hook hurt the Midlander and had him backing off. Then another right hook from Calzaghe, this time flush in the face, put Hanlon down again. He rose at the count of eight but Mr Bassett decided he had seen enough and called a halt at the 2:43 mark. – Daniel Herbert, *Boxing News*, 8 October 1993

Paul 'Stinger' Mason, a journeyman from Sheffield, only lasted until 2:29 of the first round in my second fight at Watford Town Hall. The ropes and a ring post helped to keep Stinger on his feet when I landed a hard left hook on his jaw but the referee, Richie Davies, stepped in because he was so disorientated. My dad had an even quicker win that night, before the timekeeper rang the bell. Terry Lawless was all set to be the main man in my corner, which he had engineered in Cardiff, but Dad stopped him in his tracks as we were about to go through the ropes. 'I'm his fucking trainer, so don't push me,' Dad told Lawless. 'I'm going in the ring. You stand outside on the apron!' He did and the subject was never raised again.

All of my early fights were knockouts or technical knockouts. They almost always followed the same script. I would drop my opponent, a combination of punches would then overwhelm him and the referee would jump in. Going into my third bout just before Christmas 1993 I told the local media that 'I haven't had a chance to show off my skills, only my power. I normally wear people down with speed and combinations, so I might get a couple of rounds in this fight.' I almost did. Spencer Alton from Derby, a former French Foreign Legionnaire, had gone the distance with quite a few up-and-coming fighters but I dropped him with a two-fisted combination at the end of the first round. His cornermen were worried, as was poor Spencer, but the referee had less pity for him than me.

Spencer's grimace towards his corner as he took a count of seven had more than a touch of 'Who on earth is this guy?' but he rose gamely and somehow managed to cover up until the bell. When Calzaghe quickly resumed the treatment in the second round

Alton's trainer, Jason Shinfield, winced at the onslaught and decided enough was enough. But it took him three attempts to get the towel past the ropes and then referee Roddy Evans threw it out again, waving the pair back together. Spencer's promptness in indicating the towel to the referee showed he would have been happy for the surrender to be accepted but he carried on without protest. His fate was only deferred, however, with a few more punches being sufficient to convince Mr Evans that a halt should be called after 2:45 of the round.

– Gareth Evans, *Boxing News*,
7 January 1994

After just three fights I was already questioning my decision turning pro with Duff. The turnout was disappointing at the Newport Centre and there was no atmosphere. It seemed like every time I boxed on a Frank Warren show there was a world title main event and a buzz about the place, a level of excitement which made it easy to perform. Not that I was encountering too many problems. Martin Rosamond and Darren Littlewood lasted less than a round each in my first two fights of 1994 and when I boxed Karl Barwise on the undercard of Steve Robinson's defence of the WBO featherweight title against Freddy Cruz at the National Ice Rink in Cardiff, another Warren promotion, I claimed another first-round victim. Barwise was experienced and durable. Michael Watson had stopped him in three rounds but he had been the distance with Christophe Tiozzo, who went on to win the WBA super middleweight title, James Cook, who lifted the British and European super middleweight titles, and another British title-holder, Sam Storey. I hit him so hard that he thought I had something in my gloves. 'I felt like I was hit by a lorry,' he said later with a smile. He never fought again.

I was beginning to struggle to get opponents because I was sparking everybody out, making the matchmakers' lives difficult. That was one thing Duff and Lawless did well. They were good matchmakers. Terry O'Toole, who assisted them, knew his boxing and I was always matched astutely. Sandwiched between a first-round stoppage against Mark Dawson and a one-punch knockout of Frank Minton after the Barwise fight was a second-round job on Trevor Ambrose, who was quite dangerous. He had been beating up Robin Reid before Reid caught him clean and stopped him in the fifth round. But all these guys were expected to give me rounds. They just weren't capable of doing it when the bell rang. It's a fine line that a matchmaker has to tread between babying a prospect through the early part of his career while at the same time selecting opponents from which he can learn. Frank is doing a great job so far with Amir Khan. He has the same kind of hand speed that I have but I was simply going through the guys, putting them to sleep. Unlike Amir, I wasn't on the general public's radar, however, because I hadn't been to the Olympics and my fights weren't broadcast live to an audience of millions. Nobody knew how good I was except the men I'd fought. 'This kid has everything,' Spencer Alton had said. 'He'll be a world champion, no doubt about it.' But who was Spencer Alton and, as far as the public was concerned, who was Joe Calzaghe?

In nine fights I had boxed only eleven rounds. I was blasting guys out the way Benn had done, just like Naz was doing, but to nowhere near the same fanfare. That kind of form tends to scare off opponents too, so I had to fight a cruiserweight next in order to be guaranteed a few rounds. Bobbi Joe Edwards, a squat powerhouse from Manchester who weighed 12st 10lb to my 12st 2lb, fitted the bill. His cousin was Chris Eubank, so he was of durable stock, just not as eccentric. I remember hitting him on the top of the head with a hard left uppercut in the opening round – and he didn't budge. I whacked him and he never moved. It was like punching a rock. Eubank would have strutted but Bobbi Joe just kept coming. I won every round comfortably but Bobbi Joe went all eight rounds, the first time I had been taken the distance as a pro. I felt good even though my hand was badly bruised coming out of the ring.

Joe Calzaghe almost doubled his ring experience in one night as Bobbi Joe Edwards stood up for eight threes in the chief support [to Richie Woodhall's successful challenge of Silvio Branco for the European super middleweight title]. Edwards was not really competitive, as the much lighter Calzaghe was too fast and sharp for him from start to finish. Edwards, who normally fights cruiserweights, never looked like winning a round and went down 80–75½ on the card of referee John Coyle. Only in the seventh when he clipped Calzaghe with a right cross did Edwards land a significant punch. Aside from that, Calzaghe threatened to swamp him with punches, whacking them in from all kinds of angles. But at least the 37-year-old Mancunian showed him that not everyone he hits will fall over.

– Bob Mee, *Boxing News*, 3 March 1995

Not until I fought his more celebrated cousin would I be forced to go the distance again.

Duff and Lawless were happy with my progress but I was growing more disenchanted. Once when Mickey was out of the country he rang my dad up at home, getting him out of bed at about four in the morning. Dad went downstairs to answer the call because he thought it might have been my grandad calling from Sardinia. But it was

Mickey from somewhere in the United States querying an expenses bill that Dad had put in. The phone call probably cost more than whatever discrepancy there was over the bill but Dad was advised that we should take a packed lunch and a flask to a press conference in York to publicise my twelfth fight against Tyrone Jackson. We wouldn't be getting expenses, which Dad really needed to know at 4 a.m.

Sometimes Dad chauffeured Mickey around before or after a fight. He was asked once to take him back to his hotel. Mickey wasn't sure where he was staying but he had the telephone number. They had driven to another part of the city before they realised that Mickey was staying at the hotel that Dad had picked him up from in the first place, so it's just as well Dad didn't have him on the meter.

Jackson was the second American opponent I faced in succession after Edwards. Robert Curry from West Virginia was overweight and fell in the first round but Jackson was tougher. He had several bullet holes in his body from a shooting incident years earlier and all the way through the fight he kept talking. When I hit him with a combination of punches he would say, 'You hit like a bitch, man. You can't punch. Come on, what you got?' Finally, in the fourth round, I showed him, as I caught him with a left to the jaw and five or six more hooks to his head. His hands dropped and he was out on his feet when the referee stopped it, though he wasn't quite through talking. 'Why'd you stop the fight?' he protested to the referee and at that moment I almost understood why someone might be pushed to take a gun to this guy. He was one annoying man.

Out of my early fights, my worst performance by far came against Nick Manners from Leeds. On the afternoon of the fight I ate a massive steak, which I couldn't digest and when I stepped in the ring I felt horrible, really lethargic. But I managed to stop Manners in the fourth round and this win set up a British title challenge against Edinburgh's Stephen Wilson. I was unbeaten after thirteen fights and Wilson had won twelve and lost only one on cuts. It was a good match. Wilson had boxed at the Olympic Games in Barcelona and he had a good jab. In the end he ran out of puff, but not before catching me with his head in the second round, causing a bad swelling around my eyes.

Calzaghe's performance didn't match his previous form and he was often wild and uncontrolled. He gradually wore down his opponent until referee John Coyle stepped in after 2:18 of the eighth round to declare the Welshman as the British super middleweight champion. The stoppage may have been a little premature as Wilson had not been floored and was under his first real serious bout of pressure but was understandable in the present boxing climate.

– Peter Watts, *Sunday Times*,
29 October 1995

It was great to be British champion but nothing had changed on a practical level. I stopped Guy Stanford in Cardiff in another one-round affair but I wasn't earning any more money and it began to prey on my mind. This was no excuse, however, for the disaster that nearly happened in my next fight.

Paul Samuels, my pal from the amateurs, was boxing on the same bill in Wembley. Mine was meant to be third or fourth fight on but as soon as Paul came back from a quick first-round win the British Boxing Board of Control guy knocked on the door. 'Joe, you're on,' he said. I didn't have time to warm up, or even shadow-box. I just jumped straight in the ring cold and it was almost like my opponent knew. Anthony Brooks, from Jeff Lacy's home town of St Petersburg, Florida, had never been stopped. In an early fight he lost a majority decision over four rounds to Glen Johnson, who would go on to win the world light heavyweight title and become a possible opponent for me. He was also a southpaw and he threw the hardest punch any fighter has ever caught me with. I stood in front of the guy and he got me flush, coming straight out of his corner and whacking me with a left hook that totally buzzed me. For twenty seconds or more I was badly stunned. I knew where I was but he caught me high on the temple, which throws your equilibrium. I could see stars, my head buzzed and the punch hurt. It wasn't a pleasant feeling. It was the first time I'd been stunned as a pro. Later in my career I would get knocked down by Kabary Salem and Byron Mitchell, but they were flash knock-downs which didn't hurt. I got straight back up both times and my head was clear, but through the whole of the first round against Brooks I was stunned. I probably suffered a mild concussion. Hours afterwards my vision remained blurry. I was half asleep. I still managed to make my way through the round and I dropped him with a combination in the second round but, for me, that fight was a wake-up call.

Everyone is different. Lennox Lewis used to like to go to sleep before a fight. Me, I like to be active. To make weight, I need to train. I don't have the luxury of choosing not to train. So I work out the day before a fight, ahead of the weigh-in, doing a few rounds on the pads with my dad and shadow-boxing. The morning of the fight I shadow-box and get on the pads again in the afternoon in my hotel room or wherever. I'm always on my toes. I sit down to have a bit of a rest but I quickly get up again. I need to be doing something. That's the way I am. So when the guy came to the door early all I could do was go straight to the ring and it knocked my preparation routine. I stood in front of the guy and he caught me flush with a big, crude left hand, which only goes to show how one punch, one little thing that goes wrong, might have a catastrophic effect on a career. I've never gone into a fight again without warming up thoroughly in the dressing room first.

Having survived my first real scare, I faced a benchmark fight against West Ham's Mark Delaney. He was twenty-four years old and had won all of his twenty-one fights. This was my eighteenth. The purse bids were won by Barry Hearn, Delaney's promoter, who promoted this meeting of two unbeaten fighters as 'Who's Fooling Who?' so I had to go to Brentwood in Essex to confront Delaney in what was virtually his backyard. About two thousand people turned up to the International Centre, all of them Delaney fans, and it was the first time I'd had to deal with a hostile crowd. I fed off that hostility. The adrenalin was pumping like it never had before because I realised this was a big fight. 'Jump Around' was the song I had them play for my ring walk and I danced to it as people all around me screamed, 'You're going to get knocked out, you Welsh bastard,' and other charming phrases to do with nationality. They were seething. You could see the hate on their faces. I just laughed and the atmosphere worked for me. It's great to have the fans behind you but I'm not daunted by having them against me. I discovered that night that I could box on unfriendly turf by turning the negative energy into something positive for me. I got in that ring and just fed off the crowd's hate. Eubank did the same for most of his career. He loved to feel the wrath of the crowd. Delaney's brother Gary, who was also a professional boxer, walked past me when I got in the ring and spat on the floor, never taking his eyes off me. 'You're going down,' he said. 'Bullshit,' I thought and just smiled back at him.

Delaney had been protected in the way he'd been matched and I had the clear edge in hand speed. He was strong, however, and he'd never been put down in his life, but I dropped him with a left to the chin after only twenty seconds and I floored him again before the first round was over. He was almost finished – a new thing for him – when the bell came to his rescue. He had a go over the next few rounds and I got a bit wild, but in the fifth I dropped him twice again and the victory was mine.

Bursting with self-confidence, Calzaghe set out to destroy Delaney from the opening bell. The previously unbeaten West Ham boy found himself on the floor twice from a volley of left hands and had his nose broken in the opening three minutes. Any chance Delaney had of upsetting the odds-on favourite had gone before he had a chance to get warmed up. He was also cut beneath the right eye and, with his face a mess and masked in blood,

Delaney courageously managed to carry on taking punishment until the fifth. But he was dropped three more times and referee John Coyle mercifully called a halt. Calzaghe is not a big puncher like Nigel Benn but he has tremendous hand speed and hits hard enough to hurt. Calzaghe has the talent to be the Dark Destroyer's natural successor. Co-managers Mickey Duff and Terry Lawless have produced 10 world champs between them and have no doubt Joe will be a major star. Duff said: 'I think comparing them all at this stage of their careers, Calzaghe is better than Benn, Chris Eubank or Henry Wharton. That doesn't mean Joe hasn't got plenty of faults but what he does wrong he gets away with it. Everyone knows he should have knocked out Delaney in the first round but he allowed himself to get over-excited and let the chance slip. He also drops his hands and showboats every now and again. That will have to stop as he moves up the ladder.' One thing that came through a tough test was Calzaghe's temperament. He did not allow a hostile home crowd to unnerve him.

– Colin Hart, *Sun*, 22 April 1996

At the after-show party Steve Collins, the WBO super middleweight title-holder, came up and tapped me on the shoulder. 'You're doing good,' he said. 'You were excellent tonight. I know Mark well because I've sparred with him and you've just beaten a good fighter.' Steve gave me the respect, even though he knew I could end up fighting him. The Delaney fight got full coverage on ITV but it wasn't broadcast until about 11.30 p.m. and my next two contests, neither of which was televised in full, were backward steps as far as I was concerned. First I faced Warren Stowe, a nice guy from Burnley but Warren would be the first to admit that he wasn't in great shape for the fight. He was way overweight and had a massive cauliflower ear by the time I stopped him in the second round. Brief highlights were shown on BBC's *Sportsnight*. Less than two weeks later I was back in the ring to take on Pat Lawlor, who boasted of wins over Wilfred Benitez and Roberto Duran. But Benitez was a shell of the fighter who had been a three-weight world champion when they fought and Duran was celebrating his forty-ninth birthday. Lawlor lasted two rounds with me in a bout that had no TV coverage. Frank Warren had moved his stable of fighters across to Sky TV, where all the money was. ITV were pulling out of boxing and the BBC only showed short clips. I was British champion and world-ranked but I was fighting these guys and getting minimal coverage. Frank, on the other hand, could offer me the world title fight I was looking for. When I sat and watched Robin Reid getting his WBC title fight against Nardiello I was gutted. I couldn't believe it. He didn't go the British title route at all. He went with Frank, got a title fight and even though he wasn't half the fighter I was he was a world champion and I was struggling to make ends meet. I could hardly pay off the mortgage of £45,000 on a little three-bedroom semi-detached house in Newbridge.

'When am I going to get my shot, Mickey?' I asked.

'You'll get your shot after Henry Wharton gets his,' he said.

As always, I was going to have to wait my turn. I spoke to my dad and he knew the score. I was going to have to wait and wait until I became the mandatory contender and then I would get my shot. 'No way,' I thought, so I went to see Frank, who gave me certain guarantees, the main one being that after three fights he would get me a title shot, which he did. That's what I wanted. I wanted to be in the picture. I was still under contract to Duff and Lawless, so I went to a solicitor who informed me that they were in breach of contract, because they had never shown me the contracts for my fights.

I spoke to Mickey and told him that I wasn't happy and wanted to leave. I had never had hard words with either Mickey or Terry and he was taken aback. It wasn't just about money at that stage but I had twenty-one fights with Duff and Lawless over a period of three years and nothing changed. Every time my management and promotional contracts were up for renewal I had signed new ones. I had even received a £5,000 signing-on fee but that was a loan as well. Eventually, the British Boxing Board of Control had to arbitrate and somehow it was worked out that I owed Duff and Lawless several thousand pounds. Actually, it wasn't just Duff and Lawless. At the Board of Control hearing I discovered that Jarvis Astaire, a long-time associate of Duff and Lawless, was involved as well. I didn't really know who he was. The only time I had previously met him was after asking Mickey if he could get me tickets to the Italy–Austria game at Anfield during Euro '96. Mickey said he would sort it and it was Jarvis who was there at the hotel with David Dein, the Arsenal vice-chairman, when I went to pick up the tickets for myself and a mate. We had lunch, I was handed the tickets and I paid for them. Mickey wasn't one for gifts. Actually, he did treat me once. After I beat Delaney he bought me a Chinese takeaway which I took back to my hotel room. At the hearing they argued that they were still due 25 per cent of my purses for the remainder of the contract but a settlement was reached which was later quashed.

The real issue for me, however, was that I wasn't certain where my career had been going. Frank had staged the biggest bouts in recent years in Britain and he was making Naseem Hamed into a massive crossover star. When Naz came on the scene it was like an explosion. He was able to make his name with ITV and gain a large audience on terrestrial television before he moved over to

Sky with the rest of Frank's stable and this helped him to command huge purses for the rest of his career. But it was what Frank had done with Benn and Steve Collins and even Eubank, who had mostly been promoted by Barry Hearn, that left me in no doubt about the decision I had made. I was still an amateur when I first watched Eubank and Benn and even back then I really thought that I could beat them. I believed in my ability. I was a star as an amateur, able to take my time on most of my opponents, and I was undefeated as a pro, totally in command of almost every one of my fights to date. I knew I could compete at the highest level. I just wanted the chance. I was the most exciting fighter in the country but the public didn't know me.

My dad and I decided to go to Frank to discuss the possibility of doing a deal. He knew I was unhappy with the way my career was going. I wanted a title shot and I thought it would be against Robin Reid, but Frank got me into the mandatory contender's position for the WBO belt instead.

My first fight working with Frank was in Whitchurch where I faced Carlos Christie, another former amateur star. I beat him easily inside two rounds and I felt like things were just about to happen for me. So out of the first £50,000 I made when I signed with Frank, I spent £43,000 on a new BMW M3 car. I had no more than £55,000 in the bank but it's a funny thing that when I didn't have much money I wanted to be flash. I knew I would be paid for my next fight but nearly all of the money I had at the time went into that car. At the time I wanted to spoil myself because I felt I deserved it. I'd worked hard for it and felt I could treat myself to something nice.

Straight away after signing with Frank I started to see a dividend, being paid by far the biggest purse of my career to fight Christie. It was great money and it ended years of frustration, knocking people out and doing it with pizzazz and no one taking much notice. I then knocked out Tyler Hughes, who was undefeated in twelve fights, in the opening round, before Frank brought across Luciano Torres from Brazil. He had a record of forty-four wins and just two losses, but he lasted three rounds. Then Frank held true to his promise. The match was made between me and Steve Collins for the Celtic Warrior's WBO super middleweight belt and, finally, the opportunity that I had dedicated my whole life to achieving was mine. There would be two Celtic warriors in the ring on 11 October, I told myself, but nothing is ever as it seems in boxing, so there was another twist before I was able to grab my chance.

ROUND SIX

Down in the Trenches

Steve Collins had just beaten Chris Eubank and Nigel Benn to become one of the most respected fighters in British boxing. For years he had toiled and struggled to make his name, boxing out of the same gym as Marvelous Marvin Hagler and going twelve hard rounds with Mike McCallum, one of the most underrated fighters of the era. Finally, towards the end of his career, Collins's reputation was made secure by two wins each over Eubank and Benn. He didn't need to put it all on the line against me. Steve knew the danger, so he decided not to fight me.

I'm convinced that's why Steve gave up the WBO belt he had won from Eubank and walked off into retirement. Frank had got me into the position of mandatory challenger, so Steve couldn't duck me but, deep down, he didn't want to know. He weighed up the pros and cons and probably concluded in his mind that I wasn't a big enough name to justify the risk of facing me. He'd just beaten two of the biggest names in the sport and all of a sudden he was being made to encounter a young, up-

and-coming fighter who was dangerous. So he asked himself, 'Why? Do I need to risk getting the shit kicked out of me before I retire?' The answer was straight-forward: 'No, I can just get out now.' He told people that he couldn't find the motivation but I'm sure that if they'd found another Craig Cummings for him to fight, motivation wouldn't have been so much of a problem. He had enough motivation when he stepped in the ring with Cummings only three months before and got dumped on his arse. I had also beaten up his mate, Mark Delaney, who gave Collins trouble in sparring, so the truth is that Steve knew what was coming.

I had gone to watch him fight quite a few times and there's no doubt that Steve was very good, but he also had the good fortune to catch Eubank at the right stage in his career and Benn as well. Eubank had him on the verge of being knocked out in the ninth round of their first fight in Millstreet, County Cork, but after the Michael Watson tragedy Chris never had the same instinct to finish off any opponent. So Collins was able to hang in there and win a close but deserved points decision, which he did again in their rematch at Cork's Pairc Ui Chaoimh football ground. Benn was finished after his brutal war with Gerald McClellan, who almost died as a result of his brain injuries. He won the fight but took a tremendous beating and, psychologically, those fights do damage beyond repair. So, despite his reputation, I was always 100 per

119

cent confident that I could beat Collins. I was in a bar in Newport when I watched Cummings, who was no more than a middleweight, floor him – a big roar went up – and that only increased my confidence. Even when he signed to fight me his behaviour was strange, almost indifferent. At the press conference, when Frank announced that it was on for 11 October, Collins walked in and told the press to speak to his publicist, Max Clifford, if they had any enquiries about his business. Then he just walked straight back out again. He didn't want the fight. I sensed that all along.

Time went on and he met with Frank, who told him that the fight was going to happen. Collins felt that he was being railroaded into something that wasn't in his best interests. It wasn't as if he was being offered £1 million, so it didn't make sense from a business standpoint either. I'm not going to call Collins chicken because that's one thing he wasn't – Steve was one of the bravest every time he stepped in the ring – but he's an intelligent guy also and a businessman. He calculated that if he got in the ring with this young Calzaghe kid, whom no one had ever heard of, there was just too much risk for a couple of hundred grand. So a week or two before the fight was due to take place I switched on the TV and read on Teletext that Steve had pulled out. Then he announced his retirement at the British Boxing Board's annual awards dinner. 'Joe is a good up-and-coming kid but he wouldn't fill a parish church,' he said. This isn't something I've held against him all these years. I've met him at fights and other events and I like Steve because he's a good guy who did well for himself. But he did annoy me when he said that he couldn't get up for the fight and wasn't motivated and that's when he knew he should retire. Bullshit. I know why Steve Collins didn't fight me. Every fighter and every trainer and promoter worth their salt knows how good another fighter is and Steve knew his own limitations. I think he knew he was going to be beaten and, if so, after watching my fight with Eubank he probably realised that he'd made a wise decision. He didn't make a comeback, did he?

Meanwhile, Eubank had been in training to fight Mark Prince, so about ten days before the Sheffield show Frank rang me up and told me I was fighting him.

Eubank entered the equation a year ago when he first pestered Warren about a fight deal. Early last month a deal was finalised for Eubank to box in England. On September 11 the deal was off after the pair had an argument. A week later it was back on, with Eubank allegedly in a fight against Mark Prince, from Tottenham, for the WBO Intercontinental light heavyweight title, a fight that always looked unlikely to take place. Warren wanted Eubank on the Sheffield show and last week the gap opened for him to get his way and Eubank to get the exposure he craves. When Collins went, doubts about the show taking place ended, only to be replaced by fears for Eubank's health if, as expected, he had excess weight to lose. The British Boxing Board of Control announced they would be monitoring his weight reduction methods.

– Steve Bunce, *Daily Telegraph*,
9 October 1997

Eubank had two weeks to get down to the twelve-stone super middleweight limit and there was little time for either of us to get our heads around this turn of events, but I felt I would now be involved in a more difficult fight. Overall, Eubank was a better boxer and he was fresher than he'd been for a long time, having contested just two fights in the previous two years, as opposed to six which he'd had in thirteen months coming into his first encounter with Collins. The break had revitalised him after his crazy schedule of fighting every couple of months or so during his £10 million Sky TV ten-fight deal. His batteries were recharged and he had his hunger back after going stale with one fight on top of another. His back was against the wall and few fighters were more dangerous in adversity than Christopher Livingstone Eubank. I knew he wasn't turning up for the numbers. Good fighters always brought out the best in him.

Remember when he landed that devastating right upper-cut on Watson at the end of the eleventh round? It came straight after Watson had knocked him down and looked to be on the verge of stopping him.

The only time I had ever watched him live was when he'd stopped Sam Storey in the seventh round three years earlier in Cardiff. I remember the buzz as Tina Turner's 'Simply the Best' reverberated around the arena and as I stood there watching him, the adrenalin pumping through me, all I had in my head were a few simple thoughts: *This is where I want to be. I'm going to win the world title one day. This is what I want to do and one day that will be me walking to the ring.* I always got excited about watching Eubank and Benn because I knew that I would probably fight at the same weight. In my last ABA championships I boxed at middleweight, which in the amateurs is 11st 10lb, so I knew I was going to be a super middleweight in the pros. Benn was the ultimate warrior and Eubank the ultimate showman. Chris marketed himself so cleverly. Love him or hate him, and everybody had an opinion one way or the other, he made a shedload of money because he was a unique individual, the way he carried himself, the Lord of Brighton Manor. If he had walked to the ring like any other fighter, he wouldn't have been a star. He wasn't a thrilling boxer. It was rare that I saw him in an electrifying fight. In fact, he had loads of stinkers. Benn, on the other hand, was Mr Excitement. You knew that when you sat down to watch a Nigel Benn fight it was likely to be a tear-up. He was either going to hurt the other guy or end up hurt himself. So here I was fighting one half of the most famous double act in British boxing and all I could think about was the day I had told one of my mates, as a scrawny teenager, that I could beat Eubank and how I got seriously pissed off when he laughed.

We met for the first time outside a London hotel. Eubank turned up on his Harley-Davidson motorcycle, wearing a silk shirt, a leather jacket and a pair of his trademark jodhpurs. I had never been in his company before, so I was a bit taken aback by the grand entrance. We were going to fight in a matter of days but he walked along a line of people as if he hadn't a care in the world, smiling and shaking hands while taking off his hat and his goggles. Then he came to me.

'And you are?' he asked, looking into my eyes intently.

'I'm the guy who's about to stop you and your silly walk,' I should have said back to him but instead I laughed. You just had to. That's how Eubank was, a student of amateur kidology. He also had a really strong handshake. But out of everything he said that day in the press conference one point remains vivid in my memory.

'You have a good record,' he said, addressing me directly, 'but you've never been into the trenches. I've been there and that's where I'm going to take you.'

He did. Physically and mentally, the Eubank fight drained me. I said that I was going to knock him out but that night was the hardest I've had in the whole of my boxing career. If I hadn't shown a warrior's heart, Eubank would have won back his belt. I had to dig deep just to stay with him, in the trenches, and only my heart and fitness brought me through the ordeal. It was the most exhausted I've ever been. In boxing you need to be calm under pressure but you also need immense heart because one day being able to dig deep will be your only way out.

Eubank and Benn, Michael Watson and Collins were fighters who knew how to dig. I used to love watching Benn and Eubank, in particular, and I strived to be like them. I loved Eubank's arrogance and admired his showmanship. He could be frustrating to watch against fighters he should easily have beaten, like Dan Sherry when he fought like a bum, but when he boxed the likes of Benn and Watson he showed exactly what he was about and I knew he was going to fight well against me. I was more nervous than I had been for any fight before, not because I was fighting Eubank but because it was a title fight on a big bill in Sheffield, which Frank was calling 'The Full Monty' after the success of the movie. Everything I had worked for my entire life was on the line and my nervousness showed itself in strange ways. With less than two weeks to go I brought in two local boys to spar and one of them cut me on the lip by elbowing me deliberately. I was beating up on him a little bit and he came in and caught me with his elbow. The cut was bad enough for me to need a couple of stitches. 'What the fuck are you doing?' I shouted at him. My dad tried to take away the heat. 'Right, that's it, come on out,' he told us, but I wanted to make the guy pay for what he'd done. 'No way,' I said. I kept him in there and I ripped in body shots and head shots until he went down. By now, the red mist had settled. 'Get back up,' I said, spitting out the words and, bang, I put him down again. 'Get back up.' Three times I put him on the floor because I knew he'd done it on purpose. I made sure he paid. 'Now fuck off,' I told him as we got out of the ring. It's fair to say that I wasn't in a good mood that day.

When I first turned pro I did beat up guys in the gym because I had this mentality that I was paying them £100 for sparring and they should earn it. Tony Booth, an experienced old pro from Hull, had sparred with Benn and several other top fighters and he once told me that I was the only fighter in a training camp that he couldn't wait to get away from. I beat him up for two days before he left for home. He would spend two or three weeks in camp with Benn, who hardly hit him, but he couldn't handle more than two days with me. Andy Flute, a good fighter in his day, used to spar with Benn and Sven Ottke, the long-time German holder of the IBF super middle-weight title. He always said that he was never hit as many times or as hard as he was in sparring with me. Back then I used to hit my sparring partners hard but I became more injury-prone as my career went on, and with maturity I also settled down and stopped trying to have sparring sessions that became wars in the gym. Eventually, they're not too healthy for anybody.

Over and over in my mind I kept telling myself that I was fighting Chris Eubank for a world title and the anxiety was building inside me. I'd never been in this kind of environment, surrounded by all the hype that goes with a big fight, the interviews, the photo calls, the general buzz and, of course, your own expectation. Sky TV were putting it out on pay-per-view and Naseem Hamed was top of a bill that was to feature ten title fights in all. It was a big day for sport, with England playing Italy in a World Cup qualifier – a 0–0 draw which would be Gianfranco Zola's last game for the Azzurri – and the biggest night of my career, a night when I would have to prove myself to Eubank and to everybody else.

Like Eubank, Calzaghe has a style that infuriates the boxing purists. He dances around the ring with his hands at waist height but makes no apology for that. Southpaw Calzaghe pointed out that he has finished 21 of his 22 fights inside the distance and added, 'Some people don't appreciate class. They just want orthodox or Queensberry Rules types. But I have got three or four gears. I can slow it down and bang or I can go fast. I can box, I can fight or I can showboat. The speed is natural. It has always been there and, thankfully, I can punch hard as well.' Arguably, his only victories of real significance were over Steve Wilson for the vacant British super middleweight championship and Mark Delaney in his first defence. But former champion Eubank, making another come-back, gives his opponent due respect. He said, 'Joe is undefeated in 22 fights and I should worry about that. But I have had 49 fights and nobody has knocked me out, not even the world's hardest pound-for-pound punchers, so I cannot see Joe doing it. It is very ugly and nasty in the trenches. This is the acid test for Joe and I don't think he will come up trumps.'

– David Smith, *Evening Standard*,
9 October 1997

At the official weigh-in Eubank made the twelve-stone limit comfortably, hitting 11st 13¾lb to my 11st 13¼lb. I always come to the ring twenty-four hours later weighing somewhere between 12st 10lb and 12st 12lb and when I'm at that weight I'm happy. I feel good in myself because I know I'll be strong. But I burnt so much nervous energy in the final hours before facing Eubank that I came in much lighter. I was just 12st 4lb when I went to the ring. The pressure I was putting on myself to perform meant that I didn't eat right. I just couldn't. All my life I'd worked for this moment, to challenge for a title and to win. I'd imagined it, I'd dreamt about it and, suddenly, this was the real thing. We got to the arena at about 8 p.m., which was too early because I wasn't in the ring until after midnight, and I trained for an hour on the pads, too much. I was slightly dehydrated and on edge even before I got to the ring. The adrenalin was pumping because all my life I'd worked for this moment, to fight for a world title. I'd imagined it, I'd dreamt about it, but this was the real thing and I wanted it so bad at that particular moment that I was just a bundle of nerves, so I started like a runaway train.

When the bell rang I flew out of my corner towards Eubank and hit him with a left hook, which knocked him down along the ropes. The punch hadn't caught him flush and he got up and nodded over to me, smiling. My sole purpose at that point was to go back in and try to knock him out and I thought I was going to. I kept telling myself, 'This is the big chance. Take him out now and don't blow it.' I went for it but I was far too wild and Eubank covered up well. I threw a lot of punches but I didn't hurt him again and at the end of the round, with Eubank still on his feet, I felt tired. There wasn't much in the tank. I didn't feel 100 per cent in the second and third rounds and Eubank ended the third round smiling. I knew then that I wasn't going to knock him out and that

I'd have to prepare myself mentally to go into the trenches, where he had predicted that the fight would be fought. I had never boxed for twelve rounds before. In fact, I had only gone eight rounds twice. Everybody else went inside four rounds. Now, after just three rounds, I was completely knackered. I'd hardly eaten any food and I was stressed out. I didn't know if I would be physically strong enough to last the course. Chris had been here many times and he looked across the ring before the start of the fourth round and smiled again. 'I'm still here,' he was telling me, trying to reinforce the doubts he knew would be swimming around in my head.

Eubank was always an intelligent fighter and he knew, almost instinctively, what he had to do in any particular fight. Physically, he was exceptionally strong and he moved well and covered up well and could take a really good shot, regardless of the early knock-down. Cleverly, he avoided being hit clean by moving his head fractionally ahead of being hit by a punch. He kept his chin low and he also had good power. He wasn't the biggest puncher I ever fought but he could hit. Although he never really hurt me, there were several times in the fight when he stunned me with decent shots, right hands over the top. I wasn't wobbled or in danger of going down but I felt his power and at that stage of my career I hadn't boxed anybody who could take me the rounds or anybody who was as wily as he was. If I boxed Eubank today, it would be a different story, but I was twenty-five years old and knew a lot less than the guy in the other corner. Experience only comes with the years.

We weren't even halfway when I started to ask myself, 'How the fuck am I going to come through this?' Rounds five, six and seven were decent rounds for Eubank, like murder for me. My dad had to give me a kick up the arse before the start of the seventh because he could see signs in the sixth that I was wilting. *What are you doing, Joe? Do you want me to stop this fucking fight? You've got to keep fighting this guy. Start using your jab. Box.* He always makes it more dramatic than it really is but that was my wake-up call and I started to pick it up again. In the seventh round we both slipped onto the floor and I actually found it hard to get back up. I'd hit a brick wall. Towards the end of the round Eubank thumbed me in my left eye, the only time I've really got marked in a fight apart from the Bika fight nine years later. The swelling came up around the eye and I had to lift my head in the air to see him, leaving Eubank able to catch me with more right hands. I was exhausted but I had to push myself through a hard couple of rounds. Dad was urging me on. *What the fuck are you doing? You're going to throw away this fight.* A couple of times he slapped my face and it was my sheer will and determination to be a champion that drove me on when I was past tired.

Going into the ninth round, my mouth was dry and I

started to get stomach cramps. They were painful and I was becoming seriously dehydrated. Gulping down water between rounds wasn't helping at all but, because of my general fitness and the fact that I could see the end approaching, I was able to get my second wind and finish strongly enough. For the last three rounds – uncharted territory – I picked it up again and came through some hard punches from Eubank. The experience of a long, gruelling fight must be like that of a marathon runner reaching the final mile and seeing the finishing line. That gives you the energy to see it through. I showed my fighting spirit that night. Eubank landed two good shots right at the end of the fight and I stayed on him and kept punching because that's my way. A lot of people would move around and try to stay out of trouble but that's not me. When the bell rang I knew that I'd won and I raised my hands, though I was barely able to. I'll never go through another experience like that ever again. There was an immediate feeling of joy when my dad lifted me on his shoulders but I was exhausted. The next day I struggled to even get out of bed. I just couldn't. Every muscle, from my neck all the way down to my feet, was in agony, not from the punches I'd taken but from the sheer physical toll of doing twelve hard rounds against one of boxing's true warriors.

'Joe, you're a good fighter,' he said as we walked back to our dressing rooms together after the judges' decision had been announced. 'Now I know why Steve Collins didn't want to fight you. Clever guy. Clever guy.'

At the press conference afterwards I was first in, sporting a black eye and sore all over my body. Several minutes later Eubank sauntered in, doing his strut. He had changed into a sharp suit and he looked immaculate, like he hadn't been in a fight. Even though I had won, it looked like he'd just given me a beating. He didn't have a mark on him and I was so depleted. Eubank was respectful and courteous in his comments and I remembered that he'd told me that I wouldn't knock him out. He was right about that and he was right about something else: after that fight I knew what it was to be taken into the trenches.

The harder the fight the sweeter the victory and I was so proud. The pain, the exhaustion and the hardship I went through to win the belt, which I still hold, will live with me forever. I fought a real champion that night and came through the toughest of endurance tests and I'm glad it was Eubank and that it was such a struggle because I was able to prove to myself everything that I needed to, everything that I'd always believed about myself. If I'd gone in there and knocked him out in the opening round, a guy who was a substitute opponent, it would have been a bad way to win the title. I wasn't able to beat Collins, who had been the champion, but I beat a legend who'd had more title fights at the time than I'd had fights. I was still a novice but I felt good after my first twelve-round fight.

It was quite simply one of the finest fights in British boxing history. 'Gentlemen,' Eubank said, 'the show goes on. I entertain. I crave it. I missed boxing and had time to reflect during my two-year absence. I came back and I took a gamble but it was a good gamble. Joe Calzaghe is an exceptional fighter.' As Eubank spoke, Calzaghe, his right eye closed, remained silent with a look of utter exhaustion on his bruised face. There were moments when Eubank's long right connected cleanly with Calzaghe's chin. There were other moments when a haze descended down Eubank's face after southpaw lefts landed. Every second was fought with little or no regard for the outcome of the next round. They stood with their toes touching and unleashed punches in wild round after wild round. There was a look in Eubank's eyes that was missing in many of his last championship fights and, as each failed right uppercut missed and Calzaghe blocked some that were on target, it was still impossible to rule out a Eubank win. But on Saturday Calzaghe fought like a veteran and not a novice with 22 easy wins, including 10 in the first round. The exchanges in most of the rounds were reminiscent of boxing's most brutal and memorable encounters. As the punches connected, there were gasps from the ringside area and a constant roar of appreciation from the capacity crowd. Calzaghe can do whatever Frank Warren, the show's pro-moter, wants because against Eubank he became a true fighter the hard way, the old-fashioned way, by surviving tremendous adversity to win.

– Steve Bunce, *Daily Telegraph*,
13 October 1997

Whenever I meet Chris he is constantly passing on advice. People have their own ideas about him, from what they read in the newspapers about his anti-war protests and his eccentric personality, but he's well meaning, a good man, though a very different character to me. He's extravagant in the way he spends his money but – apart from my blowout after my first win with Frank – I look after mine. I could get a bigger car or a faster car but I'm realistic enough to know that if you start chasing these things the money won't last. I'm not someone who goes seeking the bright lights or quick thrills. I live in the same area in which I grew up and my feet remain firmly planted on the ground. More than any other sport, boxing's about staying focused and staying hungry, so I never regarded my fight against Eubank as the ultimate fulfilment and I didn't change the way I live. I train with the same boys in the gym, the boys I've always trained with, and there's no superstar status around here because I'm a world champion. I walk into Newbridge and I'm just Joe. Nobody bothers me and there aren't many things here to distract me from what I've got to do. I don't have to go down the road signing autographs and I like that. I beat Eubank in my twenty-second fight and I've now fought twenty more and I'm still unbeaten and still hungry for more.

I've often reflected on the praise that was lavished on Eubank after our fight by the same people who hated him when he won. I guess it's the gallant loser syndrome that exists in this country. Maybe that's why the England cricket team can't win the Ashes more than once or why the Welsh rugby team aren't able to build on a Grand Slam. In Eubank's case the crowds used to loathe him, then he lost to me and twice more against Carl Thompson for the WBO cruiserweight title and they loved him. That's a mentality I've never been able to understand.

Eubank was an exuberant showman but he was also a good fighter and he always fought to win. I came along right at the end of the Eubank–Benn–Watson–Collins era and sometimes I regret this. Maybe I could have made £10 million in two years but been beaten to a pulp, which might have been the end of me. Instead, by staying patient and hungry, I've demonstrated my talent over a long period. I could have fought an opponent like Lacy in my first defence and made four or five defences and moved on but I had to wait for years. The way I see it, everything happens for a reason.

Naz boxed really well that night in Sheffield against Jose Badillo before he stopped his Puerto Rican challenger in the seventh round. Also on the bill, in a fight that took place several hours before me and Eubank were called to the ring, was a British light welterweight title fight between Belfast's Mark Winters and Carl Wright from Liverpool. Carl's brother, Paul, and I had been due to fight in 1996 before I injured an ankle, so the bout never happened, but Carl was confident that he could take home a Lonsdale belt for the family. He lost on points, however, and on his way home from the arena he took ill and slipped into a coma. That night he had to be operated on to remove a blood clot from his brain, and when the bad news emerged the next day, it was a shock. No fighter ever wants to hear of another fighter going through this.

It would happen again when I boxed in the same arena against Richie Woodhall three years later. Paul Ingle lost his IBF featherweight title to the South African, Mbulelo Botile, was carried out of the ring on a stretcher and underwent emergency brain surgery to remove a blood clot. Both boys have made only a partial recovery but Paul's plight affected me more because I'd known him quite well and I liked him. He won a schoolboy ABA championship the same year as me and I can remember watching him as a thirteen-year-old amateur. We were the same age and, throughout our careers, we went more or less the same route. He fought in a tremendous encounter with Hamed before getting stopped in the eleventh round but managed to win the IBF belt in his next fight. I was delighted for him, but Paul was to pay a heavy price for struggling so badly to make weight for the Botile bout.

Now we are made to do check weigh-ins by the British Boxing Board of Control in the run-up to fights, but I remember seeing Paul at a press conference seven weeks before the Sheffield bill and he wouldn't take off his top for the publicity shots. I can only assume this was because he knew that he was a bit fleshy, and I thought to myself that day, looking at him 'How is he going to make weight?' Paul could fight but I believe he was drained from the effort of making weight. It's a telling reminder to all fighters of the importance of making weight properly. I'm all for the British Boxing Board's policy of check weigh-ins four weeks before. It's a struggle for me but it gives you a benchmark and it means that you're coming down in weight in a way that doesn't leave you totally debilitated when you reach the weigh-in the day before the fight. I have to be 12st 10lb four weeks before and that's difficult as my natural walking-around weight is between 13st 10lb and 14st, but because I have to hit that mark four weeks before I always make the weight fine and I'm always strong. I prayed for Paul that night in Sheffield, as I'm sure I did for Carl. No one really knew whether he would come through. This is just a sport, so someone's health is far more important. It was Christmas as well and I felt so sorry for Paul's wife and kid. Thank God it wasn't worse, though I know he's struggled to get his life back together. It's been similar for Carl.

I never think about the potential consequences of what I do. I'm aware of them. Every fighter is aware of them, but I don't dwell on the subject. That's my defensive mechanism perhaps. I look on boxing as an art. People who are ignorant only see the brutality, but if they were to sit down and watch proper boxing, they'd begin to appreciate the skill of being able to hit and not be hit. I'm proud that I've managed to keep my features intact. I'm proud that my face hasn't been smashed and that there's no scar tissue around my eyes. Why is that? Am I really that lucky? I don't believe so. I'm just good at what I do. When I spar I always let the other fighter come to me and I get pleasure from making him miss, being slick and moving like a snake, out-thinking him and making the right moves and having the nerve to execute all that in the ring against a live opponent. That's boxing and that's the art.

It's entertaining to watch two fighters pummelling away at one another, like Marvin Hagler and Tommy Hearns did in 1985 in the car park at the back of Caesars

Palace, a tremendous fight, an absolute war. But I don't crave to be involved in that kind of fight. I don't want to be in a Muhammad Ali–Joe Frazier scenario where both winner and loser end up in the hospital and the winner describes it as 'the closest thing to dying'. When I get in the ring I just want to beat the man in front of me and come out unscathed myself. I don't want to be remembered as a crowd-pleaser, if it means that some day someone will treat me like a punchbag. Boxing's not important to the extent that I can't walk away from it. If I thought I was going to get hurt or hit about, I wouldn't do it. Boxing is as safe as it's ever been and in this country we are fortunate because the British Boxing Board of Control is excellent in the way it administrates the sport, making sure that doctors and anaesthetists are ringside at every fight. Unfortunate things still happen, as they do in other sports, in motor sport, rugby and even football. On the same day that I fought Sakio Bika in Manchester the Chelsea goalkeeper, Petr Cech, was stretchered off and underwent surgery for a depressed fracture of the skull, and then Carlo Cudicini, the substitute goalkeeper, had to be carried off as well when he was knocked unconscious. How many former rugby players are paraplegics because of a tackle or an accident that happened on the pitch? Thank God, these things haven't happened to me. I understand that in boxing the purpose is to do damage but I can only speak for myself and say honestly that I have never wanted to seriously hurt an opponent. I'm not violent, it's just the nature of what I do.

People jump on the bandwagon to ban boxing because we're inflicting punishment on another human being but this happens in other sports, not just boxing. Richard Vowles, a mate of mine, started boxing at the age of thirteen, as a featherweight. Like me, he won a school-boys' ABA title, he had a hundred-odd amateur fights, turned pro and had four fights, and the worst he ever suffered from his years in the ring was a broken nose. Richard's in a wheelchair now, paralysed from the neck down, and it happened in a friendly game of rugby. He went in a scrum, all nine and a half stone of him, the scrum collapsed and he broke his back. If he'd suffered the same kind of injury in a boxing ring, there would have been a clamour to ban the sport. It's an accident in rugby, yet in boxing it's different somehow. I know the argument about intent but, listen, I'm a fighter and I can tell you what's in my mind. I have never set foot in a ring with the express intention of inflicting serious harm on my opponent. Never. That is just not me. Look at the tapes and see my face when I'm about to answer the bell. I'm usually smiling and it's not an assassin's smile. It's just the smile of a man about to do a job I enjoy. When I got in the ring against Bika I looked down at my two sons, Joe and Connor, at ringside and I waved to them. Do you really think I turned away from my kids and immediately transformed myself into a monster who would want to kill a man? They know who their dad is and they know I'm not like that. I know I'm in a dangerous profession but I also know I'm not a sadist. I'm a father of two boys I love to bits, with the same competitiveness and the same desire to do well as the best lock forward in international rugby. I've seen their flat noses, their cauliflower ears and their gummy smiles, I've looked at myself in the mirror and all I can say is thank God I'm not a rugby player.

Boxing's a harder sport. It's the hardest sport, one-on-one combat. When you're in that ring there is no one who can help you. You're on your own, sometimes under siege. You don't have ten other teammates to help you out, or fourteen. It's you and the other guy and you can't throw in a substitute when you get injured. If you break your hand, you stay in there or you lose. If you get cut across the eyes, you're in serious trouble but you hang in there, clinging onto the hope that you can turn it all around with one punch. The ring must be the loneliest place in the world sometimes, a frightening place because your opponent is trained to beat you up physically, and if he can knock you out, he will. Cyclists, maybe, are fitter than fighters with their cardiovascular levels, but they're riding a bike, they're not getting bashed up. In the boxing ring you get hit with body shots and you get winded and you have to keep going. You get cut and you keep going. Your equilibrium goes from a shot to the head and you use your wits to survive. Then you try to get back in the fight. I have the utmost respect for cyclists because it's a hard, hard sport. But it's not boxing.

I could worry about boxing but I could also worry every time I get in the car to drive. I can't live my life worrying or eventually I would fall into a depression. When I'm in the ring I feel like I'm OK. I'm not out drinking and I'm not getting in trouble. I'm not abusing my body and eating like a pig, the way I do sometimes when I'm not fighting. I'm eating well and I'm at the peak of my physical fitness. My mind is clear and I feel more alive than I do anywhere else. Eubank said to me recently that I should walk away when I hurt an opponent. 'You know you've got his number,' he said. 'Hurt him and make the crowd laugh and cheer, then walk away.' I disagreed with him. 'I'm a finisher,' I said. But then again I haven't experienced what he and Watson, Benn, McClellan, Carl Wright and Paul Ingle have been through. And I never want to.

ROUND SEVEN
A Wake-Up Call

Just a week after beating Eubank I had to fly to Los Angeles for the WBO convention and to collect my belt. Naseem Hamed, Ryan Rhodes and Carl Thompson were all going too and I'd just arrived at Heathrow airport when someone told me I was late, that I had missed it all kicking off between Naz and Eubank. Apparently, Naz had taunted Chris with 'Do you want to look at my belts?' and Chris, who was meeting somebody at the airport, had turned round and sent Hamed's belts flying across the floor. There was a short stand-off before Naz caught Chris with an open-handed punch to his nose, just as Chris was making to slap him for the disrespect he had been shown. Security had to separate them and it was still the whole talk as we boarded the plane.

I was on cloud nine, a twenty-five-year-old lad from a small town who'd just won a world title and all of a sudden I was travelling first class on Virgin Airlines and I'd never travelled first class on anything in my life. I couldn't believe the luxury. A girl came up to my seat offering to do a manicure and I couldn't believe they did this, so I had it done. There were video games, a telephone and you could eat and drink what you wanted. Carl was quiet but I got on well with Ryan, who boxed with Naz out of Brendan Ingle's gym in Sheffield. He was down to earth and the feeling was that he was the next big thing but, unfortunately, it never happened for him. I wish he'd done better with his career. Naz was a different guy, he got on well with me but he kept slagging off Carl and I could quickly see why Eubank might have had a problem with him.

I'm not very close to other fighters. I speak to Richie Woodhall when I see him and I'm pretty friendly with Takaloo, the light middleweight from Margate. I'm big mates with Enzo Maccarinelli and I get on really well with the other lads in our gym, Bradley Pryce, Gavin Rees and Nathan Cleverly – and I talk to Barry Jones and Eubank a lot. I see Collins and Benn at dinners from time to time and there's always mutual respect. We may not know one another but we know what we do and there's a camaraderie that's forged by all of those years we've spent in the ring. We're like a large family in many ways. But not Naz. He was all right with me, though it was pretty superficial. Naz was the only millionaire among us and very money-oriented. None of the rest of us had money at all and he kept on about his money the whole time. 'Check out my rings, man,' he'd say before telling us how much he'd paid for each of them. When we arrived he ordered a limo for all of us, then we had to sit and watch his fight against Badillo and listen to his endless self-praise: 'Yeah, look at me, man. Am I good?' Actually, he was funny, you couldn't say he wasn't. He made people laugh even with his arrogance. That loud personality made him famous and he was exciting to watch, though not necessarily over and over in that limo as we drove through LA. Me and him were cool but the way he was with some of the other people on the trip was downright insulting. Brendan Ingle, his trainer, was with us and I'd always assumed that he and Naz got on well, but it was the first time I'd been around them and suddenly Naz was really having a go at him. I was embarrassed because he was so disrespectful. That surprised me, but it was the way he spoke to Carl which was especially cruel. Carl was a good fighter from Manchester and a WBO champion himself, though he had never made the fortunes Naz had and couldn't dream of making that amount of money.

'How much did you get for your last fight, Carl?' Naz asked and screwed up his face when Carl told him. 'Is that all? You should be getting more. I get that for opening up a store. I'm getting paid, man, I'm getting paid. Man, it ain't worth it. I'll sort it out.'

We went to a store on Rodeo Drive and Naz said he was going to buy a watch and, of course, it had to be a Rolex that was priced at $250,000. 'I'll give you $150,000 for it,' he told the guy in the store. I don't think he wanted the watch, he was just giving it big in front of all of us. I know that I would never go into the gym in Newbridge and say to the other boys, 'How much are you getting for your next fight? A grand? What? I wouldn't piss for that.' But Naz was all into that. Carl's a guy who keeps himself to himself but he was getting seriously wound up to the point where you could see that he wanted to rip Naz's head off. Naz was like the schoolyard bully, trying to ridicule him and belittle him: 'What you wearing, Carl? What's that on your head?' Finally, Carl snapped. 'Shut it, man. What is your fucking problem? Look at you. I don't need to see your belts because you've got ears like a trophy. I could pick you up by grabbing them. Look at you. The only reason you have a bird is because of your money.'

You could have cut the atmosphere with a knife. Everyone in the limo had fallen silent, except Carl, who wasn't finished. 'If you say another word to annoy me, I'll take you outside and I'll sort you out,' he said, looking straight at Naz. 'OK, you fucking dwarf?'

Naz was like a chastened child but the rest of us roared and laughed and clapped Carl for hitting back so forcefully.

'What you being like that for?' Naz said lamely back to Carl and that was the end of it. That's what happens when

147

someone stands up to a bully and that's what Naz was, exciting for the brief period he was at the top but a bully all the same. A lot of big punchers, deep down, are really bullies who rely on intimidation and the fear they instil as much as they do on their punch. Take that intimidation factor away from them and there's no plan B, which was the case when Naz fought Marco Antonio Barrera in 2001 in Las Vegas. As soon as he took off his gloves in the dressing room, because he wasn't happy with the way his hands were wrapped, I knew that Naz wasn't right. I could see it from four thousand miles away and I knew he was going to be beaten. Naz must have delayed the fight by close to an hour, moaning that he wasn't happy, which of course he wasn't. Naz lost the fight long before he even got in the ring. He didn't do his flip over the top rope, he just walked through the ropes, and because of the body language Barrera knew he had the psychological edge. Some men fear big punchers, so it's a powerful tool but, once he was exposed, Naz never recovered from what happened in the Barrera fight.

The same thing happened to Jeff Lacy when I beat him in 2006 and it didn't surprise me at all that he looked so bad in his next fight against Vitali Tsypko. It's difficult for any bully to recover from outright humiliation. They're just not accustomed to another man standing up to them, much less beating the crap out of them. They can't recover from it. Naz fought Spain's Manuel Calvo a year later and he was done. People booed him and walked out of the arena after a handful of rounds. Like a lot of people, I loved to watch Naz in action because he really could bang. For a period of time he was exceptional and exciting. At least he left a legacy: one of the hardest pound-for-pound punchers we have ever seen in Britain. When he hit his opponents they went.

We stayed four days at the WBO convention and I enjoyed my first trip to America, meeting and partying with the likes of Oscar De La Hoya and Winky Wright, top pound-for-pound fighters who gave a young, emerging champion like me something to aspire to.

There were six thousand people at the International Arena in Cardiff when I made my first defence of the title against Branko Sobot, a Croat who was based in Germany. For me, it was great to be boxing in front of my family and friends and a partisan home crowd as the new champion. The reception was terrific and the fight was brief, a comfortable three-round win after I dropped Sobot with a beautiful left uppercut and finished him off against the ropes. It was my first fight in the arena and the feeling was beautiful.

The packed house was singing long before the end of the first round as their man in his black-sequined trunks threatened to demolish Sobot as quickly as he had seen off so many of his previous opponents, 10 of whom fell in the first round. From the first bell there was no questioning the Welshman's superiority. All that Sobot, a late substitute for the American, Tarick Salmaci, could do was hide behind gloves held high. Calzaghe was soon delivering the most ferocious left hooks to his body in an attempt to bring them down, but it was clear that Sobot had little to offer. The best that could be said was that he had a sense of durability, but that takes nothing away from the sheer fighting brilliance of the man from Newbridge. In the second round Sobot delivered a right hook as he emerged from a clinch, and it made Calzaghe stand back for a split second but it was his only moment and he must have sensed that much, much worse was yet to come as the Welshman went looking for that winning left-hook. Instead, he had to wait until 1:35 of the third round when that same punch caught Sobot clearly on the jaw and sent him tumbling backwards to the canvas. He was soon up, albeit groggily, and referee Paul Thomas ensured he took a count of eight before allowing him to go on. It was a momentary respite because Calzaghe followed up with a flurry of punches too numerous to count as he hammered Sobot mercilessly against the ropes in a neutral corner. No answer was forthcoming and his eyes were rolling as he looked in a desperate plight before the referee jumped in and decided the Croatian had taken enough.

– James Mossop, *Sunday Telegraph*,
25 January 1998

Worryingly, I began to have problems with my right wrist during training for my next title defence against mandatory challenger Juan Carlos Gimenez, who had been the distance with both Eubank and Benn. It was a recurrence of the problem that jeopardised my career as a teenager and affected my preparations a lot in sparring and general bag work. I went to see a specialist but there wasn't much I could do except protect the hand as much as I could. Gimenez was strong and durable and it was only my superior skills which made this a routine, easy fight for me. I won every round before his corner retired him ahead of the tenth, the only time he was ever stopped apart from in a WBO light heavyweight title fight four years later. Amazingly, at forty-six, he's still fighting, winning the Paraguayan cruiserweight title in 2006. Wales's cruiserweights, I can confidently predict, will be able to rest easy when I reach the same age.

I underwent another operation on the problematic wrist, which didn't seem to do much except keep me out of the ring for the next ten months, which was terribly frustrating at a time when I was hoping to build some momentum in my career. Over the years I've tried loads of different methods to try to make the wrist better, even soaking the bandages in vinegar before I wrapped my hands, a treatment suggested by an old guy called Fred Taylor, a lovely man who used to come to the gym on a walking stick and sit himself down in a chair every day to watch me train. 'Vinegar on the hand will make it better,' he said. He was old school and it was worth a go, but it didn't help. Hand injuries are an occupational hazard in this profession, and you have to get on with it. The operation itself left me unable to throw a punch for three months, and then I injured my left elbow in an innocuous sparring session with Gary Lockett, who had just turned pro and is now one of the fighters Dad trains in our gym. I was only throwing a few jabs when I jarred the elbow but it was enough to extend my stay on the sidelines. A bout which had been planned for the autumn had to be scrapped, so I set my sights on having a better year in 1999, and having Robin Reid lined up to come out of the opposite corner in February at the Telewest Arena in Newcastle was a perfect start, if only the performance had matched.

I hadn't been sparring, so I struggled to regain my fitness and I messed up badly over my weight. The most I can be over on the day of the weigh-in is four pounds. That's the most I feel that I can comfortably lose but when I weighed myself on the official scales an hour before we were due to step on them in front of the Board of Control and the TV cameras I was six pounds over the twelve-stone limit. I had to go straight to the hotel running machine but even with thirty minutes on that I was still two pounds over. I was panicking because I'd totally misjudged it and the weigh-in was starting in just over ten minutes. The only thing I could do was throw on a sauna suit and head for the sauna, jogging up and down to shed those last few ounces. It worked because I weighed in on the button. However, it isn't a method I would recommend to anybody who's about to walk into town to do their shopping, let alone someone taking part just twenty-four hours later in a world title fight.

Losing those six pounds in such a short space of time was way too much, especially when I was tight at the weight in any case. My face was drawn and I felt horrible, so I went back to my hotel to get some food and liquid into me as quickly as I could. When we sat down in the restaurant I was so dehydrated that I had no appetite and couldn't eat but I was incredibly thirsty and decided to have an ice cream. All of a sudden I felt something hard in my mouth, which I thought was ice at first, but it was razor-sharp, so I spat out what turned out to be a piece of glass. I then discovered there were bits of shredded glass all the way through the ice cream. So what do I think immediately? Conspiracy, that's what I think, for there was never any love lost between me and Reid. The Barcelona Olympics were long forgotten, and it wasn't his fault that I hadn't been selected anyway, but I wanted to fight him when he was WBC champion and a unification bout would have made us both a lot more money. But Reid didn't even want to hear my name when he was champion. He would choke whenever someone mentioned me, he wouldn't say a word. But all of a sudden, when he lost his belt to Sugarboy Malinga, he wanted to come after mine. Why hadn't he started talking up the fight before then? He was smarmy, we just didn't like one another and the press conferences became a bit heated. I didn't hate him, and I don't hate him now, but he rubbed me up the wrong way, so I got under his skin. The week of the fight we squared up and posed for publicity shots and I had to duck down a bit because he's short.

'I've come down to his level,' I said.

'Yeah?' he replied. 'I'll make sure that in a couple of days they're carrying you out.'

He seemed insecure about his lack of height and I knew I'd succeeded in winding him up, which I like to do to opponents, but in the cold light of day, once I'd calmed down after the initial shock, I did rule him out of any conspiracy involving ice cream.

Reid has been like a scratched record over the years, shouting his mouth off that he really won the fight and he'd fight again any day. I don't think there was anyone more gutted in the MEN Arena when I did the job on Jeff

Lacy because he had clung on to the delusion that he was always as good as me, but we've had very different careers. He fought the best he could in Newcastle and I was poor, which evened things out. Every fighter has bad nights and that was one of mine. We weren't exactly in his backyard because it wasn't Runcorn, but he was an Englishman in Newcastle and I was very much the outsider, though I don't think that can explain how Paul Thomas judged Reid to be the winner by 116 to 111, which equates to five rounds, when the two other judges saw it precisely the other way round. That's a massive difference in scoring. Maybe Paul Thomas was influenced by the crowd but I definitely won the fight, even though it's one of the tapes I would gladly chuck away for good. I don't watch a fight again whenever I've boxed badly and I never watch this one. Reid was pensive in the first few rounds, grabbing my arms and even my legs and holding on for dear life. No fighter grabs your legs unless they're afraid, and he fought like that a few years later against Jeff Lacy who destroyed him in eight rounds. But Reid did fight a good tactical fight against me, he stood back and counter-punched effectively at times and managed to connect with some good right hands. It was going my way until the sixth round when I broke the metacarpal bone in my left hand and, although I could still punch, I was only able to tap with it. As the fight went on, the crowd got behind him and he fought a decent fight.

I was able to get back in the ring in June to face Rick Thornberry, an Australian, but I didn't spar a single round in training because of my hand again. Thornberry had been stopped by Henry Wharton, so I thought that I would just go through him in one or two rounds but, although I dropped him in the first round, it didn't happen. He was able to hang in there and I was uninspiring. In fact, I had reached a critical juncture in my career.

Joe Calzaghe has sacked his father as trainer just as he enters the most important phase of his career. Enzo Calzaghe began coaching his son when Joe was nine and he turned the boy into a star, forming one of the most successful partnerships in British boxing. But Frank Warren, Joe's manager and promoter, has insisted the WBO world super middleweight champion must now make a clean break from his dad after 27 unbeaten fights. Warren said, 'I have been promoting for nearly 25 years and I've had to make some very difficult decisions. But telling Joe and his father the time had come for them to part was perhaps the hardest thing I have had to do. I shall never forget the look of misery on Joe's face when I spelled out what has to happen. Joe and Enzo are extremely close and I felt bad at doing this, but sometimes you have to be cruel to be kind. I happen to feel Enzo has taken Joe as far as he can and someone else should take over. And I didn't pull any punches. I told Joe quite forcibly I think he has become complacent and, where his father is concerned, he is the one calling the shots. Enzo agreed Joe has been cutting corners in training and that simply couldn't go on any longer. Fortunately, Enzo is a sensible man and he only wants what is best for Joe. There is no suggestion their relationship won't be the same away from boxing. There is definitely no rift over this. But there's no doubt it will be a terrible wrench for Enzo after nearly 20 years to have nothing more to do with Joe's career.' The Calzaghes' gym is a dilapidated wooden shed with a postage stamp-sized ring. Joe has always bandaged his own hands, which is probably why he is always injuring them. Hand problems have been his excuse for lacking sparkle in his last two fights and his training methods came under attack when he admitted he could not spar a single round in preparation because of his damaged hands.

– Colin Hart, *The Sun*, 4 August 1999

We've had many disagreements, me and Dad, and after the fight with Thornberry many people were suggesting that I shouldn't stay with him. Frank made his position clear, so we went through a rough patch. I was having loads of injury problems and we were arguing a lot, but maybe I was looking for an excuse. My career was losing impetus and I was in danger of losing everything. I needed to find something to get me back on track. It was nothing to do with my dad really, it was about me and where my head was with all these injuries. George Francis, who worked with Frank Bruno, John Conteh, Cornelius Boza-Edwards and many other British and world champions, was being lined up by Frank to come in and train me, but I wanted him to work with Dad. My dad has always been part of my career, the biggest part, and it will never happen that he's not there in my corner. I only reached the highest level because of him and what was being written in the newspapers was upsetting for both of us. Yes, he's my trainer and, yes, we were having a bad time, but most of all he's my dad and that will never change.

We spoke and I told him that what I wanted to do was bring another trainer in and he said very simply, 'Joe, first and foremost you're my son and that's what matters. Whatever decision you make will be fine by me.' I have a lot of respect for my dad for saying that. Deep down, he would have been broken-hearted if we'd changed the way things had always been but he still wanted what was best for me. If he felt he wasn't helping me, he would have gone. If I had said, 'Dad, I can't listen to you any more because I don't respect you as a trainer, I love you but we can't go on,' he would have respected that. He would have walked away but I know that he would still have been there as my dad. That's the way he is and that's the relationship we have. He's never treated me like a little boy. He knew he was good for me, he knew that the real problem was with my injuries and he knew I was being influenced by other people. I was just going through a bad time with myself, finding it all very difficult because my career was stagnating. All I was doing was considering my options and the truth is that, from the very beginning, it's always given me more incentive and encouragement to know that my dad is there in my corner. No one can motivate me or get underneath my skin the way my dad can. He's my blood, and if I was ever in a crisis, Dad would be the first person to be at my side to bring me home safely. If I had been beaten up like Jeff Lacy the night we fought, I know that my dad would have pulled me out after eight or nine rounds. He's never told me that but I know it's the truth. I wouldn't want to be pulled out and I'd bite the head of him for doing it, but he would do the right thing, I can count on that.

People probably don't realise the way we are with one another, the fact that I infuriate him and he infuriates me, but all the time we love each other to bits. Back early in my career I went to Harley Street to have an operation on one of my knuckles. It had become inflamed and they had to tidy it up. During the surgery I was under anaesthetic but when the operation was done I left more or less straight away with my dad, who hadn't wanted to pay when he parked the car. We walked along a couple of streets and I was still half asleep, my hand heavily strapped, and I just wanted to go home.

'Where are we parked, Dad? I just need to get in the car and put my head back.'

'Don't worry, son, a minute's walk, that's all. We're just parked down the street.'

Several more streets later there was still no sign of the car.

'Dad, where are we parked?'

'Somewhere down here, Joe, all right?'

'Somewhere down here?'

Dad didn't have a bloody clue where he had parked the car.

'I could have sworn I left it here, Joe . . . Joe?'

I was already walking off in the opposite direction, looking for the nearest lamp post to kick or fall asleep against, and I muttered under my breath something about 'scatty', 'brain' and 'goat'. He became all het up and we must have looked like Basil Fawlty and son, looking for the car. Finally, we found it, about an hour after leaving the surgery. I was sweaty, cranky and my hand was throbbing, and I don't recall that it was the most pleasant journey back to Newbridge. But that's how we are all the time. My dad and I have similar personalities.

Sometimes we have little arguments in the gym. Sometimes they're much bigger. There are times when I'm pissed off and my dad will just get on my nerves and vice-versa. I'll come to the gym in a bad mood, not wishing to talk to anybody and he'll say, 'Come on then, what's wrong with you?' Sometimes it can get heated.

The day before I fought Byron Mitchell my dad drove me to the weigh-in and we were really struggling to get there on time. I hadn't eaten all day, I was irritable and I just wanted to get on the scales so that I could go home to have a drink and a meal.

'Go left,' I said quickly because he was taking a wrong turn, and he took the hump.

'Don't fucking have a go at me.'

'Aw, don't give me this, I'm getting out.'

'Well, fucking walk then.'

Dad stopped the car, I got out and walked through Cardiff on my own to the weigh-in. We have barneys, the two of us, but we always get over them. I'm moody, I can be a pain in the arse and my dad knows just how I am. We see one another every day and it's inevitable that some days he's going to be in a mood himself and won't be ready for my shit, so we'll clash. But half an hour later we'll be best friends again. We never hold a grudge. Whatever gets said in the heat of the moment is done, it's out of the way and that's the way we are.

My dad used to bandage my hands, but his hands

would get sweaty and I like to do my own bandages in any case. He'd get stressed out and his hands would start to shake and all of a sudden we'd be snapping at one another again.

'Your hands are shaking.'

'Well, do your fucking bandages yourself then.'

So Dean Powell, Frank Warren's matchmaker, has done the job for my past several fights, saving the two of us a lot of aggro and a lot of bandages.

Most of the time I'm pretty relaxed, a fairly easy-going fellow, but people perceive me as being more relaxed than I really am. I get tense before a fight because I have to lose thirteen pounds in two weeks. I half starve myself to do it and Dad understands me in that situation better than any other trainer would. I know the sport. I know about technique. I know the moves because I've been doing them my whole life. The ring has been my workplace for twenty-five years and I'm a very stubborn, strong-willed guy. But I need someone around me who knows me, who knows how to push the right buttons and knows when to push those buttons. That's so much more important to me than having someone say, 'Don't turn that way, turn this way. Don't throw that punch, hit him here and here.' Fighters are great at finding excuses and going through six or seven different trainers when the only thing that needs changing is their own attitude. There's always the bullshit way to deal with everything and, for a fighter, that way is to shoot the guy in the corner. Sugar Shane Mosley has been trained by his dad, Jack, through most of his career. He lost twice to Vernon Forrest, decided to change trainer and looked far worse. When they got back together he was effective again. I don't blame the guy for wanting to try something different but in the end he looked in the mirror and accepted that maybe it was him and, finally, that's what I did after the Thornberry fight.

I went through names in my heads, the names of top trainers, but when it came right down to it I didn't want to take that step. I'm not a conventional boxer, my style is different to other fighters and this makes me what I am. If someone came along to try to change me, would we be completely at loggerheads? Probably so, but the truth is this. I was with my dad when I started boxing and he's helped to make me the champion I am today, so there's no one who can take his place and no one ever will.

I stayed out of the ring for seven months before I fought David Starie in Manchester and, because my elbow was still hurting, I didn't spar a single round for my second consecutive bout. I just hit the bags and worked the pads and tried to get sharp, but my timing was way out. The fact that my fight was being broadcast on the Showtime TV network in the United States meant that my timing was doubly poor. This could have been a big break for me, boxing on the same card as Mike Tyson who was making his first appearance in a British ring. I wanted to put on a show to steal Tyson's thunder.

Tyson had based himself in London and everywhere he went he was mobbed. I went to train for a week at the Grosvenor House Hotel, where a ring had been set up for Mike, and it was bedlam, with hundreds of people being allowed in every day to watch him work. I tried to introduce myself one day but he blanked me, which pissed me off. Whether you're a former heavyweight champion of the world or a kid fighting in the preliminaries, every fighter's a fighter and we all want respect. I just asked to have my picture taken with him and he said, 'Yeah, yeah,' a bit arrogantly, as if it was a chore. I realised that a lot of people had been hassling him for autographs and there were women waiting to see him but I was fighting on the same bill and I thought he could make a bit of an effort. I said nothing but, of course, my dad couldn't hold back.

'Are you going to smile or what?' he said to Tyson.

'It's all right, Dad,' I muttered under my breath, a little embarrassed and more than a little apprehensive that I might have to be the cavalry in this situation.

'Are you going to fucking smile or what?' he said again.

'Hey, man, I've had a hard day,' Tyson said with a sigh. 'Lots of pictures, man, and I've had to train.'

'He's had to train too,' Dad said, pointing at me, 'and if he can smile, so can you.'

Not many people, I guess, have spoken that way to Tyson and just walked away, but later I actually sat down on a little couch beside him, out in the corridor as we were both staying on the same floor, and he was great to talk to. 'I know who you are,' he said. 'You're my friend, my brother.' This Tyson was charming. 'You got kids?' he asked and he started to talk about his own kids and he talked about Don King and how he wanted to 'rip him up' and this was the only time in the conversation when he got angry and bitter. For the most part, he was softly spoken, so I got to see the two sides to his personality, the charmer and the monster, which sadly could not be said for Julius Francis who lasted two rounds.

At least Francis tried to come forward. David Starie moved away for the entire twelve rounds, boxed as negatively as he could, and the result was a stinker of a fight, really frustrating for me. I prefer to face fighters who come towards me, that's when I'm at my best, but Starie was defensive the whole way and I was all the time in clinches or off balance. Starie was happy just to survive. He bottled it a bit and it was horrible because Frank had introduced me to Jay Larkin, the head of Showtime TV at the time, and they both wanted me to do well, as it could have made my name in the American market. But Starie was too awkward, my performance was dire and the crowd booed through most of it. When Frank Warren stepped in the ring at the final bell he walked over to me

165

and said, 'You boxed shit.' He was right but he wasn't half as devastated as I was.

Calzaghe started brightly, eager to make the most of the worldwide television exposure which could have helped the 27-year-old Welshman substantiate his claims of being Britain's best boxer. In contrast Starie, with cuts over his right eye, seemed to want to do little more than survive, and the fight degenerated into a messy, mauling bore which had the crowd loudly jeering and slow-hand-clapping from the sixth round onwards. Neither man seemed unduly troubled at any stage, which made their unwillingness to gamble all the more extraordinary. At least Calzaghe tried to force the contest. He remains undefeated and he has talent. But his excuse of ring-rustiness does not adequately explain his problems against Starie. Once his initial flurries of attacks had failed to budge the challenger he ran out of ideas and when he needed to vary his game plan he was unable to do so. Brave talk of him stepping up to light-heavyweight to meet the formidable Roy Jones Jr, the undisputed champion, seems foolhardy unless he wants one big pay-day and a painful defeat. The biggest problem facing his promoters is how to sell him as a headline act; those who jeered him while waiting for Tyson's arrival will not be rushing to buy tickets for his next outing. Calzaghe's handsome features and pleasant personality, allied to a natural aptitude for the sport, should by now be reaping rich rewards. He may be Frank Warren's chosen one but chances such as this are few and far between and on Saturday he blew it.

– John Rawling, *Guardian*, 31 January 2000

The only positive effect of the Starie fight was that it helped to persuade me to stop saying I was going to knock every opponent out. People used to think that I was arrogant, so I started watching interviews of myself and it was like I was trying to mimic Eubank or Naz mouthing off. It wasn't me. Maybe I saw the recognition they had at the time, which I was being denied, and I just thought that was the way to go. I'd said ahead of facing Branko Sobot that I was going to knock him out in three rounds and I did, but it's not my style to say those things and I felt bad when I realised I was belittling people. I never said it angrily, just matter-of-factly, all part of the hype. But it's arrogant and it demeans the opponent. Great fighters don't need to mouth off and I stopped doing this after the Starie fight. Besides, I wasn't knocking anybody out any more. I'd just gone the distance three times in a row against Reid, Thornberry and Starie and was starting to look a little silly. My strike rate at the time, it could be said, made the decision easy.

Soon there was a bigger decision to be made. Frank had put together a fight against Omar Sheika of the United States for 4 July, Independence Day, but I just didn't fancy it. I'm in constant conflict with my demons but when I'm not 100 per cent I know I'm not and I told Frank that. I was injured all the time, couldn't spar and I couldn't bring myself to watch the tapes of my fights. I could watch the Eubank tape and Sobot and Jimenez, but the Reid fight, a good one for the public, was crap for me. He shouldn't have hit me with a bag of rice because he's slow and cumbersome, flat-footed and predictable, yet he hit me with countless right hands. I couldn't see the punches coming back any more because I wasn't sparring. I should have beaten Thornberry inside three rounds but I had to go twelve again and I couldn't land a punch on Starie all night because of my balance. I told Frank that my elbow wasn't right and I wouldn't be able to fight Sheika in July, so we had a heart-to-heart.

I was quite blunt about it because I just thought it was time to face up to reality. Fighters like John Conteh and Naz suffered from hand problems in their careers and got on with it, so I said to Joe, 'It's your decision but you're either going to have to live with the problems or turn it in. We can't keep on making a show only for you to pull out, so are you going to box or are you going to quit?' It was as simple as that. I would never force any man into the ring who shouldn't be in there, but Joe was allowing these problems to get the better of him when really he needed to sort them out himself. – Frank Warren

We all need a wake-up call at some time in our lives and this was mine.

ROUND EIGHT
Where Danger Lurks

In my heart I never considered quitting boxing. Of course, I was frustrated about the injuries and the way my career was going, but I was still champion and I needed to fight. Even if only for financial reasons, there was no way I could walk away from the sport.

I knew I wasn't performing and, emotionally, this was hurting me because I've always felt good about doing what I do. I find it strange sometimes but I know I make a difference in people's lives and that's uplifting, especially when I'm training. Sometimes when I'm home and I don't have a fight to look forward to I get depressed, because climbing into the ring and standing under those shining lights, surrounded by thousands of people who are about to experience a unique kind of thrill, is the most exciting, daunting, frightening and beautiful feeling. This is who I am and people look up to me and respect me for it. But if I didn't box, what would I be? If something had to give, it wasn't going to be boxing.

At that time I lived almost next door to Oakdale Pitch

& Putt and I used to spend a lot of spare time there, almost every day. Whatever the weather, I would head out with my dad, even if there was water flooding the greens. I'm no Tiger Woods but I played the course so regularly that I was sure I had mastered it. One day I went round in two over par. I missed a hole-in-one by an inch after hitting a perfect wedge shot. The next day, of course, I was twenty over and back to being a hacker. I can't remember why but we stopped playing for about a month and my elbow started to get better. The problem might have stemmed from the chronic injury in my right wrist and swinging the club probably triggered it off, I don't know, but I was happy to give up, if it meant that my elbow would be pain-free. It was purely by chance that I had stopped going out to play golf and the elbow got better. Who would have thought that a game of golf could be so dangerous for your health?

I had not sparred for over a year at this point but I said to Frank that I wanted to carry on and I would fight Sheika, if the date was pushed back. So he set a new date of 12 August at Wembley Conference Centre and persuaded me to come to training camp in Cheshunt in Hertfordshire to get some good sparring in. Frank knew that I was much better than I'd been showing and he wanted to make sure that I was right, that I would have the best possible chance of producing the kind of performance I hadn't been able to, for a variety of reasons, since the Eubank fight. I spent two weeks in Cheshunt, the only time I've gone away to train in my pro career, and I was absolutely woeful. My timing was way out, my movement wasn't good, I was lazy because I hadn't sparred for ages and I was getting caught. My confidence was shot and it was all just dreadful. I was so out of practice in terms of sparring that I'd loaned my Reyes protector, which gives protection on the sides, to one of my mates, and had to wear one that didn't have any padding on its sides. After one session one of my kidneys was killing me and the next day I had a big, black bruise on my side where I'd been punched just below the belt. For two weeks I sparred, Monday to Friday, home at the weekend, back to sparring Monday to Friday again. Then around the middle of the second week I began to show some signs of improvement. I was timing my shots better and seeing the punches coming, so I was slipping them. My balance, which had been the most awful aspect of my performance against Starie, wasn't quite perfect but I was getting there. I was feeling more confident in myself and, most importantly, my elbow wasn't troubling me at all. I had started learning how to fight properly again and the transformation in my boxing almost made me a new man. My enthusiasm was back and I began to really look forward to the fight.

This was one of the most important bouts of my career, just behind Lacy and Eubank. I had reached a crossroads and a bad performance could have sent me off in the wrong direction. Frank was describing me as his fighter for the new millennium and great things were going to happen, but in my last two appearances I had been flat. I needed to impress again and Sheika was a dangerous boxer. He was one of the fighters I was a bit worried about and I knew that I wouldn't get away with it, if I boxed as badly as I did against Reid, Thornberry and Starie. He had lost an eight-round decision against my former sparring partner, Tony Booth, in Sheffield, but Booth had used his experience to make it a mauling match and Sheika was better than that. He could punch, having stopped thirteen opponents in his twenty wins, and that got me psyched up. Particularly in America, a lot of fight people fancied him to win. He had a big mouth and slagged me off whenever he could, even predicted that he was going to kill me, which is a phrase I hate to hear in boxing but it's a typically American thing to say. One of the guys in his entourage repeated it: 'We're going to kill Calzaghe.' You're going to kill? The thought just chills and I don't know how someone can say that going into a boxing match.

I've never had an entourage and whenever I go to a press conference or weigh-in it's usually only me and my dad, but Sheika turned up with about a dozen guys, who mouthed off just like him and we were all staying in the same hotel. I didn't fancy walking in for dinner and having to listen to their crap, so I moved to another hotel and left my PlayStation and games in a taxi and wasn't in the best of moods even before Sheika put his fist through a big poster of me during a public workout and repeated his bad-ass nonsense. If his intention was to make me as focused and determined as I possibly could be, which I doubt, he was going about it in just the right way. Another guy who annoyed me in that final week was Toks Owoh, a London fighter who'd been working with me and was putting it about that he'd wobbled me in sparring. Even though he had been stopped in four rounds by Sheika in 1998 he told anybody who would listen that he could take me. Everywhere I turned he was there, then at the weigh-in Sheika went eyeball to eyeball with me and all I heard were the people in his entourage yelling out, 'He's scared. He's scared.' Now I'm no psychologist, nor have I ever worked with one, but if I had I don't see how they could have done a better job for me than this group of comedians ahead of the fight.

Many believe that the enthralling contest against Chris Eubank in Sheffield in October 1997 was the last time that Calzaghe was at his best. Injury has not helped his cause and although he remains unbeaten, with 23 knockouts from his 28 professional bouts, he has looked far from a champion in his past three contests and is running out of time if he is to convince

Spearing my right jab into the face of Robin Reid in Newcastle. Not one of my best performances but I still got the job done.

Juan Carlos Giminez went the distance with both Nigel Benn and Chris Eubank but against me he couldn't come out for the tenth round.

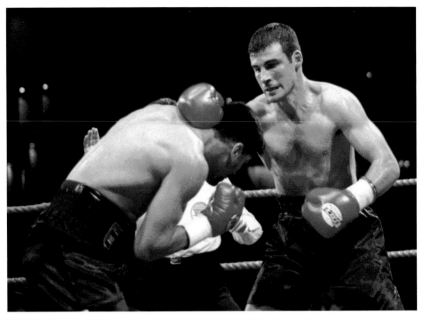

My determination to overcome Omar Sheika is evident in my face. I came out from the opening bell to stop him and in the fifth round the referee had seen enough.

From a fighter I didn't like, to a man I have the utmost respect for, two men in fact, Richie Woodhall and his dad Len. We produced a great fight.

Posing with Charles Brewer after a press conference in Little Italy in New York, a hostile place for a Philadelphian like Brewer but perfect if your surname is Calzaghe.

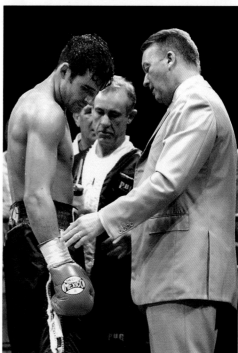

The disappointment of injury again, seen on the faces of Dad and Frank Warren. Beating Miguel Jimenez was straightforward at Cardiff Castle, overcoming my hand problems has been anything but easy.

Having been knocked down for the first time in my life in the second round against Byron Mitchell, I went straight into the teeth of the fire and stopped my opponent before the end of the round. The relief and joy is plain to be seen.

I was able to hold my left hand near my chin but unable to do much else with it against Evans Ashira after breaking it again in the fourth round at the International Arena in Cardiff, though my right worked pretty well.

Pleased to be just twenty-four hours away from the biggest fight of my life. Jeff Lacy was still sporting a beard, which Dad made him take off when we had the rules meeting. 'We want to see your chin when we hit you on it,' he told him.

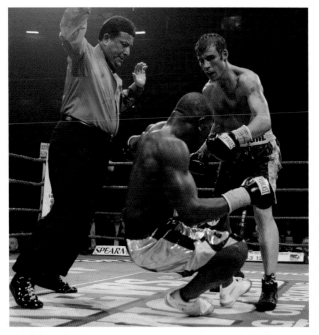

Cementing an overwhelming win on points by knocking down Lacy in the twelfth and final round. At least he had the professional pride of finishing the fight on his feet.

Roll up, roll up, circus strongman Enzo Calzaghe! Not bad for a man in his fifties as Dad carries me on his shoulders after the biggest fight of both our lives.

It was just my luck that two days after my fight with Sakio Bika, whose dirty tactics resulted in a cut by the side of my left eye and bruising on my left cheek, that I should meet one of my ring idols, Sugar Ray Leonard. Ray was one of the all-time greats and still looks in fighting shape.

the American public that he is of genuine world class. Sheika, from New Jersey, is managed and trained by Bill Cayton and Steve Lott, two former mentors of Mike Tyson. He has enhanced his credibility in the United States and Calzaghe has made only five title defences since the Eubank meeting because of hand and elbow problems. His points win over David Starie on the Tyson–Julius Francis undercard in Manchester in January was particularly unimpressive. Calzaghe is pleased that Sheika arrives intent on victory rather than survival, as his recent opponents have appeared to be. Sheika, on the other hand, is pleased that Calzaghe is fully fit so that there will be no excuses if he should lose. 'Neither fighter is going to give in, that's what I like about this fight,' Lott said. 'It's the old expression – both fighters have bad intentions.' Lott, who is sanguine about his 23-year-old charge, said, 'He's grown but he's still a baby in boxing. A fighter like Joe Calzaghe has a tremendous advantage in experience.' Calzaghe's task is to make that experience count.

– Matthew Pryor, *The Times*, 12 August 2000

I like to be on my own in the hours before a fight or just with my dad, in order to clear my mind. On the afternoon of the Sheika fight I went to the nearby shopping centre and had a meal by myself, then walked around Wembley

Stadium and imagined what might have been. When my career is over I'd like to play Sunday league football, if there's a team on the lookout for a slow, dogged ex-bruiser at that stage. I met up with Dad and we went into a bookies to have a little bet on the horses. It was the hottest day of the year, it was beautiful and my mind couldn't have been in a better place as I walked back to the hotel and prepared to leave for the arena. The theme tune from *Mission: Impossible* was turned up high as I walked to the ring, just to make sure that Sheika would hear it, but he was still busy yapping. 'Come in here,' he shouted at me. 'You're going down.' A big guy in his corner yelled across the ring, 'This is not your night, Calzaghe.' All week Sheika just didn't learn, so the only option left to me was to hammer home the lesson. His whole bullshit just made me want to smash him, which is precisely what I did.

I was bigger and stronger than him and made myself the boss in the opening round. I outjabbed him, outboxed him and outpunched him, and manhandled him completely. My timing was spot on and I did a number on him. There are probably just a handful of fights that I was completely in the zone for: Eubank, Mitchell, Brewer, Lacy and this one. In all those fights I had to perform at or near to my best and I did, Sheika provoking one of my best performances. Something seems to just click in my mind when the challenge is at its greatest and I know I've got to produce the goods at that moment. Sheika looked for big power punches from the opening bell but I outworked him. It wasn't power that beat him. My arms just moved too fast for him, he was confused and couldn't find a way to respond. He started to complain to the referee about being hit on the back of the head and there were head clashes as well but I was clubbing him on the side of the head, a legitimate punch, and he was the one who wanted to clinch. A lot of fighters neglect to punch on the inside but that shot to the side of the head hurts and I stung Sheika a lot with it. Ernie Fossie, who worked the corner with my dad in all of my fights after I signed with Frank until sadly he passed away in 2004, told me I was boxing beautifully. He always had a nice way with words to reinforce your confidence and I had a lot of respect for Ernie. Dad was urging me to finish the job, for in the fourth round Sheika began to cut up around his eyes, so I didn't let up until the referee stepped in towards the end of the fifth round. I dropped to my hands and knees because the win meant so much to me. It wasn't just that I had beaten Sheika. I was back.

As an exercise in image refurbishment, Joe Calzaghe's sixth successful defence of his WBO super middleweight title was in Premier League class. The 28-year-old Welshman, whose career had sailed into stormy waters, performed a brilliant rescue operation, stopping challenger Omar Sheika after 2min 8sec of the fifth round at the Conference Centre here last night. While it lasted it was something of a blood-and-thunder classic, which deserved a greater audience than the 1,500 or so who only half-filled the arena. It was an example of how two well-matched young men can produce a blend of boxing that is both exciting and of high quality. In the end Calzaghe, much sharper and definitely more positive than in his recently disappointing outings, had too much armoury for the 23-year-old Sheika, from Paterson, New Jersey, who was thought to be the first Palestinian Arab to challenge for a world title. When the bout was ended by the Chicago referee, Genaro Rodriguez, Sheika's features were stained with the blood of battle leaking from cuts around both eyes. The one over his left was by far the worst, the top of his eyelid almost sliced open. But damage had also been done to his other eye towards the end of the fourth round. It was announced that the referee had stepped in because of the cuts but it was confirmed afterwards that he halted it because the brave Sheika was shipping too much punishment. A fearsome flurry had him reeling, and the referee's action, despite Sheika's angry protests, merely curtailed what would have been a more painful conclusion.

– Alan Hubbard, *Independent*, 13 August 2000

I felt like I'd won the world title again, it was such a satisfying victory, particularly in the style I achieved it. 'What is happening to me?' I'd asked myself for so long. I'd beaten Eubank, a great fighter, then I made two decent defences, but I was embarrassed by my performance against Starie, and similarly angry by the way I fought against Reid. After every fight I look for the errors I've made, more than I look for what I did well, and the more I look the more errors I see and it does my head in. 'Who is that? That's not me,' I'll say. I know there is no such thing as the perfect fighter but there are so many aspects of my boxing I can make better and I want to make better. I don't delude myself that physically I can get better but, even at thirty-five years old, I know I can improve.

One weakness I had as a southpaw boxer, leading with my right hand, was that I got caught by far too many straight right-hand punches from orthodox opponents, who lead with their left. I just couldn't find a way to prevent guys with basic skills from crossing their right and nailing me. Reid was able to do it all night long in Newcastle. Boxing is like geometry, measuring angles and space and calculating where to position yourself so that you can strike your opponent and make him miss. The hitting zone is narrow but by rotating forty-five degrees to your right or left you can create a new target area for your punches while making it difficult for your opponent to retaliate. I worked out that I moved to my left more than I should and into the space where the right hands were coming. Being a southpaw, I ought to move more to my right to be able to counter across my opponent's jab. I was a complete sucker against Reid because my left hand was broken in the sixth round and I couldn't use it, yet I kept moving in a direction that narrowed the target area for my right hand and opened up opportunities for his. The right hand is the punch to throw against a southpaw and I've become savvier to this the longer I've gone in my career.

My movement on the inside developed more quickly, the slight turning of the head to slip a punch and the knowledge of those angles in close where you're vulnerable to hooks and uppercuts. People have always regarded my so-called arm punches as a weakness, ineffective, and Jeff Lacy even described them as slaps, but he was the classic example of how much these rapid-fire bursts of punches can do damage. I pick a point at which to fire three or four rapid-fire shots, *bah-bah-bah-bah*, and these baffle opponents, then *boom*, I hit the guy with a harder punch, a big one. It's unexpected because I haven't given him time to think or any warning that it's coming. I'm so busy for a super middleweight and I'm always on top of my opponent, crowding him, probing him, making him commit and luring him into making mistakes. If I stood back and threw only forty punches in a round, my opponent could think up all kinds of plans of attack but I let the punches go and I mix them up, jabs, hooks, uppercuts, crosses, so it's hard for my opponent to think when he has all of this going on around his head. He can't figure out what's happening. This was Lacy's problem, he had no time to set himself to throw his big, powerful hooks. I shocked him with my movement and he couldn't believe that I could outwork him on the inside. That was his turf, the place where he thought he'd be able to just rip into me and rip me apart because he was the puncher, but my movement was superior and so was my hand speed. I completely bamboozled him and fucked up his mind. He kept trying to land his big left hook but all of a sudden, *bah-bah-bah-bah-bah-bah*, I'd hit him with half a dozen punches, a dozen, and he could get nothing off in reply. This is what did his head in and it was the same with Sheika.

Not every punch I threw against Sheika was quality and a lot of them weren't pretty, but they confused him and this is what makes me different to other fighters. My style is unique in the way that I mix up my punches between speed shots and hurtful blows, tapping him to look for an opening and then banging in a big one. I've learnt over the years that the best defence is a good offence. It's always good to throw a punch, any kind of punch, to make the opponent think that he has to come through a minefield before he can even come close to landing a blow. Sheika couldn't do it because of my hand speed

JOE CALZAGHE
THE AUTOBIOGRAPHY

which, I believe, is my greatest asset. Even when I haven't been in the gym for a while and I come back weighing fourteen stone, my hands will still be unbelievably quick. My legs get tired but I have natural speed in my arms and I can stand and punch all day. I don't have a long reach for a super middleweight, just 73in. Lacy's a stocky guy and shorter than me, but his reach was 74in and Reid's 76in. Their arms, therefore, had further to travel to reach the target but mine are shorter and quicker because they don't have as far to come back. Maybe this is the magic formula.

Whatever it is, I am fascinated by the science of boxing. I get very analytical when I sit down after a fight, yet in the ring everything I do is spontaneous. It just happens naturally. Most fighters have to think about what they're doing when they're in there and they follow a certain plan in their head. I never go into a fight with a set plan, which means that I'm constantly alert, alive to the possibilities and ready to react. When I see an opening I go for it instinctively, I don't think about it first. I like to dictate the pace and hold the centre of the ring, make my opponent move and throw him off his game. You rarely see me on the ropes but none of this is part of a predetermined plan. When I'm at my best and most fluent I'm totally focused on the moment. It doesn't matter how fit you are, you could be in the best shape of your life, but if your mind's not on the job you're going to get caught. In this business it takes a split second and it could all be over. It's the finest of fine edges, so the only thing I always make sure I do is to concentrate and stay in the zone. Sometimes I haven't been there and I've lowered myself to my opponent's level and this is dangerous because any fighter can get caught. So I'm trying to get better all the time and I never feel totally invincible. Every day I'm champion there is somebody somewhere after what I've got.

Roy Jones was the top pound-for-pound fighter in the world and a former champion at middleweight and super middleweight, but he was already the WBC light heavyweight champion when I beat Eubank. So when people ask why I never fought him it's important to remember that we never actually boxed in the same division. I've considered moving up to light heavyweight for many years and a deal was agreed for a title challenge against Jamaica's Glen Johnson at 12st 7lb in July 2006, but a recurrence of the injury to my left hand meant that I had to pull out of the Millennium Stadium show. By this stage Jones had been knocked out by Johnson and Antonio Tarver and, although he's still active, I would never want to fight him now. He's not the same fighter and I'd have nothing to gain by beating a shadow of what he once was. Jones was a great fighter in his day and a great name, but he's been knocked out twice, knocked out cold. What would I have to gain by knocking him out for a third time?

When Jones was in his heyday, that's when I wanted the fight. He was brilliant, head and shoulders above any of his challengers at the time, and he's the one fighter I'd ever have been really worried about. Jones at his best would have been the toughest. He dominated at middle-weight and super middleweight and stepped up to light heavy to win all the belts. I loved watching him perform, I was one of his biggest fans, but you have to question why his performance level completely dipped from the moment it transpired a few years ago that he had failed a drugs test in a fight in Indiana against another American, Richard Hall. All of a sudden he fell from the Premiership to League Two, from being absolutely peerless to distinctly average. Was it age or coincidence? All I know is that after it became known that he had failed a drugs test in 2000 he was never the same fighter. Jones was like Superman when he was younger, the way he moved and the way he boxed, but suddenly he became mortal. When he fought Antonio Tarver for the light heavyweight title twice and lost twice he was rubbish. If I had fought Jones at his peak and got beaten, I would feel swindled today, knowing that he had taken steroids. It's cheating, there's no other word for it, and I don't know how it managed to be swept under the carpet for a number of years and he went totally unpunished. In athletics drugs cheats get banned automatically for two years, and if steroids can make athletes run faster, they can surely help a boxer to hit harder and to hit quicker and to hit for longer and this will enable him to inflict more punishment, which I think is repulsive. During our pre-fight medicals we get tested for drugs and it's never crossed my mind to take anything performance-enhancing. I don't have a big pot of pills that I dip into all hours of the day. In fact, I have a job just to remind myself to take my vitamins.

I would be angry if someone I fought took something that gave him an unfair advantage because this is a dangerous sport, it's not like running. In athletics it now seems almost part of the culture, just like cycling, and the whole idea is to stay one step ahead of the testing. I sat alongside Justin Gatlin, at the time the reigning Olympic 100m champion, on the BBC's *Question of Sport* about a year ago and spoke to him afterwards. We talked about the Jeff Lacy fight because he's from Florida as well and he seemed like a really nice guy and I was genuinely shocked and disappointed when he failed a drugs test last summer. Whenever I watch athletics or cycling now I have my suspicions. Some get caught and some don't but I like to think that fighters are clean. Boxing's a warrior sport and, to me, there have always been values that go along with that. If I were ever to appear in the ring with huge muscles, boxing as a cruiserweight or a heavyweight, you could assume that I hadn't built myself up on protein shakes alone, so I'd never do it.

A possible fight with Jones was being mooted when I had one of my most difficult experiences facing Richie Woodhall, for Richie was and still is a friend and it was tough to fight him at all. I first met him at Crystal Palace when we were amateurs training with the Great Britain squad and we were both managed and promoted by Mickey Duff, so I boxed on several of his undercards on the way up. Richie is a genuinely good guy and so is his dad, Len, who gets on very well with my dad. When Frank put an offer to me to defend my title against him I wasn't sure. I had to think about it because he was a mate, but in the end I thought it was right to give him the opportunity to fight for the title. The dilemma for me was being uncertain how I would react to stepping into the ring against a guy I really liked. Richie's a family man who has kids the same age as mine and at the final head-to-head press conference we asked after our families and didn't do a head-to-head pose out of respect. It was weird. I respected Richie as a fighter too. He got beaten by Markus Beyer, the German, on a bad night when he lost his WBC super middleweight title but I knew he could box and I knew he'd be up for the fight and he'd perform because this was his last opportunity.

Richie boxed really well but I lacked something essential in that fight. He was stung by a right hand to the temple in the opening round and if it had been any other opponent, I would have charged him. I wanted to win but I didn't have the same anger or fire in the belly. But Richie was really in the fight and caught me with a lot of shots. I was winning but it was competitive. Technically, Richie was an excellent boxer and he started to land cheeky right hands and enjoyed a couple of good rounds. Finally, in the eighth round, he caught me with some really decent punches and I fired back. Being a fighter is all about going against logic, going against the natural human instinct to run away from the fire. I was really maddened, so I gritted my teeth, hit myself on the chin with one of my gloves and shouted at him, 'Come on.' In my head he had crossed the line and our friendship, just for that moment, was put to one side. I could see him going back and starting to wane, so I really started to throw solid punches and he kind of became resigned to his fate. I could see by the look on his face that he didn't have much left. He came in to hold, so I used what I call busy punches, flurries of punches, because I knew it was almost over. I dropped Richie in the ninth round, used my speed to finish him and the referee stepped in. I didn't want to knock him out and I was glad when the referee stopped it. He had fought a really good fight and caught me with a lot of shots but Richie wasn't a big puncher. He's the one opponent, however, that I really felt bad for after I beat him. It was only when the fight was over that we discovered what had happened to Paul Ingle just before we got in the ring and I'm glad that I didn't know.

The 28-year-old Welshman's 10th-round stoppage victory over Telford's Richie Woodhall, in a match between present and former champions, was out-standing. The two friends had produced a memorable contest to raise the spirits of a crowd that had only minutes before been stunned to see Ingle carried out on a stretcher, and had been unaware of the full extent of the Yorkshireman's injuries . . . Calzaghe seemed deeply moved despite being denied what would have been rightful acclaim for a memorable win had it not been for the injury sustained by Ingle. Woodhall, 32, a former holder of the WBC version of the title, made nonsense of the bookies who rated him as little more than a no-hope bit-part actor in a script suggesting Calzaghe would comfortably notch up a seventh defence of his WBO title. For round after round, the two stood toe to toe giving a wonderful display of commitment and no little skill, and Woodhall's impressive combinations raised genuine hopes among his supporters that he would be capable of springing a significant upset. But the end, in the 10th, was a minor refereeing masterpiece by Roy Francis, in charge of his last world-title fight before enforced retirement at the age of 65. Woodhall was shipping heavy punches and had become an open target when Francis mercifully made a perfectly timed intervention. On numerous occasions the two friends touched gloves to show appreciation of their opponent and smiled and hugged when the fight was over. On a grim night, it was a much-needed tonic which gave hope to those who had paid to watch.

– John Rawling, *Guardian*, 18 December 2000

Lennox Lewis and Naseem Hamed were regarded as the two best fighters in the world in their different weight divisions at the beginning of 2001 but in the space of two weeks in April they both suffered crushing defeats, Naz by Marco Antonio Barrera and Lewis by Hasim Rahman, a devastating fifth-round knockout in South Africa. Just a week after Lewis lost the world heavyweight title I faced my mandatory challenger, Mario Veit, determined to stop the rot. The twenty-seven-year-old German had been at ringside to watch my fight against Sheika and, knowing he would be my next opponent, I looked into his face and he didn't seem to be too reassured by what he had witnessed. But the atmosphere at Wembley was a world away from the electrical current created by six thousand people inside Cardiff's International Arena when Veit stepped in the ring and his worry had turned to pure, naked fear. I could sense it when we came together for the referee's instructions and he refused to make eye contact. His anxiety betrayed him and this was the signal for me that he was there for the taking.

Veit was undefeated in thirty fights and a dangerous fighter but he was in the lion's den and he froze. The occasion simply got to him because he'd never boxed before in this type of situation. Usually, I'm aggressive but a touch cautious in the opening round and like to show a lot of feints, just to size up my opponent, so I stand there with a wide stance and weigh things up quickly. My dad always says that I do this in about thirty seconds. A boxer can totally wipe out his opponent by feinting him, just like Sugar Ray Leonard did to Roberto Duran in their rematch. I have a tendency to become too embroiled in a toe-to-toe fight because when I'm in that ring I never have any fear. I'm an aggressive, attacking counter-puncher, always dangerous and always in perfect range to punch. I could see that he was going to need time to get into the fight, so I made up my mind that I would jump on him, attack his body, bring his arms down, then I would hit him on the chin and knock him out. I've never been as sure of anything as I was that I'd get through this guy in a single round.

He was tall, six foot four inches, a very upright boxer but this style didn't help him when he lost his nerve. I like fighting tall guys, getting in underneath them and firing in punches over the top, but Veit was tense as well, absolutely rigid, so I jumped on him, drove some hard left hooks into his body and his hands came down very quickly. He was heavy-legged and tried to hold on but I threw a left uppercut, a beautiful punch, and he was down within the opening thirty seconds. He'd never been down before and he was absolutely gone. It wasn't long before I had him down again from a left hook to the jaw and, clearly now, he wasn't going to last. I followed straight in with a swarm of unanswered punches until the referee, Mark Nelson, stopped the fight.

I was now established as the top fighter in Britain and I wanted to take on the biggest names, like Jones, Bernard Hopkins, and any other top Americans. Showtime TV was showing my fights again in the United States so I was offered another appearance on a Mike Tyson undercard. We tried to get one of the big names but, eventually, had to settle on Will McIntyre from Louisiana who was very limited and, quite obviously, a middleweight stepping up. Every morning I came down to the hotel restaurant for breakfast, to drink only mineral water with ice because of making weight, and I'd see him already at the table eating a good, hearty breakfast and couldn't quite believe it. Just for that, I wanted to knock him out and I dropped him at the end of the third round – the first time in his career that he'd been put down – and waved to the referee to stop it. He didn't, even though McIntyre's legs were gone, but he'd seen enough and stopped it early in the fourth.

Tyson was due in the ring soon after and would knock out Brian Nielsen, the local heavyweight, but as I was settling down into my seat ahead of the main event, Shelley Finkel, Tyson's manager, came over and sat beside me. A newspaper had quoted me referring to Tyson as a bit of a lunatic and Mike had read the piece, Shelley wished to warn me. He wasn't amused. So at the press conference afterwards, I sat very close to Dad and kept myself hidden away as best I could. Knowing what Tyson can be like, I didn't fancy almost sixteen stone of him against twelve stone of me. I managed to steal away without him noticing. Lennox Lewis was lined up to fight him next and was much better equipped than me to put Iron Mike in his place, which he duly did.

I've always been closer to my dad's side of the family. His brothers, Sergio and Uccio, who is my godfather, were more like pals, brothers even. Uccio was an athlete himself, placing third in a national skills competition at Naples football stadium when he was younger. But two weeks before I boxed Charles Brewer he nearly died. I came in to my old boxing gym one day and got a cold feeling the minute I looked at my dad. He was on the phone and I knew straight away that something was wrong. Uccio had been in a car crash, his car flying across the road and finishing halfway up the bank on the side. He did manage to scramble out but the car collapsed on him and he suffered some horrendous injuries, a broken back, a collapsed lung, a broken arm and two broken legs. He was in a really bad way and it was touch and go for a period of time. I was devastated and I really didn't know going into the fight if he was going to pull through. It took him a month before he was able to leave the hospital but he's a fighter too, a strong farmer and me dedicating the Brewer fight to him gave him that extra incentive to get better.

Philadelphia fighters are renowned in boxing for their toughness, a hard edge which almost sets them apart even in the macho world of boxing. Joe Frazier was the ultimate example of their fighting spirit, but even the six-round preliminary guys from Philly fight hard because that's what they're bred to do in the gyms all across the city.

Charles Brewer lived up to this image when I returned to the International Arena twelve months later and I was made to realise why they called him 'The Hatchet'. Brewer was one of the hardest punchers I've ever fought and certainly one of the most rugged. He still carried a .22 calibre bullet in his chest after being shot in a brawl in north Philadelphia sixteen years earlier, so he couldn't have been anything other than tough.

Brewer was the International Boxing Federation (IBF) title-holder when I won the WBO belt from Eubank and had stopped Herol Graham, one of Britain's best middleweight boxers over the years, in ten rounds in

1998, but not before being floored twice himself. Sven Ottke of Germany beat him later that year in a controversial points decision, one of many that Ottke would come through in his five-year title reign. It's an interesting fact that in the nine years between my bouts with Eubank and Lacy the other titles in the super middleweight division changed hands among nineteen different fighters. Glen Catley, the Bristol boxer I beat twice in the amateurs, even won the WBC belt for a brief spell. Brewer is one of six fighters I've fought who held versions of the title, so there can be no doubt that in the last decade I've proved myself to be the best fighter in my division. From the tapes I'd seen of Brewer, I reckoned that he was chinny, for he'd been stopped three times in forty-five fights. As a middleweight, he got knocked out twice back to back, but he'd got his career going again and I could see his confidence when I went over to New York for a press conference with the American media. Fighters know, we can see it in each other's eyes, and I knew that Brewer would handle the intimidating atmosphere much better than Veit had.

In the opening thirty seconds he caught me with a hard left to the body, which slightly winded me. I didn't realise that he was a converted southpaw – a left-handed fighter, like myself – but he fought out of an orthodox stance, so he was able to land his left with real power. Body shots, in any case, are often harder to get over than punches to the chin because a good dig to the solar plexus will stay with you for a while. You can do as many sit-ups as you want but, if you're hit in the right area, you can't protect the vulnerable area of the solar plexus. There's no meat on your ribs and, if you're caught there, it stings for a while. There wasn't much in Brewer's right hand but his left jab and left uppercut were seriously hard shots. I fought the wrong fight, for I should have boxed him, but once again I got drawn into the kind of slugging match that I can rarely resist if my opponent is up for it. I stayed in there and traded punches with him and that's the way the fight progressed until he stunned me near the end of the seventh round when I walked into his left hand after being caught by a couple of jabs. Doubling the uppercut, he hit me flush on the jaw and when the bell rang I came back to the corner where I was assaulted almost as forcefully by my dad.

'Are you going to chuck this away?' he shouted at me, making things seem about ten times worse than they were.

'Is it really that bad?' I asked him.

'It will be, if you get nailed like that again. Be clever and start boxing this guy. Don't let him draw you into a street fight.'

When Dad starts to get really animated I know I need to shift up a gear and from the start of the eighth round I moved and boxed for the rest of the fight and Brewer had no answer. So many times I fight the wrong fight, and that's what happened after the hard body shot he landed early. When I boxed him I made it easy for myself because he couldn't touch me. He was very heavy-legged, so he needed me to engage him, but I was too clever for that over the final rounds. I moved well to avoid his punches and won the fight comfortably.

If his successful 10th defence of his title against Charles Brewer of the United States proved anything, it is that Calzaghe seems to have embarked on a mission to set new personal standards. Brewer, unrecognisable from the boxer who struggled to overcome Herol Graham almost four years ago, revived the legend of the tough Philadelphian but after 36 minutes of unrelenting assault and battery, the judges were left in no doubt of the outcome. That the triumvirate scored it 117–112, 118–111 and 119–109 for the Welshman was merely affirmation of a performance that must rank with the finest from a British boxer for many years.

– Martin Woods, *The Times*, 22 April 2002

Another Philadelphian was now in my sights, Bernard Hopkins, an excellent boxer who has proved himself over many years to be one of the best of his era. I respect him because he's been tremendously successful and he came up the hard way, struggling to get his dues until late in his career when he beat Felix Trinidad and Oscar De La Hoya and unified the middleweight division. He completed a record twenty successful title defences before dropping two decisions against fellow American Jermain Taylor in 2005, then moved up to light heavyweight to win a second world title against Antonio Tarver. He's not the kind of opponent I usually like to fight, as he's a defensive-minded boxer, very cagey, and I've struggled against these types many times in the past. Although Hopkins is technically very good, Roy Jones was a much more exciting fighter to watch because he had fast hands and always showed more flair. I believe I would beat Hopkins but I don't know if the gel would make for a good fight. We may still find out because Hopkins is not yet retired and I'd love to do the fight. Back in 2002 a deal was agreed and we looked all set to fight at the Millennium Stadium in Cardiff, then he walked away, which seems to be the story for me and big fights.

A teleconference was set up in my office in New York for July 30th, 2002, and on the call was myself, Don King who was in the room, Frank Warren and Bernard Hopkins' lawyer, Arnold Joseph. Along with Arnold was a woman named Linda Carter, who was there on behalf of Bernard. We asked Arnold if Bernard wanted to fight Joe Calzaghe and we asked him how much money he would want if he did. The response we got was $3 million and the fight would have to take place in the United States. After a little scratching of the head, we said, 'Okay, done.' Frank Warren agreed on the spot, Don King agreed and we agreed, so as far as we were concerned all the parties were singing off the one hymn sheet. Arnold excused himself with Linda and I can only assume it was to call Bernard. Either that day or the next day, I'm just not certain about that particular timeframe, they came with a new demand: $6 million, double the sum that had been agreed. In addition to the Calzaghe fight, we had offered him $1 million to fight Morrade Hakkar, and the winner of that bout to fight Harry Simon. Then he would have had the bout with Joe but when he came back asking for $6 million, the deal blew up. I thought that the Hopkins fight was a spectacular prospect, but it wasn't to be. Bernard's pretty shrewd, he's no dummy and has done a wonderful job of self-management in his career, but he had then and still has no desire to fight Joe Calzaghe, that much is pretty clear. Joe gets criticised sometimes for not having fought more big-name Americans, but in this case the fault has never rested with him.

– Jay Larkin, then Showtime TV Network's Senior Vice-President of Sports and Events Programming

Miguel Jimenez became my next opponent instead but it was another of those fights which I couldn't really get up for. Only the venue was spectacular, open air in the August sunshine at Cardiff Castle, though the atmosphere was like a country fair because all the crowd noise just escaped into the sky, but my focus wasn't there. I knew that Jimenez was a league beneath me and I just wasn't worried about him enough to be on my game. You always need to have a little fear of your opponent to be at your best, you have to be concerned about him. I had only two or three weeks' notice that I would be boxing him and I didn't really perform and damaged my left hand again, which came up really badly swollen. It was a voluntary defence, in which I won every round. It wasn't a great fight, however, I didn't drop him or even get him rocking, and the sight of the Millennium Stadium nearby was an ironic reminder of the big fight that might have been. So I was still searching for something that I could value as career-defining.

Tocker Pudwill didn't fall into this category for sure, though it wasn't my fault that Thomas Tate, an experienced former world-title challenger, had to pull out through injury two weeks before. I was top of the bill with Ricky Hatton, the Newcastle Arena was full and it turned out, as expected, to be a nice, comfortable defence for me, an early Christmas present. I dealt with Pudwill ruthlessly, knocking him down three times in two rounds before the referee stopped it. A lot of people disparaged the guy as an opponent, but Pudwill had gone the full twelve rounds with Sven Ottke for the IBF title two years before and was unbeaten since. I would never claim that it was like taking on King Kong but it always amuses me how wise people try to be. They said he was a bum but why was he a bum, which is a term I hate anyway? Because I stopped him in two rounds? It annoys me that there are so many people who have never laced up a pair of gloves, have spent no time in a gym talking to fighters or trainers to learn about boxing, offering sanctimonious opinions and pontificating and yet they know nothing about the sport. Pudwill wasn't a danger to me but he was no bum.

These weren't the kind of challenges, however, on which I could begin to build a legacy, and frustration was setting in, along with a trace of complacency, which was where the real danger lurked.

ROUND NINE
The Twilight Zone

You can't train for this moment or simulate it in the gym, you can never really be prepared. It's about seconds and milliseconds, yet it can determine the course of your career and maybe your life. When I hit the floor and got back up no one could help me, not even my dad who appeared to be in shock. All I could hear was silence. Then I looked across the ring and saw this big, powerful guy who couldn't have been more ready, for this is what he had trained for, and then I asked myself the question: *What are you going to do, Joe? What are you going to do?*

Byron Mitchell was a quiet guy but I noticed how strong he looked at the weigh-in. He was really big and I was surprised at how broad a back he had and how powerful he was in the shoulders. The Slama from Alabama was a formidably built guy. Just four months earlier Mitchell had engaged in a unification bout against Sven Ottke in Germany and lost by a split decision on the judges' scorecards. But Muhammad Ali would have lost to Ottke in Germany. I knew that Mitchell would be one of my most risky defences because he had stopped eighteen of the twenty-five opponents he had beaten, and his only other loss was on points against a Frenchman, Bruno Girard. I was eager to get in the ring, however, perhaps over-eager, for the fight had been postponed three times and I'd only boxed those two rounds against Pudwill in ten months. This was also an opportunity to demonstrate just how much better I was than Ottke by beating Mitchell in a more impressive way. The German's promoters had shown no interest in trying to make a fight between two unbeaten rival champions, probably because they knew what would happen. They would certainly know after this.

My intention was to box against Mitchell but the crowd got to me, like it had in the Brewer fight. From early in the opening round I became far too aggressive and very quickly we were engaged in a wild brawl. When the adrenalin is flowing, like it was that night, my instinct is to get stuck in to try to take out the guy as soon as I can. Mitchell concentrated on keeping his left hand high and on moving away from my left hand. I caught him with some solid shots in the opening round but my punches arrived at the target in more of a loop than his, which were direct. I was faster but he had shorter arms and experience had taught him how to use this to his advantage. One combination of punches I threw in the first round stunned him, but then I tried to go for the finish and my discipline deserted me, leaving me open to a quick counter. Even in the first round I was able to feel his power.

Dad kissed me when I came back to the corner at the end of that first round as if everything was all over and this was our fight. I was catching Mitchell with plenty of punches and they hurt him but he'd kept bombing forward and the fight wasn't ours yet by a long way. I was still throwing looping punches in the second round and dropping my hands, almost inviting him to step in with a big bomb, which is exactly what he did. He caught me with three decent body shots and, as I went to throw a left hook, he hammered me on the chin with a short, hard right hand. It looked to people at ringside that I might have gone down with the momentum of missing with another wild left hook because the punches we threw were almost simultaneous, but as I dropped to my knees and then got back up and wobbled it dawned on people that I'd been knocked down for the first time in my life. It had certainly dawned on me, for my head was clear and I looked over to the corner where Dad didn't react, as if he couldn't quite believe what had happened. A deathly hush came over the crowd and you could have heard a pin drop. My powers of recovery had never been tested before but anyone can get knocked down. What happens to a lot of boxers is that once they get hit they stay hit. Frank Bruno is the obvious example, for he would try to stay on his feet. Perhaps if he had been able to take a count on his knee, he could have been able to recover in fights he lost.

When I reflected later I realised that I should have worked my way back into the fight cautiously by tying up Mitchell in close and moving back out of range. But I am who I am, I don't run from danger, my heart took over completely and I stepped straight towards an opponent who was ready to rip my head off. Any champion can be a champion when they're on top but real champions fight when their life depends on it. I wasn't going to accept a beating, so I faced him and fought like this was all that ever mattered and I had to overcome. Mitchell charged me like a bull and missed by fractions of an inch with ferocious punches which would have put me down again had they landed. In the teeth of the fire I became like Keanu Reeves in *The Matrix* and threw everything I possibly could at him. If I hadn't, I wouldn't have survived. We were in a tear-up now that Nigel Benn would have been proud of and in the cluster of flying fists I landed a solid left hook to Mitchell's jaw which sent him crashing to the floor. He got back up but he was badly shaken. I could see he was groggy and I knew I was going to take him out because I've always been a great finisher. I went on the offensive and he stopped throwing punches, he was pawing. His power was gone and I threw everything I possibly could at him, but he stayed on his feet and wouldn't go down.

I looked at the referee, Dave Parris, just like I'd done in my fight with Will McIntyre, because I could see him out of the corner of my eye and expected him to dive in. Mitchell wasn't throwing any punches back and couldn't possibly survive. Finally, with twenty-four seconds left, the ref did wave it over. Mitchell was still on his feet but he was taking a beating. Some people argued that the stoppage was premature but what else did they want me to do to the guy? I didn't want to inflict any more punishment because Mitchell was beaten, there's no doubt about it, for I'd caught him with really hard combinations. He hit me with that one good shot but apart from that he got battered and outclassed in a two-round war. You could say that he nearly won the fight with that one punch but I must have hit him almost two hundred times and he never fought again.

Calzaghe was forced to climb off the floor for the first time in his career to stop American Byron Mitchell in a sensational 13th defence of his WBO super middleweight title fight at Cardiff International Arena last night. The huge Cardiff crowd were stunned when a vicious Mitchell right hand sent the champion down for the first time in his career early on in the second. But the Welshman rose and proceeded to punch Mitchell to a standstill in one of the most dramatic shootouts ever seen in a British ring.

Calzaghe, 31, showed enormous courage and heart to fight back from the brink and bludgeon his way to victory like a man possessed. Mitchell, who had been heartbreakingly close to ending Calzaghe's winning streak, had to be rescued by referee Dave Parris after 2:36 of the second. It was Calzaghe's 36th straight win. 'Maybe I went a little mad in there but the crowd seemed to love it,' said Calzaghe. 'I was shocked to go down for the first time in my entire life. I went down but got up to win by a knockout. I showed a champion's heart.' The fact that Mitchell, 29, was deemed unlucky to have dropped a split decision against Sven Ottke, the WBA and IBF titleholder, in March, was a tremendous spur for Calzaghe to outdo his German rival with a spectacular triumph and cement his claims of being the king of the 168lb division.

   – Mike Lewis, *Sunday Telegraph*, 29 June 2003

It was an incredible night, one of the best wins of my career because I had faced genuine adversity and responded in the way a warrior should. 'In the nineties I promoted Nigel Benn, Chris Eubank and Steve Collins and I think that even at their peaks, Joe would have beaten all of them,' Frank Warren said later. Jay Larkin from Showtime TV in America was adamant that a deal could still be done with Bernard Hopkins to give me a genuine superfight. 'A fight against Hopkins is a natural for Wales and we would like it to take place here,' he said. Once again nothing came of it. Instead of Hopkins, I fought the new mandatory challenger, Mger Mkrtchian, in my first fight of 2004. A Russian-based Armenian, I'd seen him fight Freeman Barr of the Bahamas and he looked quite good in a three-round win. He was tough and Eastern Europeans were becoming a force to be reckoned with, so Mkrtchian definitely wanted it but I outboxed him comfortably. I didn't want to be fighting him toe to toe because he was five foot nine, strong and squat, and that would have been his only chance to do damage. By using my jab and moving, I won every round until the seventh when I stepped it up with hard combinations and two straight lefts which floored him and persuaded the referee, Paul Thomas, to save him from any more abuse.

Another mandatory challenge met, another routine defence notched on the belt, but I wanted something more out of boxing than this. However, I wasn't as focused as I should have been on achieving the impetus I needed, for there were other things going on in my life that needed to be addressed first.

I got married to Mandy in 1994 and our two boys, Joe and Connor, are really the centre of my world. It's difficult for me to talk about the breakdown of my marriage because there are children involved, but by 2004 me and Mandy had drifted apart and were getting divorced. Although boxing was the last thing on my mind, as I seemed to be in court all the time, I was scheduled to fight Glen Johnson in June. He hadn't beaten Roy Jones or Antonio Tarver at this point, so a win over Johnson wouldn't have had the same kudos, but it would provide an entry to the light heavyweight division where I thought my career needed to go. Making the twelve-stone super middleweight limit was becoming more of a problem and I figured also that I needed a new challenge. Physically, I was in good shape; mentally, I don't think I was into it and fate moves in mysterious ways sometimes.

In the final thirty seconds of a hard, flat-out twelve-round sparring session I threw an uppercut that missed and fell down on the canvas in absolute agony. I'd suffered back spasms before, most recently three hours before I fought Jimenez. Barry Jones had come up to the room, so I got my dad to put the pads on, I put on the gloves and I started to show off a bit. Suddenly, I felt like I'd been shot in my back. The whole of my left side just seized up and I knew I had a serious problem. I didn't know if I could get a physio quickly enough because it was almost time to head to the arena. So my dad started rubbing it and the pain eased but it didn't go away. I wasn't able to warm up properly in the dressing room and when I got to the ring I didn't shadow-box. When your back is in spasm you can't put any leverage into your punches and I was hindered in the fight, but the adrenalin kicked in and I wasn't too conscious of the problem. This was different, though, because I really couldn't move and for days I was hoking around until I had to tell Frank that there was just no way I could fight against Johnson. I'd seen a specialist in London and underwent lumbar puncture treatment but it did me no good. It was disappointing to lose out on the fight, though I always look at the positives. With everything I was going through I could have been all over the place, if I'd got in the ring. The same thing happened to John Ruiz when he fought Roy Jones. He was going through a divorce, had all sorts of problems because of it and his mind wasn't on the job when he had to answer the bell. Although the timing was terrible, maybe my injury was just meant to be.

The divorce was making me angry and depressed. When kids are involved and there's money involved and then lawyers come along and take over and you're not talking to one another, it's not easy. Everything started going through solicitors' letters, it became tit for tat and all of this wells up inside. You're not just mad about that, you become angry with the world and boxing had to take a back seat as the court case dragged on for over twelve months. Everything was about money and the amount of money I had to pay in the end was unbelievable. When we reached a settlement it was out of court but we'd still been dragged through the whole legal process for that length of time because we weren't talking and, psychologically, I got into a bad place. My personal life had become a distraction but I'd been boxing such a long time that I felt I could just turn up in decent shape and win, a terrible delusion.

Deep down I knew differently. My boxing career wasn't moving in the direction I wanted it to and I wasn't getting a big fight. Hopkins wasn't biting, there seemed to be no one else on the horizon and I needed an opponent who was going to get me motivated. I was becoming disheartened and hadn't been training with my normal fire and dedication. I wasn't pulling my weight in the gym and was out drinking and socialising more than I should have been. At that stage I don't know what I was really thinking. I was just going through the motions and needed a good kick up the arse, which is when a mysterious woman appeared in a car park just as I stepped out of my car around five o'clock on a Sunday afternoon. My kids were with me and hers was the only other car in the vicinity.

'I knew I was going to see you today,' she said. 'Things are pretty bad for you at the moment but it's all going to be OK.'

I turned back towards my car because I thought this woman was crackers. She said she was a clairvoyant and claimed she had heard from my great-grandad and had this message to deliver from him.

'At the moment you're going through a traumatic time but don't worry, it's going to get much better for you. You need to set a training goal and he's saying to me, "Don't let it go, everything that you've worked for. Don't let it go." This is what he's telling you, Joe.'

She could have read about my injury in the newspapers but she couldn't have known that I wasn't bothered about my training because of the divorce.

'You get up in the morning and you don't want to run or go to the gym,' she continued. 'You're becoming depressed and you want to do nothing. You're not training properly. When are you fighting again?'

My next fight would be against Kabary Salem in October.

'You need to focus.'

It was like something from *The Twilight Zone*. The woman had been burnt down one side of her body when she was a kid and had almost died from her injuries. She said that the experience had left her with this gift. She described my great-grandad in appearance and then she left, just as suddenly as she had arrived.

I went home and told my dad, who was sceptical and laughed it off, but he did say that his grandad looked exactly the way she described. I kept an open mind about it because her message did mean something to me. I do believe that there is life after death and that the people in our lives who pass away probably keep an eye on us. I was brought up a Catholic, though I no longer go to church every Sunday, in fact I haven't been for a while, but I believe in God and I believe in Jesus and that's the important part, the spirit and faith that's inside you. I do believe that I'm being looked after and I've always thought that's reassuring. When I go in the ring I feel safe because God is looking out for me. As a kid, I prayed every time I boxed, before and afterwards, even if I got beaten, and I always cross myself and give thanks that I haven't been hurt or my opponent either. I don't just pray to win, I pray that we'll both come through the fight healthy. I'm fortunate that I've been given so much in my life, my beautiful kids especially, and I'm not wanting for anything. I'm no angel, I swear a lot and I do a lot of things that I know I shouldn't, but we all go through bad times. Who knows why that woman appeared when she did? All I do know is that what she said was right.

Kabary Salem, an Egyptian based in New York, had a reputation for being one of the dirtiest boxers in the world. In his previous bout against Mario Veit, who beat him on points by a split decision, he had even allegedly headbutted the referee, but he wasn't half as big a pain in the arse as his trainer, Nettles Nasser, who had worked Omar Sheika's corner. Nasser started on about the belt and I said, 'The only belt you're going to get is if you go to

Top Man and buy one.' Of course this only made him more annoying and he got so carried away with himself, predicting I was about to have my last fight, that my dad got into the slanging match.

'You went home crying the last time after the Sheika fight and you'll do the same again,' he said. 'Salem has a better chance of running across the Sahara Desert barefoot than he has of beating Joe Calzaghe. I'm fed up with all your yapping, you're like a fucking goose, so take a tablet and shut up.'

Whatever the clairvoyant had said to reassure me back in Newbridge, the omens in Edinburgh were not good. We were heading to the weigh-in at our hotel and on the way down from the room Dad decided to clown around in the elevator. 'This lift doesn't look very safe,' he said, as he jumped up and down, testing the floor. Suddenly, we came to a halt. 'What have you done now, Dad?' I shouted, pressing the ground-floor button. Nothing happened. I was thirsty, hungry and tetchy and I was stuck in a lift with my dad at the moment that I should have been stepping onto the scales. 'What? I didn't know,' he said. We must have been an hour in the lift before, finally, the security guys were able to open the doors wide enough for us to crawl out on our hands and knees, with me that embarrassed and pissed off that I was almost ready to throw Dad back in.

We arrived for the weigh-in twenty minutes late after I stopped off to do a bit of skipping because I was a few ounces over the twelve-stone limit. When I jumped on the scales I was smack on the weight, so I jumped off again and took a sip of my drink. As soon as I did, Nasser started up again. 'You didn't make the weight,' he shouted. 'You are two pounds over, Joe. I demand you get back on the scales.' The Board of Control official told him, 'No, he's twelve stone,' but Nasser got up on a chair to continue with his protest. 'There's no fight,' he said. 'They're cheating. He didn't make the weight.' When I went to walk past him he stood right in my way and I really wasn't in the mood at that point. I must have shoved him six feet through the air into a wall, for he had got on my nerves. 'We're going to kill you,' he shouted out as he walked away with a stupid grin on his face.

That night I was only able to get an hour's sleep because of the noise from the nightclub that was joined on to the hotel. There were people shouting and scream-ing at all hours. I rang reception to see if I could change rooms at midnight but the hotel was full and I tossed and turned until 5 a.m. when I got up because I couldn't sleep. I was stressed about the lack of sleep, which I wasn't able to catch up on, and going to the arena I was yawning and worried that it might not take a punch to put me to sleep.

The Salem fight was the most disconnected I've ever

been, not because of the opponent but because of myself. I just didn't turn up on the night because my preparation had been quite poor. The guy was awkward but, once again, I didn't have much respect for him and I didn't fear him in the slightest. I thought I could do whatever I liked and I walked to the ring as if I was walking down the aisle of a shop. I felt no nerves and no buzz. It was like I was in a dream.

When we walked through the ropes my uncle Serge, who is usually uptight when it comes to fight time, carried the belt all the way across to Salem's corner where Nasser spat out, 'That's ours. We'll have that.' My uncle was so incensed that he dropped his head on him and it all nearly kicked off. Passions run high whenever two men are about to fight but almost the last thing you would want as a boxer is for your uncle to have to leave the ring in case he starts slugging before you.

Salem was gangly and awkward, arms everywhere, just a horrible fighter. He was dirty too but that's no excuse because I was poor. I just wasn't there that night and it became a bad-tempered street fight. I slammed him at one point and we even headbutted one another. I've never been a dirty fighter but that's the kind of fight it was, scrappy and tense. In the fourth round he dropped me with a good right hand. My hands were down, I wasn't concentrating and was wide open to it, though I wasn't badly shaken. It wasn't the kind of punch that

Mitchell had caught me with, so I got up and moved around and tried to box more cleverly but it turned into an awful fight, another one that I'm embarrassed about. When he went to the press conference afterwards he wrote me off and Salem wasn't the only one. I was thirty-two years old, having fought only four fights in over two years, and was most critics said that I was past it, even Colin Jones. I loved to watch Colin as a kid, a proud Welshman also who fought the best boxers of his day, guys like Milton McCrory and Don Curry. He said that I was clearly past it and should retire now. But I'd only had one bad fight. How many bad fights did Ali have? What about Leonard? Even great fighters aren't at their best all the time. Colin wasn't alone in his criticism but all that negativity actually made me want to fight to prove people wrong.

Calzaghe is the best of British and that's official. Yet the fact that the Welshman doesn't mean a bag of leeks across the Atlantic is reflected in the list of the world's top 100 fighters ranked by *Ring* magazine. Despite being the longest-reigning world champion in any division and the most successful super middleweight ever, 32-year-old Calzaghe is down the list in 27th place . . . His performance against adopted American Kabary Salem would have done little to earn him promotion up the *Ring*'s fistic league table. It was, on his own admission, a disappointment, an unkempt, scrappy if unanimous points victory which contained only the second knockdown of his career. 'A bit embarrassing, really,' he acknowledged. It was, by his own unblemished yardstick, probably the least distinguished of his 38 victories, certainly of his 16 WBO title fights dating back to his acquisition of the belt from Chris Eubank in October 1997, whose record number of defences he has now equalled. But when he was floored in the fourth round by a right hand counter which would have KO'd more fragile-chinned men, it seemed as if Calzaghe might have encountered a seven-year hitch in his title career . . . The Scottish audience of 6,000 endured the sort of brawl more commonplace on a Saturday night in Glasgow than a Friday in Edinburgh. 'That was the worst you will see of me,' said Calzaghe. 'It was a bad day at the office.' So what now? No more messing around, according to former world champion Barry McGuigan. 'He needs a career-defining fight.' McGuigan says it is incredible that a champion of Calzaghe's calibre has not captured the attention of a wider audience, not least in America. 'He has the looks of a matinee idol, can box and punch, is undefeated but has not lit many fires outside of the British boxing community. It is time he did.' Calzaghe's trouble is that he has had too many fights against mediocre opposition. He knows he needs a really big fight.

– Alan Hubbard, *Independent on Sunday*, 24 October 2004

The embarrassment continued in March 2005 when I was scheduled to face Brian Magee in Belfast. Complications developed on the eve of the fight because Mario Veit had become my mandatory contender for a second time, so I would have to fight him again. It had been agreed that I could meet Magee in a warm-up bout, then defend against Veit, but his promoter, Klaus-Peter Kohl, won the purse bids to stage the fight and suddenly the goalposts were shifted. The Germans were able to call the shots and lobby the WBO to strip me of their title if I fought Magee first. Frank assured me that they were working on a solution that would see Veit receive step-aside money and a guaranteed title shot within ninety days. But the German camp really wanted me stripped because Veit couldn't have been relishing the prospect of facing me again. The uncertainty continued until the night before the weigh-in when I had to pull out of the Magee fight because I realised what was likely to happen. Although my back was in spasm that day, I was more concerned by the tactical game being played by Veit and his promoter. It was almost as if they were daring me to go ahead with the Belfast show and then they would play their hand.

There's no way I was going to jeopardise my title just to make a voluntary defence.

Boxing's not like football, rugby or cricket, where you get paid anyway. If there's no fight, there's no purse and that's the end of it. That's why most of the time fighters go ahead and box even when they're injured. I could have my hands insured but it would be ridiculously expensive, especially with my track record, costing me maybe the whole of my purse. So anyone who might think that I just pull out of fights without a legitimate injury are crazy. I didn't get a penny for the Magee non-fight and all the training came to nothing. I was out of pocket and angry, but had a few beers on the Thursday night before flying home. The Veit rematch was set for May 5 and the whole process of getting prepared began again.

When it comes to getting myself ready to fight I realise that there's someone out there who's going to try to take my head off and take away all that I've worked for, so a little voice activates inside my head: 'Joe, it's time to go back to work.' I train with the same intensity every time and I know the markers as they come along, twelve weeks, eight weeks, four and so on. A dozen weeks out from the fight I start light training, jogging and a few rounds here and there to get my general fitness built up. The first week or two is like anybody else going back to their work. It's hard to get back into it. You get pulls and aches and little niggles and you're tetchy, but within a week of being back

219

in camp I don't mind the training at all. I enjoy it when I'm in full flow and love the sensation of being fit because it makes me feel almost invincible. Eight weeks out I step up my training. I run in the morning and go to the gym in the afternoon, putting real effort into it, and I watch my diet and take it all very seriously.

Eating is my big vice when I'm away from training, I love my food. When you've finished a fight and you've been so strict about the preparation, you need a release, so I go out to eat curries, Thai food or Italian, my favourites. I'm a big meat-eater and enjoy a pint like any other guy when I'm not in the gym. My diet deteriorates the longer I'm out of training and I barely see a salad or vegetables. I eat absolute crap, anything, sweets, chocolate, cakes, crisps and I eat loads. The only thing that saves me is a high metabolism. I always stay a little active and don't become a complete couch potato. I play football and get out with my kids and I run as well because I enjoy it. I don't go on a bender and hit the drink day after day and totally pig out, but I enjoy a few drinks with the lads. I'm not bothered about having a drink or socialising when it's time to train. I'm not a big socialiser in any case, I just go out mostly with my girlfriend, Jo-Emma.

Six or seven weeks from a fight I cut out all the shit and I really have to start losing weight. I'm an evening eater, which is the worst possible thing. I love to scoff at night and that's probably the continental influence because I've always been the same. I'm never hungry in the morning, so I have to consciously change my routine to eat some porridge or Weetabix for breakfast. I change from one sugar in my tea or coffee to sweeteners and put Canderel on my breakfast instead of sugar. For sweet things, I take diet yoghurts. Eventually I get on to skimmed milk and generally eat more healthy meals, with plenty of vegetables and fruit. I have to be careful of my sweet tooth but I do it all gradually, over a period of six weeks. I'm watching my weight constantly, being sensible about it. For a boxer, taking weight off quickly and right at the end is the most dangerous thing. I try not to eat at night and I cut out the bread, the crisps and the chocolate. It's not difficult, it's just getting yourself into the mindset, but after all these years I'm so used to it.

Four weeks before a fight the British Boxing Board of Control conduct a check weigh-in. This is a good innovation, recently brought in, because it stops fighters from trying to crash-diet down to the weight at the last minute. I like to be no more than ten pounds over the twelve stone limit and it's easier then to get down to twelve stone than it would be from a higher weight.

After all these years of making the twelve-stone limit I no longer have to write down what I eat on a piece of paper because I know my body. Apart from a couple of lapses, I make the weight perfectly and I'm always strong when I get in the ring, which is the whole objective. In the last few weeks I'll eat high carbohydrates in the day and protein to repair my body in the evening. I'm able to spoil myself a bit at weekends by eating a nice steak or going out to a restaurant, which is good for me psychologically because it means that I'm not being too monastic or being driven nuts by a strict, overbearing regime.

My gym sessions are short but they're high-intensity. If I do twelve rounds on the bag or the speed ball, I throw maybe 200 or 300 punches per round. When I'm on the pads with my dad we work throughout the entire three minutes of the round, throwing dozens of punches in combination, working on sharpness and timing. Sparring usually starts about four weeks before a fight but I keep it very light now, working mostly on defence. I don't use weights because, for me, boxing's about speed, not building up muscle. I just need my stomach muscles to be as solid as I can make them to avoid getting winded by body shots, so I do sit-ups while my dad stands over me throwing a medicine ball into my belly. All of my training is basic, very old-school, and I'm able to do my running around where I live, mostly five-mile or six-mile runs at a good pace. It's the greatest of feelings when it's all going well, I feel more positive and I know I'll be ready to perform in the fight. I don't get distracted when I'm training. Morning, noon and night my mind is consumed by boxing. That's all I think about, getting ready

From the left, Connor, Jo-Emma, me, Uncle Manlio, Auntie Alba and little Joe at a restaurant in Sardinia, a great place for great food, not so great if you're trying to make twelve stone weeks later.

Three generations of Calzaghes, with my dad and granddad. My first championship belt rests proudly in Giuseppe Calzaghe's home in Sardinia.

My two biggest fans and my pride and joy. Connor had just won a medal playing football while we were on holiday at CenterParcs in Wiltshire.

My mum and dad with Joe and Connor on Christmas morning, Joe looking like a chip off the old block already.

A night out last Christmas with Jo-Emma, looking gorgeous, and she's not looking bad either!

My two sisters, Sonia, who has baby Louisa on her lap, and Melissa, feel my strength.

My grandmother Victoria with my granddad and Dad on one of her few visits to Newport. Sadly she passed away not long after I won the title from Eubank.

My nan Rebecca and grandfather William, a miner from Markham, on their wedding day.

From the first time I met Lennox Lewis on the set of Ian Wright's TV show, where this picture was taken, Britain's former heavyweight champion has offered me only encouragement. He's a great guy.

In Miami with my mate, Enzo Maccarinelli, and the Golden Boy, Oscar De La Hoya, where I collected the WBO Fighter of the Year award for 2006. Over the years De La Hoya has been great for boxing and he's another good guy.

Jake La Motta fought Sugar Ray Robinson so often, he jokes, that Sugar gave him diabetes, but the Raging Bull also handed the greatest boxer who ever lived his first defeat. They say Jake had the best chin in boxing, some boast at a time when fighters fought once a week.

Mike Tyson wasn't delighted to have to pose for yet another picture during his stay at the Grosvenor House Hotel in London, but Dad made sure that he did – and here's the evidence.

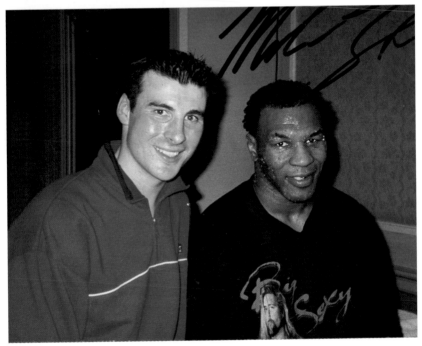

Sylvester Stallone and me squaring up for a publicity shot for Rocky X, to be released in 2026! Actually, we met before the premiere of *Rocky Balboa* in London and chatting with him about all the Rocky movies was great.

A Legend of the Welsh valleys, Tom Jones came to see me the day before I fought Bika in Manchester, and his advice was that I should follow him and try to make my name in America.

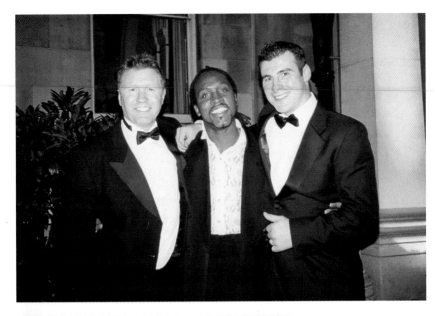

Steve Collins and Nigel Benn were two of the great names in British boxing at the start of the 1990s, when I was dreaming of reaching the top. Steve's always been a great guy and Nigel is simply one of the most exciting fighters ever to come out of this country. We were all at the premiere of *Ali* starring Will Smith.

Normally I'm moody when I'm in the gym but me and Dad have happy days at work too.

physically and mentally to step in that ring in the best condition I can possibly be in.

When you're only fighting twice or three times a year at the most, as it has been for me for many years, you have long gaps out of the ring and there are only so many holidays you can go on, only so many restaurants you can eat in, so I get bored and lazy. I'm happiest when I'm training because life has more meaning sometimes. People say that I could start a business but, if I did, I'd feel that I had to put my whole mind into it and I couldn't do two jobs together once the training started again. When I train that's all I do and I don't want my mind preoccupied by other things because that's when you come unstuck. One day there will be a lot of time in my life for business and other stuff. The kids relieve the boredom and we go to the pictures, along with Jo-Emma. I throw the occasional little party but life here is quiet, ideal for me. I'm out of the way and I'm left alone. The house in Blackwood is only temporary and I could buy a better house, but do I want to go spending twice as much money to go to live in Cardiff? I'd be further away from my gym and my family and I'd have nowhere to run, so this is fine for now and perfect for a fighter.

Boxing's a lonely sport, it's not like a team sport, you're on your own. I used to run with my dad but he's getting older and can't keep up as well as he used to do. The old legs aren't the same. So going to the gym is something to look forward to because I have Bradley Pryce, Gavin Rees, Nathan Cleverley and Enzo Maccarrinelli all there for company. We have a good camaraderie, the guys in our gym, but most of the time it's lonely and I get edgy. I'm very moody, especially coming up to a fight when I can't eat and it's constant solitude. I squabble easily and argue, mostly with my dad but he understands. This is a difficult game, a hard sport, an angry sport. There's a constant drain on your physical and emotional resources and in your head you can begin to feel under siege. My kids and my girlfriend relax me and put me at ease and when I'm happy I'm able to leave here and go away to perform. I live like a fighter almost all of the time and like a champion when I'm not training, but once the training starts I revert to challenger mode very naturally.

When the Magee fight fell through, the rematch with Veit was set for seven weeks later. I was already in great shape, so I went to Rome for a few days with my girlfriend to chill out, then was straight back in the gym. I knew Veit would be a different proposition than he was four years earlier in Cardiff and I'd have to go to Germany where he'd feel less threatened and more confident. I knew he was going to be up for it. I expected the worst in terms of how I'd be treated because I'd heard all these bad things about the tricks the Germans might play, but they were fantastic from the moment I arrived until I left, very hospitable.

Dad got up to his usual antics at the weigh-in, which was held in a big car showroom where all the undercard fighters weighed in first before the main event fighters. I'd made up a one-litre bottle of my Diaralite drink, a mineral replacement fluid, and I was on the weight of twelve stone but absolutely gagging for some liquids, in one of my 'don't-speak-to-me' moods. Dad was holding the bottle and I was getting more anxious the longer this charade went on.

It took forty-five minutes of hanging around before I weighed in along with Veit. The scales were up on a raised platform and all the WBO and German boxing officials were on the stage. Finally, they called my name and up I went, followed by Dad and Sergio. But Dad, of course, tripped going up the steps and spilled the whole bloody drink over Paco Valcarcel, the president of the WBO, who was wearing a black tie and tuxedo. My dad's face turned beetroot red with embarrassment but I was too dehydrated to be the same colour with rage. He picked himself up and started rubbing Paco's jacket. 'It's okay, Paco,' he said. 'There's a dry cleaners here somewhere.' Then he saw my face, like I was about to kill him, so he ducked down to pick up the bottle. Totally stressed, he dropped it again and only managed to save the dregs. I jumped on the scales, stepped off and sucked the last drops of my precious drink. Dad was mortified and it was only later, after he'd got me some water to drink and we'd returned to the hotel for a meal, that we saw the funny side of it and had a good laugh.

Veit did fight better the second time around but no fighter can forget the kind of experience he went through in Cardiff. The demons were bound to be affecting him, even though he boxed well for a couple of rounds. He knew what to expect from me and he moved better, but once my jab began to work I boxed a lovely fight. He caught me with a few good punches but never troubled me and I stopped him early in the sixth round.

It was then that the prospect of a fight against Jeff Lacy in November materialised. He had won the IBF title against Syd Vanderpool of Canada in 2004 and looked quite good, but I wasn't impressed when he struggled with Omar Sheika in his first title defence. We came face-to-face for the first time in the lobby of the Lowry Hotel in Manchester, ahead of a press conference the day before the Ricky Hatton–Kostya Tszyu world light welterweight title fight. It was before he fought Robin Reid and, I have to confess, I hadn't been too bothered by him, so it was all very friendly as we chatted and he seemed all right. Gary Shaw, his promoter, was there and he said, 'We'll come over here to fight you. Jeff's going to beat Reid and I know Frank well, so we'll get the fight on.' It was said with smiles all round and I didn't really believe that the big fight would happen because it had stayed elusive for so long. Two months later I watched on TV what he did to Reid. Even though Reid was past his best, the manner in which Lacy destroyed him was impressive. He knocked him down four times, so I knew this guy was dangerous, and he rose in my estimation after that fight. I wanted to box him but I insisted on a warm-up fight first.

ROUND TEN
The Best of British

Someone called it the 'The Curse' and maybe that's the best way to describe the problem with my hands, for it struck again to threaten my superfight with Lacy, which was scheduled to take place on 5 November 2005. Evans Ashira's only claim to fame was that he had boxed for the vacant WBA middleweight title but lost in the second round. He was strong and squat and had a style of bending right down into a crouch that made him about three foot tall, virtually a dwarf. I could hardly hit the guy.

Then in the fourth round I threw a left uppercut which landed on the top of his head and at the moment of impact I knew my hand was completely gone. From my schoolboy days, I'd been protecting my left hand with loads of bandaging so that I could use it to punch. I'd had it operated on and I'd nursed it through a succession of fights when all I could do was slap with my left glove, just to score points, but this was the worst injury I'd ever suffered, pure agony. Whenever we clinched the pain was like a bolt of electricity shooting through my hand and up my arm. I couldn't throw the left hand at all, I just had to use my right, grit my teeth and suffer. The metacarpal bone was broken and I had to box for eight rounds more. How many fighters could win a fight one-handed? Some people in the crowd started booing and I was frustrated by their reaction but I understand that a lot of people didn't realise the extent of my injury. I could hear the boos, though I was winning convincingly, but this didn't satisfy some people. The mentality in Germany is different. Watching Sven Ottke box was like watching paint dry but every punch he threw – and he only threw about six per round – he was cheered to the rafters. He won, that's what mattered, and the German crowd appreciated a winner. I felt like taking the ring microphone between rounds and saying, 'Excuse me, ladies and gentleman but I have a slight problem in that my left hand is fucked,' but I got on with it and did the best job I could with the tools I was given. If I'd been fighting Lacy that night, he would probably have won.

The real frustration was that it became a crap fight after I'd boxed well in the first few rounds and I'm sure I would have stopped him if the hand hadn't gone. Luckily, the fracture was clean and neat because I hadn't punched any more with it. If I'd continued to throw punches, the doctors would probably have had to operate. All they did was put on a cast and tell me to keep it elevated. I had a holiday booked in the Caribbean, one of those all-inclusive packages, flying out on the Monday but I couldn't go. I was in agony with my hand and I couldn't sleep for two days. I tried to get the dates changed on the insurance but couldn't do it because I'm a boxer. They said I was fighting, so they wouldn't pay out and I lost quite a bit of money, missed the holiday and now the Lacy fight was off.

Calzaghe was last night accused of ducking a multi-million pound world super middleweight unification clash against Jeff Lacy. The WBO champion broke his left hand as he laboured to a points win over journeyman Evans Ashira in Cardiff on Saturday. It forced him to cancel a November 5 clash with IBF king Lacy, bringing a furious rap from the American. Lacy said: 'Calzaghe damaged his left hand? I think he is trying to worm his way out of the fight between me and him. Is he really hurt? There is a track record of Calzaghe pulling out of fights. I was afraid this would happen and those fears have come true.' Plans were well advanced for Calzaghe to get the fight he had been demanding. A press conference with Lacy was staged in Manchester six weeks ago. Lacy's promotor Gary Shaw was due in London next week to finalise plans. But Calzaghe's hand, injured in the sixth round, will remain in plaster for a month. Lacy added: 'I don't think he should have taken the fight against Ashira. Why take that kind of risk when a big fight, no, a HUGE fight was already agreed? Now it seems as if I might have to go in another direction.' Shaw was even more scathing. He raged: 'Calzaghe wanted a way out and he has found it. He and his promoter Frank Warren no longer tell us where and when to fight. They had better get their passports ready because now it will be in the USA.'

– Pat Sheehan, *The Sun*,
12 September 2005

Frank Warren sent a photographer into my dressing room to take a picture of the injury so that he could email it out to Florida but I was annoyed that I should have to explain myself. I'm sure that neither Lacy nor Gary Shaw, on examining the evidence, considered picking up the phone to say, 'Poor Joe, you were right, we're sorry,' but I still believed that the fight would happen. Lacy went on to destroy Scott Pemberton on 5 November instead and looked pretty good, though Pemberton was fragile, the perfect opponent for Showtime TV to be building up their new Mike Tyson.

It was eerie that I should have encountered the psychic woman for a second time a couple of months before the Ashira bout, in the Asda supermarket in Newbridge. She had warned me again of taking my eye off the ball and I had felt like I could beat Ashira without being at my best, almost one-handed. Maybe the injury was another warning.

Sometimes I'll be on the pads, hitting them sweetly, *bah-bah-bah-bah-bah-bah*, feeling beautiful, like a million dollars. My dad really brings it out of me on those days. He'll get the pads out because he knows I'm on form, that I want to do it and he'll say, '*Bah-bah-bah,*' as I'm hitting them and make me feel good. 'You're brilliant today,' he'll say. He always tells me when I look brilliant and never tells me when I'm bad. When I'm bad he knows it's because I'm not in the mood and he's going to have a fight if he says anything, but he knows, more than anyone, that when I'm myself no one can beat me. That's why he was more confident than me for the Lacy fight. He knew what I could do but sometimes I don't realise my own capabilities. I lack confidence. Considering everything I've done, I'm not really a confident guy. This is a good thing, for it causes me to worry about my opponents. I should walk straight through some of them but this is a dangerous mentality to develop because it breeds complacency and complacency often leads to a bad night down the line. The night I stepped into the ring with Lacy I felt like the gladiator who goes in the arena, kneels down and rubs sand through his fingers. I'd gone through all the nerves and negativity, all the fears and worries, so I was able to look myself in the mirror and say, 'Lacy's been brought here for you and you know what has to be done, just do it.'

The signals from Lacy were a little different and I took heart from them, for example from seeing him by his girlfriend's side all the time. You shouldn't need to have your girlfriend constantly by your side when you're near a fight. I know that I never want to see Jo-Emma the day of the fight or even the day before. I don't think it's good to be with your girlfriend when you're trying to build a different kind of mindset, but Lacy was with his, holding hands as she mollycoddled him at the weigh-in when he appeared to be subdued, kind of melancholy. Wherever he was, she was. When I went over to do a Showtime press conference in November, four months before the fight, at Times Square in New York, she was there. When we had a conference call on the telephone with the media she was there. Coming off the plane at Manchester airport, she was there, and even at training she was there. The night of the fight I saw him on a TV monitor arriving into the arena and he was hand in hand with his girlfriend, which wasn't really the sort of entrance to intimidate. We were fighters about to go into battle and, to me, it's just too comfortable to be arriving hand in hand with your girlfriend. It makes you relaxed and takes your mind off the job. When you go in the ring you're going to hurt somebody. You don't need to be angry or too psyched up. I'm always calm and I have that cold-eyed state of mind.

When I'm in the ring I know what's about to happen and I like the guys around me, guys who know boxing, to have a laugh. But I took Lacy's demeanour and the fact that he and his girlfriend were holding hands coming into the arena as a sign of weakness. The cameras followed them into his dressing room and I watched them sit down in a corner, all loved up. I was hoping they might keep it going and maybe she'd take away all his strength a few minutes before the fight.

Maybe it meant nothing but, as a fighter, you always like to pick up on some sign of weakness in the opponent: looking away when we do the head-to-head staredown; not very assertive in his answers to the press; a bit pensive in how he says everything. These little things give you confidence and when he looked at me at the weigh-in, then looked away, I could tell that he wasn't 100 per cent. He was tight going into the fight because all the pressure was on him. It was the first time he would face a fighter who'd been a champion for nine years and the roles were reversed. Suddenly, he wasn't the main man, he was in Manchester, my place, and the crowd were amazing. Their support and some of the things I'd seen around Lacy encouraged me greatly and I felt like I'd won the fight before the bell was even rung.

If body language counts for anything at pre-fight press conferences, the dour demeanour of the normally affable Jeff Lacy, when he faced the media alongside Joe Calzaghe in a Manchester hotel yesterday, suggests he is feeling the pressure before their world super middleweight title unification fight at the MEN Arena in the early hours of Sunday morning. Lacy, 28, the IBF champion, had earlier refused to appear with Calzaghe on the set of Coronation Street for a series of publicity shots to be shown on last night's ITV News and in selected newspapers. He was then close to monosyllabic in his response to questions after his rotund promoter Gary Shaw described him as a cross between Mike Tyson and Evander Holyfield and as 'the most exciting boxer in the world'. By contrast Calzaghe, 33, who is now quoted as an 11–10 outsider by the bookmakers for the division's biggest fight since Roy Jones Jr faced James Toney 11 years ago, seemed relaxed and showed a confidence befitting a man who has been the WBO champion since 1997 and is about to figure in his 19th world title contest . . . Lacy restricted himself to a 'we'll see in the ring on Saturday' style of publicity which has proved a frustration to would-be interviewers since he arrived in Britain last week. The American, who is undefeated in 21 fights, was at least lucid when asked about the effect of Calzaghe's huge level of support. 'It doesn't worry me. I've always been the underdog,' he said. 'I like this event and that's why I've come here.' Calzaghe's father and trainer Enzo, a diminutive man who never suppresses the opportunity to spill out a thousand words or so when assessing his son's chances, says he spotted a chink in Lacy's psychological armour when the two fighters finally stood head-to-head for publicity pictures. 'Joe got right in his face and stared into his eyes and Lacy didn't want to know,' he said. 'He looked away and I think it was the moment he realised exactly what he is up against.'

– John Rawling, *Guardian*, 3 March 2006

On the evening before the fight I was sitting in the restaurant of the Lowry Hotel, eating some pasta, when I got a call on my mobile from some guy with a Manchester accent. 'Lacy's gonna get you, Lacy's gonna get you,' he started chanting. 'In round seven he will fuck you up.' Charming. I don't know how he managed to get my number because I never give it out to anybody but I laughed at him before he hung up. My mind was in the perfect place and some idiot making a crank call wasn't going to knock me at this stage. I just felt so at peace. All these years this is what I'd trained for and I'll always respect Lacy for coming to Britain to finally make my big fight happen. He could easily have priced himself out, like a lot of fighters do, then they pretend that they were willing to fight. I didn't price myself out of the fight, that's for sure, but to me it wasn't about money. This was about legacy, I needed a big fight to establish my proper place in history and, finally, everything was slotting into place.

Even the Ashira fight I was able to turn into a positive in my mind. I had no regrets at all that I fought him because my destiny all along, I told myself, was to fight Lacy on 4 March. Because I broke my hand in the fight, I was able to get my right hand working, my jab, and the same thing when my left hand went in training mid-February. When I got back in sparring I used my right and worked on speed and the jab became lightning quick, the perfect weapon for a pressure fighter like Lacy. Being a fast-punching southpaw, I can win a fight by simply keeping my right foot on the outside of my opponent's left and jabbing his head off. He can't punch me, he can't do anything and that's the way it would turn out against Lacy. His stock had risen because of the way he destroyed Scott Pemberton on our cancelled date in November. I may have still been the favourite after his stoppage of Reid but the way he ripped through Pemberton made me an 11-10 underdog in the betting, which spurred me on. After all those fights where I was expected to win and had nothing to gain, suddenly I was in a great position. The pressure was off and the psychology was completely different. I just knew what Lacy would be thinking: *I punch harder than that guy, I'm going to knock him out, he's shot. He got put on his ass by a journeyman two fights ago, then he couldn't even beat up a middleweight. Reid I knocked down four times and this guy only beat him on a split decision. Calzaghe's mine.* The fights with Salem and Ashira were blessings in disguise all along.

The morning of a fight I usually eat a large bowl of porridge or seven or eight Weetabix because they're full of slow-releasing carbs, not the fast-releasing carbs in sugar for instance. But I made a mistake the night before the Lacy fight, I ate too much steak and pudding and couldn't sleep when I went to bed because I felt bloated. When you haven't eaten big meals for a long period and you've trained every day your stomach shrinks. But the next day I was fine, just knackered from the lack of sleep, though I never sleep well before I fight and I can't have an afternoon nap either. I watched a comedy film called *The 40 Year Old Virgin* in my hotel room, which chilled me out and relaxed me, then I went for a walk. One of the Showtime TV guys couldn't believe it when he saw me walking around the hotel alone. In all his years in boxing he had never seen a fighter on his own so close to a fight.

Those few hours by myself are when I get my mindset just right. I've already watched my opponent on tape, though not a complete fight. I might pick two or three rounds from one bout and that's it, I know the guy and he's in my mind. I don't sit down and study with my dad because Dad scrutinises the guy's style and his opinion means more to me than anybody's when it comes to boxing. He knows what's good for me and what's bad, what kind of fighters will inspire a good performance, the kind of fighter that will give me a nightmare. Dad's watched practically all of my fights, amateur and pro, and he knew that Lacy had a perfect style for me. Sometimes he'll say to Frank, 'No, we don't want to fight so-and-so,' and I'll trust his judgement, but I go away on my own to think about the fight ahead of going to the arena. I think about walking into the ring and about what I'm going to do to counteract my opponent's style. I picture what I'm going to do and it's very vivid. I don't think about the punches I'm going to throw, that's all natural. I just think about what the other guy is going to do – maybe he's going to run or come looking for where to land a big right hand? – and I think about what I'm going to do in terms of my movement. The main thing for me, as a southpaw, is to determine in which direction I'm going to move, whether it will be mostly to my left or to my right. A southpaw should move to his right most of the time, but not always because you can't be predictable. Normally, I move to the left, which leaves me open to the right hand but Lacy was renowned for his left hook. I couldn't think why because he didn't knock people out with the left hook, from what I was able to see, so I figured that if I circled to his left that he wouldn't be able to handle it. He would be off balance constantly and I saw that clearly in my mind.

The only slight concern was that I started to get leg cramps late in the evening, which were really bad. I tried to stretch my legs, but I still had the cramp, so I went for a walk with my mate, John Salerno, at about eleven o'clock and, luckily, the cramp went away.

I got back to my room just before it was time to go, went down on my knees to say a prayer and that was it, there was a switch in my mind, I was the warrior at that moment. My kit was ready and I put my earphones in, I was 'there' already.

We walked across from the hotel, me, my dad, Sergio, and I was so relaxed. I felt serene because the waiting was over and all I wanted to do was get in the ring.

I arrived at the MEN Arena and you wouldn't have believed it was me who was fighting. I smiled and talked to people and did an interview for Showtime TV. Frank Warren looked at my dad and said quietly, 'Is Joe all right?' He was worried because I was so relaxed. I got to my dressing room, put on my music and danced around, then chilled out while my hands were taped up. It's the same ritual every time but you don't always feel the same. I didn't feel like this when I fought Salem or Thornberry or Starie, and I knew on those nights that I wasn't going to perform the way I know I can. You can't make yourself become worried, the opponent has to do that for you. I've been boxing for twenty-five years and it takes a lot for me to become aroused. When I saw Lacy smashing up Reid, that got me excited and made me nervous. 'I wouldn't like to feel those right uppercuts,' I thought to myself. 'They lifted him clean off the floor.' Lacy could hit and he had a body on him that made me train and made me get up in the morning. I trained so hard that as it got closer to the battle I couldn't sleep. I was nervous, yet at 2 a.m., as I was about to leave my dressing room after stepping out of a cold shower, I just felt invincible and it's the only time I've ever felt this way.

Lacy was already in the ring, prowling around, when I got in but there was nothing he could have said or done at that moment to make me fear him. Prodigy were belting out in the arena and the crowd were electric. Psychologically, I was so strong and so ready physically and mentally that it wouldn't have mattered if he'd brought a gun into the ring. He started flexing his neck muscles and tried to look mean, just like Tyson used to do, but to me he looked more like Huggy Bear out of *Starsky and Hutch*. I was quite amused by his jacket and by his big pimp daddy friend in the corner, who was wearing a fur coat and kept shouting, 'Yeah, yeah.' When Lacy took off his jacket his body looked like it was chiselled out of marble, whereas I'm lean and I don't have a big chest. If you had asked a hundred people who knew nothing about boxing which guy they'd rather have on their side, no one would have picked me. I was being told a different story though. I didn't take my eyes off him but he couldn't bring himself to look at me. He kept glancing away, looking down and looking out into the crowd. The build-up and the whole incredible atmosphere had started to get to him because he'd never been here before. He looked wary, almost like he was caught in headlights. I'm not saying he bottled it and that's why he lost – I would have won the fight whatever his frame of mind – but the way he felt and the way I jumped on him were a perfect combination.

I knew what Lacy had expected to do when the bell rang, he thought he was going to roll over me. In the opening round he hit me with what turned out to be his best punch, a wicked right hand to the chin, but it did nothing. My head snapped back but I just stood there and he knew he had no more for me. When you're as psyched up as I was you can take a heck of a punch and I expected him to hit me hard. I anticipated a war, so I was ready to march through a wall. When he hit me with one good punch I didn't get too excited about it. I outworked him from the first bell, bombarded him with punches and his game plan was gone. As soon as he got outworked on the inside he had nothing left. His strategy, his only hope, was to beat me on the inside. I did him in on the inside so what was he going to do?

Barry McGuigan had warned me, 'You don't want to

get inside with this guy.' Barry was right but I was just so pumped up that it didn't matter. I ripped him up on the inside too. My ability to fight inside is underestimated. I'm not the biggest puncher but I have fast hands and my movement makes me awkward inside. I knew he wasn't going to catch me clean because my reflexes were quicker and I was able to smother him. I always try to get a sense of the ring because even though I'm an offensive fighter I'm naturally cautious. So my hands were high and I wasn't looking for big left hands, I just picked him off with my jab and on the inside I made sure he wasn't getting any free shots. But I fight when I want to fight and he realised this very quickly.

Round One, John Rawling, ITV commentator: 'There's a right hand, the best shot from Lacy so far. That's the danger punch.'

Duke McKenzie, ITV co-commentator: 'That shook Calzaghe!'

Rawling: 'Oh, great work from Calzaghe. Good head shots.'

McKenzie: 'This is what you get from Calzaghe when he's hurt. He's like an out-of-control windmill, he just starts throwing shots.'

(Bell rings.)

Rawling: 'Well, that's the first round to Calzaghe but he did take a big right hand.'

At the end of the round I put my hands in the air. I wasn't being cocky but I could tell by looking at his face that he had no confidence at all now and knew exactly what he was up against. He got caught with as many punches in the first round as he'd taken probably in his entire career before then. Although my hands were low, the speed and volume of my punches just overwhelmed him. He tried to load up with his punches but I just stepped to the right and threw my jab, so that he could never get set. When my right hand was on the outside of his I was in charge of the fight. I was also quicker than him on the inside and landed my left uppercut at will and this became tremendously demoralising for him. He thought he was going to come in behind that right and start to dictate the terms of the fight, he thought it was going to be a quick night. Everybody had been falling at his feet but he was in a different league now and all he got from me was a smile and half a dozen hard punches in his face.

Lacy had come into the fight with a false sense of security because people told him that I was old and washed up, but there was just no way that he was going to come over here to do a number on me. I turned him constantly, which is what I worked on in the gym, lateral movement. In sparring I was jabbing and moving to my right and making my sparring partner look like an idiot, so I knew I could do the same against a guy who was confused by my movement and low on confidence because I was hitting him hard and often. He made it easy for me because he didn't throw combinations and I was first to the punch all the time.

Round Three. Rawling: 'Oh, this is good work from Calzaghe, quality work, but can he keep this sort of intensity of performance, this sort of speed and work rate going for twelve rounds? He had to do it a few years ago against Charles Brewer down in Cardiff. That was a great fight that night.'

McKenzie: 'I think he can, John. He just needs to box sensibly now and he's boxing fantastically well so far.'

Rawling: 'He's making Lacy look ponderous in there but we know Lacy has fitness and strength, and blood is still seeping from Lacy's nostrils. Good right hand from Calzaghe, if he is the slapper that Jeff Lacy says, he slaps hard.'

McKenzie: 'This was meant to be the hardest fight of Calzaghe's life but right now he's boxing the fight of his life. Lovely combination and then spins off to leave Lacy hitting thin air . . . Lacy's become very pedestrian, very one-paced. Punchers like him rely on setting their feet to get those big punches off and while he's doing that Calzaghe's outboxing him.'

Rawling: 'I've always thought Lacy was one-paced, Duke, but the thing about it is that he does bang, that big right

245

hand, and as Calzaghe tires, if he can't get Lacy out of there, that could be more of a factor. Look at that hand speed from Calzaghe, that is exceptional.'

At the end of the third round, when I came back to my corner, Dad was very animated. We knew that Lacy was a slow starter, so I had gone out at a terrific pace while staying conscious about not burning up too soon, but I got so excited that all I could do was throw punches. My dad was worried that I was going to burn myself out, that no one could keep up that pace.

'Just rest this round, Joe,' he urged. 'Take a breather, just take your time.'

'Dad, I'm all right,' I said. 'He's nothing. He can't punch shit.'

The adrenalin was pumping and I felt like Superman. My conditioning meant that I was able to box for all twelve rounds up on my toes, I just felt so good physically. Lacy was bleeding around both eyes from all the punches he had taken and his face was turning into a mess. I began to smile at him because I was having fun. It was like an exhibition for me, with me showing what I could do, but I was doing it against a world-class fighter. The only danger was that I could maybe go through a lull, which normally happens for me around about the seventh round. But I was aware before the fight that Lacy gets better the further it goes, so I never let up.

Round Seven. Rawling: 'Marvin Hagler said he deserved to be ranked in the best six in the world pound-for-pound and Jeff Lacy was supposed to be the coming star. He doesn't look like one now. It's been all Joe Calzaghe.'

McKenzie: 'I've got Calzaghe winning everything, he's absolutely boxed rings round Lacy, given him a boxing lesson.'

Rawling: 'Lacy has been battered from pillar to post for eighteen minutes and blood is flowing across our commentary position, coming from the eye of Jeff Lacy . . . but now here comes Lacy, desperately trying to wing hooks. There's his girlfriend, Jennifer, in the corner, trying to urge her man forward but Calzaghe doesn't box his way out of it, he tries to get into a trading session.'

McKenzie: 'Calzaghe's obviously learnt from his mistakes because when he starts his combinations he keeps his chin down. As he starts to throw his shots, look where his chin is, in his chest. He doesn't want to hang it out to dry. He's boxing a great fight . . . Lacy's getting worked over and he doesn't like it.'

Rawling: 'Calzaghe, I think, is starting to tee him up for the big finish . . .'

McKenzie: 'Oh! He's got him!'

Rawling: 'I think he might be looking to take him out here, big left hands and Lacy is on the receiving end of a barrage of punches. Calzaghe wants to get him out of there.'

McKenzie: 'His legs have gone, John, he's all over the place.'

Rawling: 'Somehow Lacy has seen it through to the bell . . . Lacy has never been down but, my goodness, he nearly went then. He came so close to being put down by those two left hands.'

I had prepared myself to face something more than Lacy, I was prepared to take the hardest punches I've ever been hit with in my life. My brain sent me messages all night, reminding me that I was going to get hit, so be ready. I was prepared and Lacy wasn't. He only prepared himself to come over to Manchester and take apart some old man who he thought couldn't do it any more. He didn't prepare himself and, suddenly, in that ring he knew he was in a real battle. But you have to prepare yourself. It's too late when the cannons start. Within the first couple of minutes he was suffering from shell shock and by the seventh round, psychologically and physically, he was smashed, for he'd been hit by clusters of shots. Lacy was in great shape, he trained for three months and you could tell that by looking at him. But he didn't fear me until he arrived and saw exactly the kind of man I am. Then it was too late because he didn't have enough time to overcome his fear and channel it positively into his performance.

After eight or nine rounds Lacy had taken such a one-sided beating that many people said the fight should have been stopped. All I can say is that I'm a fighter and I don't just mean by profession. A top fighter has to be a fighter inside as well because in the end that's what it will come down to. There are many qualities that a fighter needs: ability, a natural ability to perform, dedication, conditioning. I've seen a lot of fighters with all the talent but they're not dedicated, and I see boys with all the dedication but they'll still never make it. When I watch a fighter go down and stay down, even though he could have got back up, I can never understand it because that's just not in me. That's what makes a great fighter, I believe, his heart and desire and willingness to go to the bottom of the well. I hope to God that it never comes down to this but I would never, ever think about quitting in the middle of a fight. People still ask me about the Lacy fight, if I think it should have been stopped. I'd be happy, if I was Lacy, that it wasn't because I would want to go the twelve rounds and at least go out on my shield. So I don't think that the fight should have been stopped and Lacy showed that it didn't need to be. He lasted the course.

Round Twelve. McKenzie: 'He got in again, beautiful shots, this has been an absolute masterclass from Joe Calzaghe.'

Rawling: 'Last few seconds of a superb, wonderful boxing display. He has silenced the doubters and is boxing his way to a magnificent points victory, quite outstanding. Oh! How is Lacy staying up there? How is he staying up? A peach of a

249

right uppercut from Calzaghe, the bell is about to sound, Calzaghe's still picking his man off and Gary Shaw is shouting across at the Lacy corner to pull him out but it's all over. Lacy comes forward and embraces Calzaghe. Let the doubters be silenced, Joe Calzaghe is absolutely, utterly top-notch and is now getting a rightful embrace from his father and trainer, Enzo Calzaghe, because I don't really think that it gets very much better. That was quite outstanding.'

McKenzie: 'I can't remember seeing such an impressive victory over a really good champion. Lacy's a puncher but Calzaghe nullified him from start to finish.'

Rawling: 'Calzaghe has gone to all corners of this Manchester arena and shouted out to the crowd, "Who's best?" That is the performance of the best fighter in Britain for me, no question.'

When the bell rang to end the fight I collapsed back onto the floor, not out of exhaustion but relief. I could have boxed for fifteen rounds easily but I could also have gone my entire career and never experienced pure elation, as I did at that moment. It wasn't just that I won the biggest fight of my life, it was the way I won it. That's what had clicked in my mind when my dad was saying in the weeks beforehand that I had to fight this fight, regardless of the injury to my left hand. 'It's not the winning or losing,' he said. 'It's how you fight and it's the fact that you fought.' I had been pulling my hair out only two weeks earlier, thinking, 'I can't fight, I can't fight.' Even if I'd lost, I'd have got more respect than if I hadn't gone through with the fight. If I had walked away with an injury, I would never have forgiven myself, it would have been torture. I would probably have disappeared off the radar and people would have called me every name under the sun. Then if I'd retired undefeated, people would have said, 'So what? Big deal.' But just one fight changed everything because of the way I fought. I couldn't have written a better script.

What a fight. What a fighter. Joe Calzaghe's brutal dismantling of Jeff Lacy is right up there with Randolph Turpin's victory over Sugar Ray Robinson. It ranks alongside John Stracey's win over Jose Napoles in Mexico and Lloyd Honeyghan's beating of Donald Curry in Atlantic City. I raised eyebrows in Saturday's column claiming Calzaghe was arguably Britain's greatest champion. There won't be many who disagree now. Lacy arrived in Manchester with the highest reputation and in possession of the IBF world supermiddleweight title. He started favourite with the bookies and most experts. Yet Joe made him look like a cab rank fighter. I had forgotten that Calzaghe could box like that. Memories had been dulled by the Kabary Salem bout and the fight against Evans Ashira, where he was utterly demotivated and dealing with the break-up of his marriage. This was the old Calzaghe, the fighter who had Chris Eubank on the seat of his pants when winning the WBO world title eight and a half years ago. The footwork, hand speed and combinations all returned. And with them the confidence. There will be the inevitable temptation to re-evaluate Lacy's credentials after this. That would be an insult to Joe.

– Barry McGuigan, *Daily Mirror*,
6 March 2006

So many reports prior to the Lacy fight suggested all sorts of sorry ends for me. He was going to pulverise me and beat me to a pulp, then after the fight he was suddenly overrated. Who overrated him? The people who said he was going to beat me up? The truth is that I made Jeff Lacy look like an ordinary fighter by boxing as well as I could possibly box. Ultimately, it's not about how good Lacy was anyway. For several years Floyd Mayweather has been regarded as the best pound-for-pound boxer in the world and he's one of the few I believe to be genuinely superb. Technically, he's tremendous, but I could find ways to slag him off and say negative things about his record. If people think Lacy was overrated, what about Carlos Baldomir? He had lost nine times before he ever fought Mayweather and Mayweather became the tenth, big deal. It doesn't take a bright man to think up a negative line but it takes a special man to go out and accomplish something that not many other people think he can. There are still people who say that Lacy was overrated, Lacy was nothing, but they didn't say too much before I fought him.

It meant a great deal to me to be presented with *The Ring* championship belt, which was on the line as well as my WBO title and Lacy's IBF belt. There's a lot of confusion in boxing today about who the proper champion is in each weight division because there are so many titles and so many title-holders, but very few fighters have worn this belt. It's the toughest to win because you have to be the bona fide champion of your division and I'm proud to be the first super middleweight in history to win *The Ring* belt. No one can take it away from me. Someone else will be the champion one day but I have that belt now, just like Joe Louis and Jack Dempsey, Sugar Ray Robinson and Muhammad Ali. This was the icing on the cake to finally be acknowledged as the proper champion and have that recognition from an influential voice in American boxing. There will always be doubters when there are rival champions. An undefeated record means nothing if there aren't good names on the record. Without Lacy on mine, people would have put me down as another Sven Ottke, an undefeated world champion nobody really gave two hoots about.

Calzaghe finally established himself as, arguably, the best boxer of his generation and one of the very best in British boxing history when he produced a flawless display to win every second of every round against the previously unbeaten American Jeff Lacy. 'If Joe had beat somebody like that on the street, he would have been charged with GBH,' his father and trainer Enzo said, while Frank Warren, Calzaghe's promoter, added: 'That was the best performance I've seen from any fighter in all my years in the sport.' Dan Birmingham, Lacy's trainer, agreed. 'I've never ever seen a better performance anywhere in the world,' he said. Even Calzaghe's most biased fans failed to predict such an astonishingly easy victory . . . To say that Lacy was simply overwhelmed is to suggest that Calzaghe arrived in the ring better prepared. That only tells half the story because on Saturday night Calzaghe's plan was quite brilliant. Lacy, his cornermen and his large entourage did not know how to respond.

– Steve Bunce, *Independent*, 6 March 2006

Finally, people are giving me my dues, almost as if I've just arrived on the scene when, in fact, I'm now a thirty-five-year-old veteran and a world champion for ten years. My record speaks for itself, that's why I beat Lacy the way I did and now I don't feel like I need to prove much more.

If I have a bad fight, it's because I'm only human and sometimes I just won't be able to get up for the guy, but that night against Lacy I showed balls. They brought over this knockout merchant from America, who'd been smashing the shit out of everybody, and they reckoned he was going to do the same to me. He was the younger, stronger and more fancied fighter but I was invincible that night. It took courage to do what I did and my speed was my power. I love to hear people say to me, 'That was a great fight.' It's nice and it doesn't happen all the time because in some of my fights I've been ordinary. But it's always the first thing I ask my dad: 'Was it a good fight?' I didn't realise how good my performance was until I overheard some people talking as I walked out of the ring.

'Was I really that good, Dad?'

'You were brilliant, Joe, fucking brilliant.'

ROUND ELEVEN
The Man in the Mirror

It's 7 p.m. on a Saturday night in Manchester and I'm stood in front of the bathroom mirror in my suite at the Lowry Hotel. I'm stressed out, I've just been sick, everything's going tits up. My girlfriend, Jo-Emma, rang to say that she's delayed flying over from Jersey and she'll have to go straight to the arena and my routine is screwed up too. I'm going to have a fucking bad night tonight, I just know.

I'm a creature of habit, I like to do things at a set time and follow a set routine, but it started to go wrong when I had something to eat about four o'clock with Enzo Maccarrinelli. Normally, I just have my Dioralite drink and my own little thing but Enzo ordered spaghetti bolognese, so I decided to have the same. As soon as I ate it I realised I'd made a mistake. It was up around my chest and I just couldn't digest it. I went back to my room to lie down on the bed, picked up my CD player to have some music on and realised that I'd forgotten my earphones. I rang my dad and was a bit moody: 'Dad, get me some earphones.' I'd been really picky with Dad all week and I felt a bit sorry, so I said we'd go out for a walk together with Sergio. We headed out of the hotel but some people recognised me – 'Calzaghe' was written across the back of my tracksuit top – and I didn't want the attention. 'Do me a favour, Dad, try to find a shop that's open and get me those earphones. Here's sixty quid.' I went back to my room and waited.

'What the fuck are these?' I asked my dad when I saw what he'd come back with.

'They're the earphones you wanted me to get you and don't fucking start on me.'

I'm edgy and I'm trying to chill out but my dad has bought the cheapest set of earphones that had to be on sale in Manchester.

'How much were these?' I'm looking at him with contempt.

'£9.99,' he says. 'That's all they had. What the fuck could I do?'

I plug them into my CD player and I hear the tiniest, faintest sound and my dad leaves the room before I go ballistic. I lie down on the bed, stressed out and feeling sick, when all of a sudden I get up, grab hold of the CD player and throw it as hard as I can onto the hard floor, smashing it to pieces. Bits of it fly everywhere and I'm on my own in the room. 'Shit, I'm going to cut my feet next.' So I get down on my hands and knees and I start to clear the mess, I'm feeling sorry for myself and I break down in tears. I'm so fucking stressed.

'You idiot, now I haven't even got my CD player,' I tell myself.

The bolognese is still in my stomach, it won't digest, so I go over to the toilet and stick my fingers down my throat to bring it up. God, do I feel horrible? I'm puking up everywhere and the worst thing of all is that I'm boxing at 10 p.m. against a big brute of a guy called Sakio Bika. But I'm a world champion boxer about to make my nineteenth title defence, so you wonder why I'm looking at the mirror? Why? It really shouldn't be like this, it fucking shouldn't.

How have I got into a state like this? After all these years tonight should be a bloody walk in the park, but I've struggled to make weight for this fight more than any other. What was it Monday? A little porridge in the morning, trained and ate an apple, trained again in the afternoon, came home to a bit of pasta, light sauce and a low-fat yogurt. That was dinner. Tuesday similar, trained twice wearing a sweatsuit, drank plenty of water and a mint tea. Came to Manchester Wednesday and spoilt myself, I had a few jelly beans, had trained with the sweatsuit in the morning, did the press conference in the afternoon, then went on the running machine for twenty minutes and shadow-boxed. Was hungry, only ate a starter portion of risotto and a green salad with no dressing in the evening. Trained Thursday morning and again at night in the sweatsuit and felt weak, didn't eat one morsel of food because it was the day before the weigh-in and it was all *about hitting twelve stone. Got up Friday morning and jumped on the scales, three pounds over, no problem. I put on my sauna suit and went for a light jog on the running machine and shadow-boxed for fifteen minutes, came back to my room, got on the scales again and was smack on the weight, twelve stone, was even able to sip a little water, an egg-cupful, felt OK. I've felt worse in the past, but my legs, they didn't feel as strong as they should be.*

There's nothing worse than feeling hungry and knowing that you can't eat or drink. It drives me to the edge, makes me angry inside, this is me at my most agitated, I don't want to speak to anybody. Richard Maynard, Frank's publicist, lovely guy, look at the way I spoke to him. Yesterday he tells me I have a HBO interview at 4 p.m. and before that at 3 p.m. a picture with Tom Jones, who's in town gigging. So I snap.

'When am I going to have some food, Richard? You know not to book things without speaking to me first, next time speak to me.'

I don't mean it and I know Richard understands but right before the weigh-in is when I'm at my narkiest. Then I hear him talking to Dad.

'Enzo, can you speak to Joe and tell him?'

'You'll have to speak to him yourself, Richard, I'm not speaking to him.'

'I don't want to speak to him, he nearly bit my head off.'

Jesus, am I really that bad? Dad, poor bugger, always

bears the brunt of it. 'I don't need this shit,' he tells me. 'I'm stressed enough as it is.' But so am I, Dad, so am I . . .

'Hello . . . I'll be five minutes, Dad, just getting my things . . . OK, see you in the lobby.'

. . . Come on, get it together, Joe. This guy's going to be strong. He's never been put down and never been stopped, he has a good chin, seems like a capable guy. But he's never been in the ring with Joe Calzaghe. He'll think he can win until he gets hit. I'm faster, more powerful and twice the boxer that he is. The guy's got no chance.

So you're going to come back here a winner?

Course I am.

I was still feeling the euphoria from my victory over Lacy when I agreed to move up in weight to challenge Glen Johnson for the IBF light heavyweight title four months later, which was really too soon after the March date. I couldn't give 100 per cent commitment to training for the fight and my hand wasn't 100 per cent either, so rather than take the risk I pulled out. My ideal fighting weight, I believe, would be 12st 7lb, the light heavyweight limit. Maybe I'd be facing stronger opponents if I did step up, but I would be stronger too. I've been a super middleweight boxer, weighing in at twelve stone for fourteen years. Between fights my natural weight is 13st 10lb, which is a very good weight for me, though I've gone up to about 14st 4lb by being greedy. Getting down to the super middleweight limit is difficult. Does it affect my performance? Does it weaken me? I think it does, I'd be a better fighter at light heavyweight because of the strength I would gain from not having to torture myself to make twelve stone. If it was the same today as it was a decade ago when weigh-ins were held on the morning of the fight, there is just no way that I'd still be fighting at super middle, I just wouldn't have time to hydrate my body again properly. But thirty-six hours between the weigh-in and the fight gives me the necessary time to do this.

Moving up in weight would all depend on the fights that can be made at light heavy. I wouldn't be interested in giving up my title for a non-title fight in that division. It would have happened had Johnson beaten Clinton Woods of Sheffield in September 2006 in Bolton, for Frank Warren had already negotiated the deal with Johnson's people. But Woods won the fight to scupper the plan. Fighting Woods would seem to be an obvious move but it isn't going to happen because of the politics. Frank would be willing to put on the fight on one of his promotions but Woods's promoter, Dennis Hobson, wants to promote his fighter and there doesn't appear to be room for compromise. Antonio Tarver was another possibility, for he was *The Ring* light heavyweight champion and Frank was negotiating with his team until he got beaten by Bernard Hopkins in June 2006. Many of the fighters who have been successful in stepping up in weight have had one common denominator: speed. Sugar Ray Leonard and Tommy Hearns were fast punchers, though Hearns had power too and he carried that power from welterweight, 10st 7lb, through to light heavyweight, 12st 7lb, like Leonard capturing titles at each weight. But speed was just as crucial. Roy Jones, who had the quickest hands maybe of any fighter in my era, was able to move from middleweight to heavyweight. Speed is everything and I would have the same speed at light heavyweight as I do now at super middleweight and more power and it's a move I may make before my career is over.

A month after withdrawing from the Johnson fight my hand felt better and my appetite was back, so it was time to get in the ring again. Sakio Bika, a Cameroonian fighter based in Australia, had just failed in his WBC title challenge against Markus Beyer in Germany. Beyer was on his way to a defeat, I believed, until a headbutt by Bika opened a bad cut over his eyes and the fight was declared a technical draw. Bika went in with his head a lot, which should have been a warning to me, but I didn't have the same focus or intensity going into this fight as I had ahead of fighting Lacy.

Maybe this was inevitable, but it's been a pattern in my career that for every good performance I seem to produce a very average or poor performance in my next fight. I thought about this going in, that I wasn't due a good fight, but I still couldn't channel that thought into finding my focus or concentration during training. I guess this is part of who I am, I'm unpredictable unless everything is on the table, then you can bet your life that I'll perform. The brilliance is there but it takes the right circumstances to bring it out, I'm just not a robot.

I trained the same way I always do and I was just as fit, but I wasn't as psyched up or intense. My left hand became a problem again when I damaged it in sparring with Nathan Cleverley, who's fast, talented and quite a bony lad. I was a bit too relaxed when I came in and threw a left uppercut that hit him right on the top of the shoulder and the hand just flared up straight away. I ended the session, went to see a doctor and was sent to have an X-ray at the accident and emergency at Abergavenny. Thankfully, it wasn't broken, so I just put the ice pack on it, but I was down. 'Not again,' I thought, and the truth is that it was a worse injury than the one that had prevented me fighting in July. If I hadn't pulled out of the July date, I wouldn't have gone through with Bika on 14 October. But this is the fight game, so what am I going to do? Pull out every time I have a problem? I'm thirty-five years old and I might as well retire if I'm going to keep pulling out of fights, so I took the risk because I felt that with my boxing ability I would beat Bika comfortably. I had a cortisone injection from a specialist in Harley Street and for a week I didn't use the hand in sparring. It never got 100 per cent better but I was able to start tapping with it after a week, though I didn't spar well and wasn't able to work hard on the pads with Dad. I could throw my left but not with full power and I completed maybe forty or fifty rounds of light sparring, just flick punching with big gloves on. Overall, however, I was in great shape and the positive feelings that came flooding back when I arrived in Manchester three days before the fight were great encouragement.

It's been like déjà vu seeing the same guys on the door of the hotel and stepping into the same room, I'm even starting to think about what I did every day before Lacy. If everything stays the same over these next few days, it couldn't be more perfect. I've been out of the ring for a long time and it's a beautiful moment when I get in there. I'm looking forward to experiencing the familiar old feelings of nerves, anxiety, adrenalin and, most of all, winning.

I came up by train again, though this morning was wet and miserable, no snow, but I feel a good aura here. If I was to look for other differences, the biggest between this fight and my last fight is that Lacy had something to lose, Bika has nothing to lose. He gets a phone call a few months ago and he has a shot at the title. What has he got to lose? An opponent like this is dangerous and I know this guy is tough. He'll be relaxed because he knows the worst that can happen is that he suffers a defeat. He's expected to lose – I'm 50-1 on in the betting, which is a ridiculous price – but he has an opportunity which has suddenly been handed to him. All the pressure is on my back. Against Lacy, I was the underdog and this took the pressure off and made me relax and perform. I wanted to stick it up to everybody. Now there's not the same kind of thing to shoot for.

I know I'm not as focused as I was for the Lacy fight but I've never been that focused in my life. The guy was so intense that from the first bell I knew I'd have to stand and fight. Everything I'd achieved in my career was on the line. If I'd failed, the American critics in particular would have been pouncing on me, saying, 'Told you so, he was a protected European fighter all along.' They were all ready to jump on the bandwagon but I shut them up. The way I won the fight was brilliant and yet I still have bigger and better things that I want to do. I still have the same burning desire to win because I love being champion. The guy's saying that I'll be less hungry after the Lacy fight and that will make a difference to the way I fight. That's what he hopes. He doesn't understand that he's fighting a guy who's been champion a long time but I'm still hungry, more hungry than he is because I've always been a winner. I'll find a way to win because I want to win, I need to win. I don't even think about losing because it would be the most terrible thing in the world, like a death. Something will have to go hugely amiss for me to lose this fight.

In the Lacy fight I set myself a standard and I want to

keep fighting at that standard for the rest of my career. It's about me and everything I bring to the ring and I'm ready to perform. If I turn up and fight the opponent the way I can, it's not a race, it only becomes a race if I'm complacent. Nothing is written before you step in the ring, however, no fight is a foregone conclusion and the only time you can really tell anything is when you're in there, staring across at the guy. That's the moment all is revealed, you know how your mindset really is and you can sense how he's feeling and what he's thinking. I'm experienced enough to know what I need to do because I've done this countless times.

But I'm excited about Saturday and about fighting on HBO for the first time. This is long overdue. Naseem Hamed got it as soon as he jumped over the top rope but I came slowly through the back door, never really given the respect I deserved. Even Ricky Hatton got his fight with Kostya Tszyu and was straight onto HBO. Now that I've finally got here I hope I can go on for another eighteen months because I deserve every penny that I'll earn for working my arse off for years. I'm not even thinking of the last thirteen years, I'm thinking of the amateurs when I trained and didn't get paid and starved myself through most of my teenage years. I killed myself to make weight just to win a trophy, there was no money at the end of it, just a plastic cup. Fighting back then was harder than it is for me now. This is what I'm programmed to do and I'm good at it, I've been through it.

So I feel quite relaxed, though I'm a bit agitated and tired.

I'm making the weight and that drains me. I'm 12st 1lb after training but I've had two training sessions in which I lost half a stone. I haven't even touched those grapes on the table. The waiting around now and the press conferences, these things make me edgy. As soon as I make weight I know the tension will go and I'll be happy, that will be the first part of my fight over with and I'll start to build up my strength again.

Bika's a potential banana skin, I don't really know how tough he is but I want to go in the ring and give the same kind of performance as seven months ago. He has never been scared before, he says, but he's never fought me either. I'm 100 per cent confident because I can't let him destroy what I'm creating. All of these fights are going to be my legacy and I can't afford to fail. That's what keeps me motivated. I don't feel fear for Bika but I know the world will be watching and that's something to be apprehensive about. I've not had the eye-of-the-tiger feeling I had for Lacy but my mind hasn't been totally elsewhere. Regardless of who your opponent is, he's still going to try to knock you out and I'm never so relaxed that I'll allow that to happen. I got knocked down against Kabary Salem because I wasn't focused but that was a cheap imitation of me, that was me at my worst. I never want to fight like that again and I feel like I'm at my peak.

It's difficult to compare how this guy has fared against other fighters with what he might do in the ring against me.

My hand's not perfect but when is it? I still have the means to win and right now I'd far rather be me with one hand than him with two.

Much as I wanted to make the fight about me, every fight is about two fighters and how they gel and Bika was one of the most awkward customers I could possibly have faced. Rough-house would be a kind word for some of the tactics he used. He was also stronger than I thought and, in hindsight, was the wrong opponent because he got under my skin and I tried too hard to impress to make it a good fight for the TV audience, especially in America. Any super middleweight in the world would struggle to look good against him because Bika came to spoil. He was dirty, used his head a lot and I got cut around my left eye for the first time in my life in the fourth round, luckily by the side of the eye rather than on the eyelid. I just totally lost my composure because some of his fouling was sickening.

I would never hit a guy when he's down but he tried to do just that when I slipped to the floor in the third round. In other rounds he took big swings after the bell and hit me with cheap shots to the back of the head. I turned him in one of the rounds and tapped him on the back of the head when I could have banged him if I'd wanted to, as he had done to me. I'd have got away with it probably and could have resorted to other foul tactics because I was the home fighter but that's not my manner, my means has never been to injure a guy unnecessarily. I did rub my head against his but that was to stop him from banging into the cut near my left eye. I tapped him on the belt with a borderline shot but he threw a low blow. He knew he was losing and just didn't care. It was almost like I was fighting under Marquess of Queensberry Rules and he was one of the bad guys out of the WWE. Bika crossed the line.

My plan was to try to move onto my right side because my left hand wasn't perfect, I wasn't able to throw it with a lot of clout. Normally, I'm a good worker on the inside when my hands are free, but when my left hand became free in a clinch I didn't really want to throw it because it hurt, so I tapped with it. I wanted to be on the other side of him so that I could hit him hard with my right hand but the cut to my left eye made this impossible, for the injury would have worsened rubbing against his head and shoulder. He was crude and he knew exactly what he was doing, that's why he was willing to work away on the inside. I kept waiting for the referee to break us up and got angry because I just couldn't get my hands free from his clutches. 'He's pulling my arm and hitting me with rabbit punches,' I tried to explain to the referee in the seventh round, but Bika clipped me mid-sentence, he didn't miss a single trick.

Dad was stressed in the corner. 'What the fuck are you

doing, Joe?' he yelled. 'You didn't need to get cut, I told you to watch this guy's head. You're fighting the wrong fight, Joe, throw long punches. Stand off the guy, just box and he won't be able to touch you.'

I knew I could make it easier for myself and I knew what I should have been doing, but I wasn't listening to my dad because I was too embroiled in the wrong fight. Sometimes you get caught up in a situation that you just can't escape from. I was angry and allowed my heart to rule my head. I just wasn't clever enough on the night, Bika never came forward and I fell into his trap. I was too eager and kept falling in but it's difficult to stay composed and impress against a fighter who's constantly on the back foot. He pulled and leant on me, so I was tired towards the end. I knew I wasn't going to knock out the guy because my left hand wasn't strong and I began to count down the rounds, I just needed to get through the fight. I knew I was winning by seven or eight rounds and I never got worried about the cut because the blood wasn't running into my eye, it was trickling down the side of my face. I felt a sharp pain every time he hit me near the eye but pain's a thing that you can block out. So I got bashed up a bit and needed seven stitches in the cut, which I was disappointed about. But I shouldn't have been, scars are medals in this business and I deserved a medal for that fight. It was even entertaining.

Victory took Calzaghe's magnificent unbeaten streak to 42 fight after the judges scored it 117–110, 117–110 and 116–111. It was also the 19th successful defence of his WBO belt – but unlike his superb victory over American Jeff Lacy, this was a bloody struggle. Calzaghe won the first three rounds but was rocked in the fourth when a shuddering headbutt smashed into his forehead, opening a gaping wound over his left eye. Calzaghe was still seeping blood at the start of the fifth and Bika, nicknamed the Scorpion, targeted the wound. But referee Mickey Vann deducted the challenger a point for illegal use of his head as Warren protested vehemently from ringside at the Cameroon-born Aussie's dirty tricks. The fighters exchanged terrific lefts and rights but Calzaghe came good in the seventh, unleashing a two-fisted barrage. Vann warned Bika about his nut once again and gave him another in the 11th for a low blow which sent Calzaghe down. But the Brit clung on in the 12th to get the verdict.

– Fred Burcombe, *News of the World*,
15 October 2006

Lennox Lewis, who was over to commentate for HBO's *Boxing After Dark* show, came to the hotel afterwards and congratulated me. He wasn't scintillating every time he got in the ring, that is impossible, but Lennox was an excellent champion and always a class act. I had just been in a messy fight but he told me that no one can be perfect every time and the most important part I got right: I won. Lennox got banged up a couple of times himself and knows what it's like at both ends of the scale. He even got wiped out by Hasim Rahman and Oliver McCall, but he came back and won and I've always admired that about him. It says a lot for a guy that he can stand across the ring from an opponent who has already knocked him out and go back to war with him – and then win. He stopped Rahman and McCall in rematches and always showed heart. I'm glad he hasn't been tempted to get back into the ring now that he's in his forties. He's achieved far more than any other British heavyweight and he's left a legacy that will stand the test of time, which is what I'm now trying to do.

Two days later I met Sugar Ray Leonard, one of my heroes, at a hotel in London. I had grown up watching and worshipping him as a fighter but I found out that he's just as impressive as a man, completely down to earth, and he offered some interesting insights. I turned up half embarrassed about the state of my face, with my black eye and loads of bruising – not the way to impress him with my boxing skills, I thought. But he put me completely at ease and told me how he had been drawn into the wrong kind of fight several times. It happened to him early in his career against Roberto Duran, and it happened on other occasions, but the most important thing, he said, is that a fight like that shows character. Sometimes you won't win pretty, he said, but you still have to win. I was proud of what he said about my performance against Lacy, he called it 'perfect' and 'masterful' and told me that if I fought like that every time, nobody would beat me. I believe that too, but hearing it from Ray was the ultimate compliment and a great boost to my confidence. Fighters know best. We know because we're in there and Leonard emphasised that you can't make yourself fear an opponent, fear has to be there.

'I had bad fights too,' he said. 'When you don't have that fear factor it's hard to bring out your best. You have to have tunnel vision, you have to be so alert that you know what punches he's going to throw before he throws them, but when you don't fear the guy it's hard to put yourself in that place. That's just human nature.'

I knew Bika was a decent fight but I didn't have that extra edge that would have come from fearing what he could do. Deep down I knew I would beat the guy – my boxing ability is so much more advanced that even when the going got tough all I had to do was stand on the back foot. If I had moved, he wouldn't have been able to lay a glove on me but I engaged him at his game, I made a bad choice. The HBO people were happy, however, because I'd shown resilience and come through and won, and Ray was tremendously reassuring, not just about this but about all the injuries I've had in my career. He had a lot of problems with his hands too, but he said that he just had to grin and bear it. Ray still looks like he could grin and bear it today, for he can't be seven pounds above his best fighting weight. He always made me feel good watching him in the ring and I came away from the hotel in London feeling a lot happier, though funnily enough I'd felt proud when I'd looked in the mirror on Saturday after the fight.

You look like you've been run over by a truck, in fact you almost look like a fighter now. Hey, this is the fight game. Guys get split open, busted up, battered and bruised, one day it was bound to happen, even to you.

Yeah, but you know what? I came through. I won and that's what it's all about. He wasn't a good fighter technically, but he knew what to do to make it a difficult night: throw the right hand, grab my arm on the inside – the guy must have a few friends round here on Moss Side. I underestimated the guy, I thought I could beat him with one hand, but I wasn't as switched on as I should have been and he wasn't what I thought he was going to be. I've never looked good against guys who don't come to fight. I like to engage and I like a fast work rate. Maybe opponents are aware of that now. Sometimes I'm too easy to draw in because I feel the need to throw punches. But you never stop learning in boxing. The perfect fighter has never been born and never will be born. I learnt a lesson, which will stand me in good stead for a bigger fight some day. When I meet an opponent who stands back, fuck it, I'll just walk away. I should have sat back, let the crowd boo if they wanted to, and done that for twelve rounds. But that's not me. I'm slick, I have skills and I can box, but when it gets right down to it I'm a fighter. It's in my DNA. I have a big heart and my nature is to fight. Maybe I was foolish to fight that way and in future I'll try to stay more composed. If I fought that way against a better fighter, I could get caught and maybe it could turn out worse.

I left myself too open. I went with the flow, got mad, and that's the way I fought. I dropped my hands and tried to be flashy for TV but I tried too hard. I wasn't fighting for me. I should have just fought my fight. I thought I had to finish the guy by throwing a thousand punches per round. I was excited and I just wanted to show people what I'm capable of. Anyway, these Africans are always hard guys. He didn't have a mark on his face. In his whole career he'd only lost once and he was unlucky to lose on a majority decision. He wasn't a bad fighter. The guy was in the fight. He should have beaten Beyer for the WBC belt and this would have been a unification fight. Mikkel Kessler's just taken the credit for that tonight, knocking Beyer out in the third round, they said. I knew he'd beat Beyer. He was a guy just looking for one last payday. I knew Kessler was going to smash him up. Beyer was shot, yet I bet I'll get criticised for going the distance with a 'journeyman'. He's not the best fighter I've fought but he wasn't the bloody easiest. I'm always down on myself when I don't perform but anyone who knows anything about boxing could see that Bika was no fall guy. He was dirty but I stuck it out in the trenches and showed I'm not a pitter-patter paper champion who just wins when he's on top. It was just never going to happen against this guy. If I fought him again, it wouldn't happen. The next time it would be a boring fight. I'd box him and land ten punches a round, like Bernard Hopkins does. Just like Marco Antonio Barrera did against Rocky Juarez when they fought a rematch. Barrera's had so many wars but he just stood off him and won every round. Maybe that's the intelligent way. Maybe this was a good fight for me, a good experience. If I go on to fight Hopkins, this fight will have stood me in good stead. I'll think twice about being impatient after what happened tonight, that's for sure.

This could even coax a few people into fighting me, like Jermain Taylor or even Hopkins. If I'd done what Enzo Maccarinelli did to Mark Hobson, knocking him spark out in the first round, who would want to fight me? Jesus, my body's sore, my kidneys feel sore. Did he hit me there too, the bastard? I know he hit me on the back a couple of times. He caught me with those sucker right hands too but they were clumsy and I should have avoided them. And now look at

*me, massive swelling on my left cheek, seven stitches over my
left eye, so much for the career in Hollywood.*

Yeah, but you've still got one as a fighter.

ROUND TWELVE
The Ring and Beyond

> Joe Calzaghe, having produced by far and away the most dazzling performance by any British sportsman or woman in this largely barren year of 2006 [has earned his] rightful chance of being voted the BBC's Sports Personality of the Year.
> – Jeff Powell, *Daily Mail*, 8 December 2006

I was exaggerating to make a point when I said that this country gets behind losers when it comes to the BBC Sports Personality of the Year award, or maybe I just got out on the wrong side of the bed that morning. Making weight for the Bika fight, which was a week away when I made the comment in a radio interview, had affected my mood perhaps. Whatever, I wasn't exactly holding my breath about a TV show that made a winner out of Greg Rusedski, who has never won a Grand Slam tournament in his life.

It wasn't my intention then to come across as bitter over the Sports Personality award and it isn't my intention now. I really don't care. I had never watched the show before I got invited to take part in December 2006 because I'd been nominated. I'm not a fraud, I'm the real deal. I've been champion for almost ten years, the longest reigning British world champion in any sport, and it's not as if I've cheated my way onto the big stage by parading a meaningless belt in front of people, a plastic piece of nonsense. I beat a British boxing legend in Chris Eubank to become champion and I've beaten six former world champions. Watch those fights and tell me which one of those wasn't a world-class performance. Everybody thought Lacy was going to come over and wipe the floor with me but look at what happened to him. Can he not fight either? All the top fighters that America has sent over, I've sent them packing, simple as that; yet after all these years as champion I've not been given the proper recognition. It's a joke and I laugh about it, what else can I do? If I was a footballer or a golfer or a tennis player and as successful in one of those sports as I am in boxing, it would all be different.

Even so, Darren Clarke thought I should have picked up the award. 'I think Joe Calzaghe should get it because he's a world champion and a proper sportsman,' he said. Darren was the odds-on favourite in the betting and he didn't have to say this. He'd had a terribly traumatic year, losing his wife Heather to cancer, but he came back and played magnificently to help Europe win the

Ryder Cup. He's a proper sportsman too and a proper man but, despite Darren's support, I wasn't on tenter-hooks about the award. I kept an open mind but, deep down, never really thought I was going to win, even though I picked up the BBC Wales award a week before going to Birmingham for the kind of event that is not really my thing. Darren, Zara Phillips and Beth Tweddle all had long segments at the start and boxing and cycling were the last sports that they came to, just before the public voting closed.

Coming off the stage after being interviewed, I walked past Seb Coe who shook my hand and said, 'I want you to win, you should win.' Maybe if boxing had a higher profile, I would have, but who cares? I don't know much about Zara Phillips as an equestrian rider but she's done great to become a world champion and good luck to her for winning the award. Having the acknowledgement of top sportspeople gives me enough pleasure, I don't need a trophy to show off on my mantelpiece and I certainly hadn't gone there with a speech planned. It would have been good for boxing, if either Ricky or myself had got in the top three, but I haven't lost any sleep over it. Picking up *The Ring* belt is worth a lot more than Sports Personality of the Year in my book.

My twentieth defence of the WBO title was confirmed the next day for 7 April 2007 at the Millennium Stadium in

Cardiff against Peter Manfredo, a guy who had made his name on the TV reality series, *The Contender*.

I was a fan of the first series of the show and followed the personalities. Peter was prominent as he finished runner-up but, to be brutally honest, I didn't think much of him and when I was told that I was fighting him I thought it would be comfortable, an easy fight. I didn't anticipate any danger but I was still able to get excited because 35,000 people were expected to come to the Millennium and the fight would be broadcast live on HBO in America. Over the years I've not been so fussed about boxing in the United States, I even went through a period shortly after 9/11 when I didn't want to fly there, or anywhere else for that matter because I'd had several experiences of going through heavy turbulence and I didn't like it. I remember a press conference in New York ahead of my fight with Charles Brewer and I was stressed out, I didn't want to go. When we got to the gate I took one look at the plane and said to Richard Maynard, 'I'm not going on that.' It wasn't a jumbo, so in my mind it wasn't going to make it and Richard didn't know what to do when I had my bags taken off. But, after calling Frank Warren, he made another booking and we headed from Gatwick to Heathrow for a flight six hours later – on a jumbo. Eventually, I changed my mind again about flying and about fighting in America and facing Manfredo was a way of opening doors to some bigger American names.

I even changed my view on Manfredo because of the two fights he had at super middleweight after *The Contender*. Scott Pemberton was past his best but Peter had a good three-round win against him and another against Joe Spina, who was undefeated. In *The Ring* ratings he was ranked number ten, so he was a legitimate challenger and I had respect for him as an opponent. Fighting in my national stadium in front of all those people – 35,018 to establish a European record for a boxing match held indoors, for they closed the roof – made me even more determined not to repeat the mistakes I made against Sakio Bika.

Seeing a hero of mine, Sugar Ray Leonard, in the Manfredo camp was strange but I can't say I was disappointed because it was business. *The Contender* is Ray's show and he had to show faith in his man but he actually believed that Manfredo had a chance. Barry McGuigan told me after the weigh-in that Leonard had said to him, 'I think Manfredo can win this fight.' Barry insisted there was no chance that he could go more than ten rounds, so they bet on it and shook hands, Leonard insisting that it would at least go the distance. It was turned out to be shorter because this was a different reality for Manfredo. The atmosphere was electric as I walked to the ring but, honestly, it could have been 5,000 people at the International Arena because my focus was on one man on the other side of the ring. Manfredo looked relaxed and calm, he didn't look afraid. I think his plan was to counterpunch me because he expected me to come wading in all wild, like I was against Bika, but he hadn't prepared for my speed and awkwardness. I didn't allow the emotion of the occasion to get to me and made a conscious effort going into the fight to box for the first few rounds, just stay relaxed and use my jab. I was taller and much bigger than him and it worked perfect. I used my jab and threw fast combinations and he really had no answer.

From the opening bell, I was able to find my range, my distance, my speed and my jab, everything was there. For two rounds I outboxed him and when I stepped it up in the third after hurting him with a body shot, a hard left under his ribcage, I showed that he wasn't in my league. I must have hit him on the top of the head or on the elbow because I felt my left hand go – an x-ray two days later confirmed a scaphoid fracture, on the thumb side of my wrist – so I had to throw speed punches. I was waiting for him to fire something in retaliation so that I could step back and hit him with one big shot but the guy was throwing nothing. He held his hands up and I kept punching, maybe 30 or 40 unanswered shots, before the referee, Terry O'Connor, stepped in.

For me, it was a bit premature and this took some shine off the win because it left Manfredo with an excuse when really there was none. He said I didn't punch hard and never hurt him but, if I didn't hurt him, why didn't he hit back? Why take 40 punches without responding, even with one shot? The guy had trained for twelve weeks and it was a world title fight, so maybe he was entitled to get knocked out before the referee stopped it but it was inevitable that it would have happened, if not in the third round then certainly by the fourth. Manfredo couldn't hit me, he was slow and deep down he knows that. He can say whatever he wants but, as far as I'm concerned, I sent another fighter packing and 20 title defences is a milestone which says everything you need to know.

So what is left for me now? I've had my career-defining fight and I might never fight that well again because you can only fight as well as the opponent or the occasion allows you. I could fight the Danish boxer Mikkel Kessler, who holds the WBA and WBC super middleweight belts, and a Celt against a Viking might stir some old passions, but it wouldn't be the same as the fight with Lacy. The way the Americans had built him up and the way the fight turned out, how can it ever be the same? I might never produce a performance like that again, so should I give up? Very possibly, and maybe it's not good to admit this to myself. If I think I could quit now and walk away, maybe I should. Some of my motivation for continuing to fight is financial and money can be an unhealthy incentive in this business. Muhammad Ali came back because the money was too good to resist for a fight with Larry Holmes and, despite what he says about his desire to retire as heavyweight champion, Evander Holyfield has got to be fighting on at forty-four for money reasons too. I never want to end up like them and I've always remembered a piece of advice that Nigel Benn once gave me: 'Don't fight for the money, fight to win.' You get paid anyway, so it shouldn't be your motivation. But what could possibly be better than where I am at this moment? How do I improve? By fighting Kessler? He's possibly as good a fighter as Lacy was, maybe better, but I don't think that he's a big enough name in America, so the fight would mean nothing there.

The way I feel now, I could fight until I'm forty. I'm thirty-five but I'm still at the top of my profession and it's a case of how long I want to keep fighting. My mum asks me more and more when I'm going to retire and she wants me to and I definitely want to get out at the top, I don't want to become one of these guys who hangs on too long, chasing some lost glory. Some days I really feel like I want to give up and other days I realise that if I did, it would suddenly hit me, 'Why did I retire?' I still feel fresh, even after ten years of being champion, and freshness is vital to a fighter's longevity. What I've achieved in my career is tremendous but if I let it go now by having one fight too many, it's not going to be the same. I want to get out at the top, that's my goal because I have the ability to do that, and if it doesn't happen, it will be my fault. Inevitably, I'll get beaten sometime, if I just keep fighting. It's about getting out at the right time and I don't look past my best at this moment, nor do I see anybody around who can beat me, even Kessler who's largely untested. He's fought good fighters, ex-titleholders like Eric Lucas of Canada and Australia's Anthony Mundine, who came into boxing from rugby league, but he's not beaten or even faced anyone exceptional. I do like him and I watched him on the night we both boxed on the undercard of Mike Tyson–Brian Nielsen in Copenhagen. He was early in his career and I thought he would go far, he impressed me, but there aren't any other super middleweights who get me excited.

So the reality is that after another three or four fights, that will be it, time to leave. I want to pass the milestone of ten years as champion, which I'm only a few months from doing, and then I'll see. These next twelve months will be everything, so I want big fights, another super-fight, I don't want routine title defences because it's hard psychologically to keep getting myself up for each fight. I'm aware that my opponent is always dangerous, and I know that if I underestimate him I could get beaten, but it's difficult to be constantly motivated for defence after defence unless the opponent can light my fire. I'm not always intense in the ring but I can't make that happen, it's either there or it's not, though, physically, I'm always in good enough shape to win. Of course, it's harder each time I go back to the gym to start training, and it's been that way for several years, but that's only natural. Fighters like Kabary Salem and Evans Ashira were beatable, I could beat them with one hand and I actually did in the case of Ashira, but I got caught with silly punches that I wouldn't normally get caught with, especially against Salem. I made mistakes because I wasn't as sharp as I would be if I had felt real fear while preparing for the fight. Against fighters like Sheika and Brewer I prepared myself with much more enthusiasm because I knew they could punch, I knew they were going to be dangerous and, if I wasn't on form, they could beat me. Physically, getting prepared is no harder now than it ever was, apart from my hands, which are more brittle because I've been boxing for twenty-five years. I do worry and I do get stressed about them and there are enough little anxieties going into a fight without being worried about injuries to your hands too. But the hardest part now is finding the motivation to get me going, which is why being written off against Lacy worked so much in my favour. It gave me incentive to prove myself again, which I did, so I ask myself, what is there for me now?

Sometimes it's difficult for me to answer that myself. When I'm out of the gym for a few months I begin to feel comfortable and I feel like I could easily retire. As I say, if I had millions in the bank, I probably would. So why am

I fighting and battling to get down to twelve stone all the time? Maybe it's as simple as this, nothing gives me the natural high that I experience in the build-up to a fight. The physical and mental edge, the nerves you feel from walking out in front of tens of thousands of people, the pressure and all that adrenalin, money can't buy any of this and that euphoric feeling of victory makes the sacrifice worthwhile. But there can be a flip side to all of this. I experience an unbelievable buzz through boxing, so when I come down there's not much there to take the place of that excitement and for weeks on end I feel that I'm not really doing anything. My personality becomes very up and down, I become tetchy and uninterested and I can be a proper pain in the arse. Boxing is a profession in which this can very easily happen because of the long breaks between each fight, so you end up trying to find other ways to entertain yourself. I could go out, get drunk, come home and do the same the next day; other fighters do this and it passes the time. I can be OK one minute and the next minute I can switch.

Boxing's such an extreme activity that the strain on your emotions is huge and I've developed different characters because of this. I'm not a straightforward guy. All of a sudden I can switch from being a nice guy to a guy whose blood is boiling, or I can just become cold. Most of the time I'm placid, but I can become extremely argumentative, very passionate and fiery. Yet when it's time to fight I'm not angry at all. If somebody were to call me a dickhead as I'm about to step in the ring, I'd laugh at them, my heart wouldn't miss a beat. It's when I'm between fights and not channelling my aggression or my energy into something positive that I get moody and allow things to fester because I'm bored. So I start an argument and then another one erupts. I can row the whole bloody time. If I'm not rowing with my girlfriend, I'm rowing with my dad, and in some strange way I almost need that in my life, a bit of disruption and mayhem. Dad asks me why I can't have two days that are just smooth, but if things stayed normal for two days, I would think that I've got to say something to cause some strife. I've always been that way, up and down. I'm a different person when I fight, an extrovert and totally in control. As soon as I put in my earphones and walk to the arena, nothing on earth could shake me. Deep down I know that I'm shy, which is strange, because I can go out and perform in front of these tens of thousands, yet I get nervous when I have to stand and speak in front of a dozen people. Dad is the same because he was able to sing in front of large audiences but he's uncomfortable even with small public engagements. For me, I'm most confident when I put my gloves on, I'm ready to entertain.

So I wonder what I'll be like when I retire, what it is that will keep me on an even keel. I think I'll be OK. Having two boys, Joe who is nearly a teenager and Connor who is eleven, and being a full-time dad takes up a lot of my time, so I don't think I'll be too bored. But boxing is in my blood as well and I do see myself staying in the sport. Maybe I'll manage a few fighters or join Dad as a trainer, not for the money but to be able to pass on my knowledge. I've always wanted to travel the world and I'd like to read more. I'm always taking a book whenever I go to my hotel ahead of a fight but I end up watching TV instead. I'm just not one of these people who likes to sit and contemplate, I'm spontaneous, I get up and I want to do something. I don't like my own company too much. Sometimes I'll have a quiet afternoon but I don't enjoy being on my own. I can't get up in the morning and listen to the peace and quiet and just chill, I've got to turn the TV on because I like the sound. I just like noise, a constant buzz.

All of this worries me because one day I'll have given up boxing and I won't have a fight around the corner to give me my next fix. I could do dinners, get fat and get drunk and babble on about my past glories like a lot of ex-sportsmen. It's a nice little earner, pays the bills though because I'm too shy and introverted I don't particularly enjoy speaking in public. I can do it but I just don't feel comfortable in that environment. Ricky Hatton is good at it but I'm not people-wise when it comes to speaking to an audience and cracking jokes. Maybe I'll be one of these fighters who come out of retirement, who can't get away from the sport. I've been buying some properties in Eastern Europe and building up a property portfolio abroad, but that will only generate some income, it won't replace the excitement that boxing has brought into my life. Is it all going to be an anticlimax? I really don't know what I'm going to do. I didn't think about it before but in the last twelve months I've been concerned about it more, as I've started to realise that some of these fighters who I thought were getting on in years are actually younger than me. Maybe I'll retire and miss the buzz so much that I'll make a comeback, like Leonard did and Ali and a whole host of fighters, but I hope I'll be wiser.

A few years ago I was offered the opportunity to do a shoot for an ad campaign, modelling Marks & Spencer underwear. I was a bit reluctant and my ex-wife was very adamant that I wouldn't be doing it, so I turned down the offer. Then on holiday in Sardinia I thought some more about it and couldn't see any harm in doing the pictures, so I rang up Frank Warren's office and told the people there that I'd do it but by that stage Marks & Spencer had gone and chosen somebody else. Later on, Freddie Ljungberg, the Arsenal footballer, made a big name for himself wearing Calvin Klein underwear and sometimes I smile when I see one of those big posters of Freddie in his underpants and think, 'That could have been me.'

It's been difficult at times to persuade Joe to do some

of the extra-curricular stuff that might have raised his profile sooner. The Marks & Spencer offer was a real case in point because Joe would have been the face of their rebranding campaign and they wanted him to model men's underwear. I remember him saying to me, 'I don't want pictures of me just wearing pants plastered all around the place,' and I laughed. 'Joe,' I said, 'any time the public sees you you're half-naked anyway in a pair of shorts.' By the time he decided to go with it, the chance was gone but he's got better over the years with the self-promotion. I don't think it's really in his nature to court attention but he knows now that it's part of the business he's in, an important part.

– Frank Warren

I haven't turned down a load of opportunities but I don't show up to open envelopes, which is my prerogative. If I'd got myself involved in that side of things, I might not be champion today because it's a distraction and, if I did everything I was asked to do, when would I train? I know I've been criticised for not making more of myself, but I'm not one of these people who seeks the attention, I prefer to slip into the crowd. Over the years I've become a bit savvier but boxing is difficult to sell. You're big news when you beat a guy like Lacy, but there's a lot of time between fights and it goes quiet again, people forget.

It's not like football where they're in the newspapers and magazines and on TV every week. If they got beaten 4–0 last week, they're useless so-and-sos, but it's OK because they won 3–0 today. The people at Ringside were very good to me early in my career and I wore their gear, but I haven't really been able to exploit any commercial opportunities since the Lacy fight and I suppose I'm disappointed. Jasper Conran wanted me to be the face of their aftershave and I met some of their marketing people, but time went on and after a few months everything was forgotten. Maybe these kinds of opportunities will kick off for me after boxing.

When I first challenged for the title I had to win. I beat Eubank and started making more money and I've done even better as I've made more title defences. If I didn't box again, I wouldn't have to work straight away. I don't make millions but I do well, so a certain motivation goes, because I live comfortably in a big house and I drive a decent car, I eat in the best restaurants and I don't have to worry about paying the bills. I don't live an extravagant lifestyle and if I invest my money properly I wouldn't need to work again. So what keeps pushing me back in the ring? It's simple, this is who I am, I'm a champion and the thought of losing rips me up. Even when I fight bad and win, I'm not happy, I'm down on myself, and it would be a hundred times worse if I lost. I believe that when I'm at my best I can beat any boxer in the world and I don't want to leave the sport with any regrets, so there are still a few fights out there before I'll be totally fulfilled. Maybe then I'll be able to walk away happy and stay away for good.

I've remained in this part of Wales for all these years, right in the heart of the valleys, because it keeps my feet on the ground. That's the way people are here, down-to-earth, and I think that's why people respect me, for I'm just one of them and they can see that every day. I'm Welsh and I'm Italian-Sardinian and both of these cultures fill me with pride. Wales is a small country but just in boxing we've produced Jimmy Wilde, Tommy Farr, Howard Winstone and other really good fighters. Through my boxing, I've put the town of Newbridge on the map, but still no one bothers me, which suits me fine. I like the familiar surroundings and I'd still be training in that old, blue shack, if they hadn't thrown us out to knock it down. Sometimes I can close my eyes and still breathe in the musty smell, but we've done the new gym up nice and I know where I'd prefer to be training.

For young people in the area, it's a good place to go and keep fit and boxing still has an important role to play in society. It encourages discipline and respect and teaches people that there are no shortcuts to the top. If you don't put the work in, boxing will find you out very quickly. Unfortunately, the numbers in amateur boxing are nowhere near the level they were at twenty years ago. I

remember the first time I boxed in the ABA championships I had to go through a regional set of qualifiers and
there were maybe ten or fifteen boys at the weight. I was
even made to box twice in one day and after stopping the
first boy I had to come back later to stop the other one.
Now you have boys getting byes all the way to the finals of
the Welsh championships. The sport isn't as popular
today as it was when I was growing up. I played football
and there was a boxing gym and that was it, whereas
today kids can play golf, tennis, all kinds of sports and
there's also PlayStation. They don't want to go to a boxing
gym any more, they would much rather play a boxing
game on the computer.

But the biggest thing that counts against boxing today
is all the internal politics. There are too many titles
and not enough top fighters and this has taken away
from the prestige of winning a world title. All these Intercontinental titles, what are they and who cares? The only
Inter I knew growing up was a football team in Milan and
I never liked them either. Intercontinental belts mean
nothing, they're for fighters ranked between twenty and
fifty in the world or whatever it is and they diminish the
value of a real title. When I won the British title I went on
to challenge for the WBO title, but television want to put
on title fights that make the public switch off. The IBO,
WBU and IBC and all of these other organisations just
confuse people. Their belts tarnish the sport so that the

average man in the street doesn't know what a legitimate title is any more. Go back twenty or thirty years and being a world champion meant something, it was a big deal, but now people don't know who the real champion is in any division.

The heavyweight division is the perfect example. Being heavyweight champion was like being king in the time of Rocky Marciano, Muhammad Ali and Jack Dempsey, but today the majority of people couldn't name the heavyweight champion of the world, even sports fans. Most people would probably say that it's Lennox Lewis or Mike Tyson. The heavyweight division is so bad that, if I was a stone heavier, I would give away the rest in weight to fight some of those guys. James Toney was once a middleweight but now he fights with his belly hanging out over his shorts. How can a blown-up middleweight become a legitimate heavyweight contender? It demeans the sport. Boxing has suffered in America because a lot of guys are playing other sports like basketball or American football. It's easier than getting hit on the head and they get more money for playing those sports, tens of millions of dollars.

I've never liked the heavyweight division because most of the time it's vastly overrated. Tyson was exciting for a year or two and he dominated when the division was shit, beating up on the likes of Pinklon Thomas, Tyrell Biggs and Tony Tubbs, a poor bunch, though I enjoyed the Riddick Bowe–Evander Holyfield–Lennox Lewis era. It was interesting then but it hasn't been interesting for years. If you were to take away Tyson, Lewis and Holyfield, Larry Holmes and a few others, the heavyweight division has been crap since the 1970s. There were guys like Thomas and Trevor Berbick, Tubbs and Bonecrusher Smith, then Tyson came along and destroyed everyone. Was Tyson that good or was the division just crap? Would Lewis have destroyed all of them too? Of course he would have, maybe just not as explosively. The division was average, as there were no other great heavyweights. The bigger they are the more average they seem to be, which probably hurts boxing overall. I only watch about half a dozen fighters who entertain me, like Marco Antonio Barrera and Manny Pacquiao of the Philippines, who are both super featherweights but there aren't too many fighters around today who make me think, 'That boy can fight.' All these Intercontinental and Intergalactic title fights don't interest me one jot.

Amir Khan can fight, he can move well and his fast hands will be a great asset as the level of competition he is facing improves. Will he go all the way? It's probably too early to say but, if he's matched in the right way, he has a chance. Ricky Hatton has done really well for himself and British boxing and I'm pleased for Ricky, who's a down-to-earth guy. He's gone to America to fulfil his dreams and I'm happy for him.

My future, I hope, will be in America. I'm in the last leg of my career now and it's about cementing my legacy. My dad reckons that I'm getting better with age, like a fine wine. I don't take any unnecessary punishment in the gym by taking part in wars because the body can take only a certain amount of wear and tear. With a lot of ex-fighters, you can detect a difference in the way they speak and their movement slows. I spoke to Nigel Collins, the editor of *The Ring*, when he presented me with my championship belt and he brought up the sad case of Meldrick Taylor, who was a terrific fighter from Philadelphia, fast hands, brilliant boxer, had an unbelievable war with Julio Cesar Chavez. He actually beat up Chavez when Chavez was at his best before the great Mexican stopped him in the final seconds of a classic fight. Now Taylor is almost like a ghost and he can hardly speak. Nigel talked about the way he sparred, he had wars in the gym, Philly wars, they call them because that's the way they were brought up sparring in Philadelphia. From fourteen years old, he was in the gym having wars. Eventually, they will catch up on any man, as much as the fights in the ring.

My sparring sessions now are all about speed and timing, mainly due to my fragile hands which I need to protect but this is why I'm still sharp and why I still feel that there are other big fights ahead of me. For many years I never really had the urge to go to America to fight at

Caesars Palace or one of the other venues along the Las Vegas Strip or at Madison Square Garden in New York. This is where I live and my attitude was always that they could come over here to fight me. I've never felt like I had to go there for the history, I'm not too bothered by that and I don't think my career could ever be classed as a failure or a disappointment if I never fought in America. I've beaten every top American that they've had to offer and I just haven't been given the respect for being nearly ten years a champion. No other boxer in the world today has achieved that level of dominance.

I do think there's a bias within the American boxing media and the wider American market. They're slow to recognise the achievements of sportsmen from other countries because it's an insular country. If you don't do it there, you might as well be nobody. So people have always said that I need to go and box in America, that's the holy grail. But the truth is this, I would fight Bernard Hopkins, the light heavyweight champion, and Jermain Taylor, the middleweight champion. I would fight Winky Wright who boxed Taylor to a draw, I would fight all of these guys tomorrow. But Hopkins is too shrewd a businessman and he simply doesn't want to fight me, so he's going to fight Winky in July 2007 at a catchweight around the twelve stone super middleweight limit. Yet in a recent interview with *The Ring* Hopkins said, 'If the money is right, I would fight Joe Calzaghe, but not at one hundred and sixty-eight pounds. Calzaghe would have to move up to light heavyweight.' Hopkins still considers me too dangerous, I guess, or he wouldn't be changing the rules. Taylor has been talking about moving up in weight from middleweight but he, too, shows no desire to get in the ring with me. It's almost like those fighters have their own little clique and they fight among themselves to make as much money as they can but don't allow anyone else in, particularly somebody who could beat them. Hopkins is the biggest fight out there for me, along with Taylor, and I'd just be too strong for Winky Wright. I have no interest any more in Roy Jones and no interest in Antonio Tarver. Jones is washed up and Tarver was never that good anyway, he just caught Jones when Jones was shot and Johnson did the same. Then they got on their little merry-go-round and everyone began to say Tarver and Johnson were great fighters but, if they were so great, why was Johnson losing a dozen fights during the prime years of his career? Why was Tarver fighting nobody? He fought like he was scared and did absolutely nothing for twelve rounds against Hopkins, a middleweight moving up. That's why I'd like to fight Hopkins, *The Ring* light heavyweight champion against *The Ring* super middleweight champion, it's a natural. I don't think it would be the most exciting fight in the world because of his style but, technically, it would be terrific, a fight for aficionados and I'd go to America to make it happen.

'Joe Calzaghe, he could fight,' that's what I'd like people to be able to say. 'Look how long he was undefeated and when will somebody else do that?' I'm not a person who craves attention and thinks, 'Look at me, look at me.' I like my privacy and I probably couldn't handle it if I was a footballer or a film star and had paparazzi trailing me everywhere. I'd be one of those people who would have to move away from the spotlight because I wouldn't like it. I just don't crave it. I get invites to movie premieres but I don't go and I get offers from agents, 'You have to do this, Joe, and you've got to go there . . . Open this envelope and you'll get publicity . . . Just go to be seen at this new place, see who's coming and go rub shoulders.' I'm a fighter and all I crave is respect for being a fighter. Maybe ten years down the line when people look back I'll be more appreciated, this tends to be the way. I'd like to fight in America too, even once, just to show them that there's been a great fighter in the Welsh valleys all these years. It doesn't bother me if the man in the street recognises me or not over there but there have been occasions when it might have been handy.

A week after the Bika fight I flew to Miami for a couple of days to collect the Fighter of the Year award at the WBO convention, where Dad was also honoured as trainer of the year. Enzo Maccarrinelli came with me as well as Dennis Gilmartin who works in Frank Warren's office. I don't like flying, so it was good to have the company, especially when we went out to experience Miami's nightlife. The first bar we went to, however, was a bit unfriendly. I went to the toilet after ordering a round of drinks and when I came back some guy had nicked my seat. I asked for my seat back, very politely, but the guy had real attitude and, of course, he felt big surrounded by a few of his mates. Dennis had been talking to the guy's girlfriend who told him, 'Don't worry, my boyfriend won't beat up Joe. It is Joe, right?'

Dennis laughed.

'Have you heard of Jeff Lacy?' he asked her.

'Sure, he's from here in Florida, I know him,' she said.

'Well, that's Joe Calzaghe who beat the shit out of him about six months ago, so I really don't think your friend's going to beat him up either.'

I'm not sure what she said to the guy, but all of a sudden I found myself back in my seat being asked, very politely, if I would like another drink. The atmosphere lightened up considerably.

We stayed for a while, then somebody suggested we should go to a club called Mansion, which was once owned by P Diddy, so we thought it would be a good place. It was packed when we got there but we managed to get some drinks in before a guy came up to me all of a sudden, right in my face. I had just managed to avoid trouble in the other place and I didn't want any here but he just looked, smiled at me and said, 'You're gorgeous.'

I turned in shock and walked away and by the time I found Enzo and Dennis to tell them what had happened, the guy was over with them and the situation was getting heated. Apparently, he had taken the liberty of pinching Enzo's ass, which was a bad mistake because Enzo sent him flying with a push about twenty feet across the floor. 'What's wrong with you guys?' he said in his most camp voice and it was then, as we looked around, that we realised we were in the middle of one of the biggest gay bars in Miami in the most recognised gay area in the city, South Beach. Now, if only somebody had recognised me, they might have been able to put an arm on my shoulder and say, 'Joe, I don't think this is your place.'

LAST WORD

'For all that Joe's achieved, he is one of the most down-to-earth people you could possibly meet and, as a father, that's what I'm most proud of. He's not changed one bit from the boy who first put on the gloves, he really hasn't. There are people who seek to be the centre of attention, they embrace it and they think they've reached the peak but Joe's not like that. It's strange but everything I tried to achieve as a musician, fame and all the rest, he's not really fussed about. He wants his achievements to be recognised but he couldn't care less if he's recognised or not. After a fight he just sits down with his family and a few of the friends he's known for years for a few drinks. As a matter of fact, after he beat Peter Manfredo in his 20th title defence, a landmark night, he didn't even stay in the hotel for the party. We all just went home and had a few beers there. That's the real measure of Joe, his modesty' – Enzo Calzaghe

'My grandad takes me training and sometimes my dad

shows me a few moves. Maybe I'll be a fighter one day, I'd like to be. Me and Connor, we're proud of what Dad's done, he's done great. We stayed up to watch his fight against Jeff Lacy on TV and we were up on our feet, shouting and throwing punches. I'm nervous at the start when I watch him fight but once I get into it I'm fine. Connor kept jumping up and down, then he turned to me and asked, "Is Dad winning?" I said, "He's doing very well." So he started jumping up and down again and it was like that for the whole twelve rounds' – Joe Calzaghe Jr

'I'd like to see Joe go to America, just as I did when I beat Doug DeWitt and Iran Barkley, and beat someone like Bernard Hopkins or Jermain Taylor over there. But what he's achieved over the past decade is phenomenal, he's beaten every opponent he's faced in his career and no fighter can do anything more than this. Joe is one of the legends of British boxing and, as I've said before, if he'd come around in my era when Eubank and Collins and Watson were fighting too, he might have beaten all of us, who knows?' – Nigel Benn

'I had never been knocked down in the first round before Joe hit me with a powerful left-hand punch, which I never saw, and within half a minute of the bell ringing I was having to pick myself up and deal with the realisation that

I was in for a long night. That punch really hurt and thereafter it was a tough fight. We battled each other in the trenches, Joe had very fast hands and was really awkward. It was a good fight and Joe has since gone on to prove himself a worthy world champion, one of the best we've seen. Unfortunately, he hasn't established a rivalry with any particular opponent in the way that Nigel and I held the public in thrall but he has been a magnificent boxer for many, many years. I'm particularly glad about this because it means that I was beaten on that night by no ordinary fighter, no ordinary Joe, but by a man of real class' – Chris Eubank

JOE CALZAGHE — AT A GLANCE

Alias:	Pride of Wales/Italian Dragon
Birth Name:	Joseph Calzaghe
Country:	British
Hometown:	Newbridge, Wales
Birthplace:	Hammersmith, England
Division:	Super Middleweight
Age:	35
Born:	23rd March 1972
Stance:	Southpaw
Reach:	73"
Height:	182cm
Manager:	Frank Warren
Trainer:	Enzo Calzaghe

Date	Opponent	W-L-D	Location	Result	Score
7.4.2007	Peter Manfredo Jr	26-3-0	Cardiff, Wales	W TKO 3	≈
	WBO Super Middleweight Title			1:30	
14.10.2006	Sakio Bika	20-1-2	Manchester,	W UD 12	117–110,
	IBF Super Middleweight Title		England		117–110,
	WBO Super Middleweight Title				116–111

Date	Opponent	W-L-D	Location	Result	Score
4.3.2006	Jeff Lacy	21-0-0	Manchester,	**W** UD 12	119–105,
	IBF Super Middleweight Title		England		119–107,
	WBO Super Middleweight Title				119–107
10.9.2006	Evans Ashira	24-1-0	Cardiff, Wales	**W** UD 12	120–107,
	WBO Super Middleweight Title				120–108,
					120–108
7.5.2005	Mario Veit	45-1-0	Braunschweig,	**W** TKO 6	
	WBO Super Middleweight Title		Germany	0:42	
22.10.2004	Kabary Salem	23-3-0	Edinburgh,	**W** UD 12	117–109,
	WBO Super Middleweight Title		Scotland		118–107,
					116–109
21.2.2004	Mger Mkrtchian	18-1-0	Cardiff, Wales	**W** TKO 7	1:05
	WBO Super Middleweight Title			1:05	
28.6.2003	Byron Mitchell	25-2-1	Cardiff, Wales	**W** TKO 2	
	WBO Super Middleweight Title			2:36	
14.12.2002	Tocker Pudwill	39-4-0	Newcastle,	**W** TKO 2	
	WBO Super Middleweight Title		England	0:39	
17.8.2002	Miguel Angel Jimenez	21-1-0	Cardiff, Wales	**W** UD 12	120–107,
	WBO Super Middleweight Title				120–107,
					120–107

Date	Opponent	W-L-D	Location	Result	Score
20.4.2002	Charles Brewer **WBO Super Middleweight Title**	37-8-0	Cardiff, Wales	**W** UD 12	118–111, 117–112, 119–109
13.10.2001	Will McIntyre **WBO Super Middleweight Title**	29-2-0	Copenhagen, Denmark	**W** TKO 4 0:45	
28.4.2001	Mario Veit **WBO Super Middleweight Title**	30-0-0	Cardiff, Wales	**W** TKO 1 1:52	
16.12.2000	Richie Woodhall **WBO Super Middleweight Title**	26-2-0	Sheffield, England	**W** TKO 10 0:28	
12.8.2000	Omar Sheika **WBO Super Middleweight Title**	20-1-0	Wembley, England	**W** TKO 5 2:08	
29.1.2000	David Starie **WBO Super Middleweight Title**	22-1-0	Manchester, England	**W** UD 12	118–110, 120–108, 116–113
5.6.1999	Rick Thornberry **WBO Super Middleweight Title**	23-2-0	Cardiff, Wales	**W** UD 12	120–107, 119–108, 119–109
13.2.1999	Robin Reid **WBO Super Middleweight Title**	26-1-1	Newcastle, England	**W** SD 12	116–111, 116–111, 111–116

Date	Opponent	W-L-D	Location	Result	Score
25.4.1998	Juan Carlos Gimenez	51-8-3	Cardiff, Wales	**W** TKO 10	
	WBO Super Middleweight Title			0:01	
24.1.1998	Branko Sobot	14-1-0	Cardiff, Wales	**W** TKO 3	
	WBO Super Middleweight Title			1:35	
11.10.1997	Chris Eubank	45-2-2	Sheffield,	**W** UD 12	116–111,
	Vacant WBO Super Middleweight Title		England		118–110,
					118–109
5.6.1997	Luciano Torres	44-2-0	Bristol, England	**W** TKO 3	
22.3.1997	Tyler Hughes	12-0-0	Manchester, England	**W** KO 1	
21.1.1997	Carlos Christie	13-22-1	Bristol, England	**W** TKO 2	
15.5.1996	Pat Lawlor	21-8-0	Cardiff, Wales	**W** TKO 2	
4.5.1996	Warren Stowe	17-2-0	Dagenham, England	**W** TKO 2	
20.4.1996	Mark Delaney	21-0-0	Brentwood,	**W** TKO 5	
	BBBofC British Super Middleweight Title		England		

Date	Opponent	W-L-D	Location	Result	Score
13.3.1996	Anthony Brooks	11-6-2	Wembley, England	W TKO 2	
13.2.1996	Guy Stanford	16-11-1	Cardiff, Wales	W TKO 1	
28.10.1995	Stephen Wilson **Vacant BBBofC British Super Middleweight Title**	11-1-0	Kensington, England	W TKO 8	
30.9.1995	Nick Manners	9-3-1	Basildon, England	W TKO 4	
8.7.1995	Tyrone Jackson	7-9-1	York, England	W TKO 4	
19.5.1995	Robert Curry	33-34-0	Southwark, England	W TKO 1	
22.2.1995	Bobbie Joe Edwards	5-9-0	Telford, England	W PTS 8	
14.2.1995	Frank Minton	26-21-1	Bethnal Green, England	W KO 1	
30.11.1994	Trevor Ambrose	10-13-0	Wolverhampton, England	W TKO 2	

Date	Opponent	W-L-D	Location	Result	Score
1.19.1994	Mark Lee Dawson	7-9-0	Cardiff, Wales	W TKO 1	
4.6.1994	Karl Barwise	14-28-3	Cardiff, Wales	W TKO 1	
1.3.1994	Darren Littlewood	1-1-0	Dudley, England	W TKO 1	
22.1.1994	Martin Rosamond	10-15-1	Cardiff, Wales	W TKO 1	
16.12.1993	Spencer Alton	12-23-3	Newport, Wales	W TKO 2	
10.11.1993	Paul Mason	5-7-3	Watford, England	W TKO 1	
1.10.1993	Paul Hanlon	7-16-0	Cardiff, Wales	W TKO 1	

RECORD TO DATE

Won 43 (KOs 32) Lost 0 Drawn 0 Total 43